Book 10 in the Durvile True Cases Series

INDIGENOUS JUSTICE

TRUE CASES BY JUDGES, LAWYERS &

LAW ENFORCEMENT OFFICERS

Book 10 in the Durvile True Cases Series

INDIGENOUS JUSTICE

TRUE CASES BY JUDGES, LAWYERS & LAW ENFORCEMENT OFFICERS

Lorene Shyba PhD &
Raymond Yakeleya, *eds.*

Foreword by
Chief Justice Shannon Smallwood
Supreme Court of the Northwest Territories

DURVILE &
UpRoute Books

DURVILE IMPRINT OF DURVILE & UPROUTE BOOKS
CALGARY, ALBERTA, CANADA
DURVILE.COM

Durvile Publications Ltd.

DURVILE IMPRINT OF DURVILE AND UPROUTE BOOKS

Calgary, Alberta, Canada
www.durvile.com

Anthology copyright © 2023 Durvile Publications
Individual stories © the authors

ISBN: 978-1-990735-26-4 (pbk) | 978-1-990735-28-8 (audio) | 978-1-990735-27-1 (epub)

LIBRARY AND ARCHIVES CATALOGUING IN PUBLICATIONS DATA

Indigenous Justice: True Cases by Judges, Lawyers and Law Enforcement Officers
Shyba, Lorene and Yakeleya, Raymond: Editors
Smallwood, Shannon: Foreword

1. True Crime | 2. Indigenous
3. First Nations | 4. Truth & Reconciliation | 5. Criminal Justice

Book 10 in the Durvile True Cases Series | Series Editor, Lorene Shyba MFA PhD

The following stories are republished from earlier Durvile Reflections or True Cases series books:
Morrison, Nancy, "Kamsack: Thursday 10 a.m." and "The Sublime Blanche MacDonald."
Both stories from *Benched: Passion for Law Reform*. 2018. Stories are revised.
Vertes, John Z., "The Case of Henry Innuksuk," from *Tough Crimes*. 2014.
Pate, Kim, "The Story of S," from *Women in Criminal Justice*. 2016. Revised.
Rudin, Jonathan, "The Death of Reggie Bushie," from *More Tough Crimes*. 2017.
Dunn, Catherine, "Silent Partner," from *Women in Criminal Justice*. 2016.
Briscoe, Jennifer, "Fly-in Justice in the North," from *Women in Criminal Justice*. 2016.
Louttit, Ernie, "There is No Law Against It Constable," from *After the Force*. 2021.
Bourque, Sharon, "A Full-Circle Experience," from *After the Force*. 2021.
Heckbert, Doug, "I Know Who Killed My Brother" and "Get FPS# Off Our Backs," from
Go Ahead and Shoot Me! and Other True Cases About Ordinary Criminals. 2020. Both stories are revised.

Book and jacket design: Lorene Shyba

Printed in Canada | First edition, first printing. 2023

Durvile Publication Ltd. is committed to reducing the consumption of nonrenewable resources in the production of our books. We make every effort to use materials that support a sustainable future.

Durvile Publications acknowledges the financial support of the Government of Canada through
Canadian Heritage, Canada Book Fund and the Government of Alberta, Alberta Media Fund.

With gratitude, Durvile & UpRoute Books recognizes the traditional lands of
Treaty 7 Peoples of Southern Alberta upon which our studios rest:
Siksika, Piikani, and Kainai of the Blackfoot Confederacy; Dene Tsuut'ina;
Chiniki, Bearspaw, and Wesley Stoney Nakoda First Nations; and the Region 3 Métis Nation of Alberta.

This book is for
legal and law enforcement professionals
who dedicate themselves to providing
compassionate and reliable services to Indigenous
accused clients, offenders, victims,
witness and family members.

CONTENTS

Foreword
Chief Justice Shannon Smallwood
Supreme Court of the Northwest Territories . ix

Introduction
Lorene Shyba and Raymond Yakeleya
Mindful of Culture and Tradition 1

PART I The Judges and Senator 9

1. The Hon. Justice Thomas R. Berger
The Mackenzie Valley Pipeline Inquiry 11

2. The Hon. Nancy Morrison
Three Stories 35

3. The Hon. John Reilly
Baret Labelle and Restorative Justice 51

4. The Hon. John Z. Vertes
The Case of Henry Innuksuk 67

5. The Hon. Kim Pate
The Story of S:
A Study in Discrimination and Inequality 81

PART II Lawyers 103

6. Eleanore Sunchild KC
Treaty Lessons:
The Killing of Colten Boushie 105

7. Jonathan Rudin
The Death of Reggie Bushie
and the Eight-Year Inquest 117

CONTENTS

∂

8. Catherine Dunn
Silent Partner.. 133

9. Joseph Saulnier
Justice in Hazelton: One Family,
Two Murder Trials, a Hundred Years Apart ... 147

10. Brian Beresh KC
A Life's Journey for Indigenous Justice............. 163

11. Jennifer Briscoe
Fly-in Justice in the North................................. 175

12. John L. Hill
Carved in Stone:
The Mistreatment of Inuit Offenders.............. 189

**PART III Law Enforcement and
Parole Officer** 201

13. Ernie Louttit
There is No Law Against It Constable.............. 203

14. Sharon Bourque
A Full-Circle Experience 217

15. Constable Val Hoglund
The Unwitting Criminal 225

16. Doug Heckbert
I Know Who Killed My Brother 241

17. Doug Heckbert and Jennifer Bryce
Getting FPS# Off Our Backs 257

Index *282*

FOREWORD

Chief Justice Shannon Smallwood
Supreme Court of the Northwest Territories

I WAS HONOURED TO be asked to write a foreword for this book, *Indigenous Justice: True Cases by Judges, Lawyers and Law Enforcement Officers.* I have read and enjoyed many of the preceding books in the Durvile True Case series and the topic of Indigenous Justice is one that is near to my heart.

As a child growing up in Fort Good Hope in the 1970s, Indigenous justice and the debates swirling around the prospect of oil and gas development in the Northwest Territories were not concepts that I had any awareness of or any notion of their importance to the people of my hometown or the Northwest Territories in general. The impact of the Mackenzie Valley Pipeline Inquiry, as discussed by the Honourable Justice Thomas R. Berger, was one that resonated with my community and for Indigenous Peoples throughout the North. For many, the impact of the Berger Inquiry Report, *Northern Frontier, Northern Homeland* lent credence to the idea that Indigenous voices could and should be heard and taken into account in decisions that affect Indigenous Peoples and their lands. More than 40 years later, development on Indigenous lands continues to be a challenging issue facing Canada and Indigenous People are regularly consulted throughout the process.

The chapters in this book touch upon the involvement of Indigenous persons in the Canadian justice system as told by judges, lawyers and law enforcement officers who have dedicated their careers to working in the justice system and who, as a consequence, have regularly dealt with Indigenous persons.

Anyone who has a passing familiarity with the criminal justice system is well aware that Indigenous Peoples are greatly overrepresented in Canadian prisons. Almost 25 years ago, the Supreme Court of Canada in *R v Gladue* considered the circumstances of Indigenous offenders in the justice system and recognized what had been said by the *Royal Commission on Aboriginal Peoples* in 1996: that the Canadian criminal justice system has failed the Indigenous Peoples of Canada.

The issues facing Indigenous persons involved in the criminal justice system, whether as accused persons, offenders, victims, witnesses, or family members are highlighted in the chapters of this book. Indigenous persons frequently meet challenges navigating and understanding the justice system and often encounter barriers like racism and systemic discrimination, which many other groups do not face.

Since the Supreme Court of Canada's decision in *Gladue* in 1999, the over-representation of Indigenous People, particularly Indigenous women, in Canadian prisons has only gotten worse. It is a situation that has persisted despite the directions given to sentencing judges by the Supreme Court of Canada in *Gladue, R v Ipeelee* and other cases.

At the same time, awareness of the issues facing Indigenous Peoples has greatly increased and entered everyday conversation in Canadian society. The *Report of the Truth and Reconciliation Commission* (TRC) brought the legacy of residential schools to the forefront. The need for reconciliation with Indigenous Peoples is widely recognized across Canada.

Reconciliation will require that we each play a role. No one group, organization, institution, or government can effect reconciliation on their own. It will take society as a whole to ensure reconciliation occurs in Canada. Within the justice system, every judge, lawyer, law enforcement officer, and others involved in the justice system will need to do their part.

Reconciliation will take time and commitment; it will not occur in my lifetime. As the TRC said in their final report, it will take many heads, hands and hearts working together at all levels of society in the years ahead. It took a long time for the damage to be done, so, it will take a long time to fix it. As the daughter, granddaughter, and niece of residential school survivors, the legacy of residential schools is one that casts a long shadow.

There are different views about what is required to achieve reconciliation and the TRC calls to action provide some guidance. The path to reconciliation and what is required may differ for some. Indigenous People themselves might have different views amongst themselves about what is required. Every Indigenous group comes from a different place, from a different traditional territory, from a different language and culture, with many shared experiences from residential schools and the impacts of colonialism but every Indigenous person has experienced these things in their own, unique way.

Reconciliation will require that we become aware of what has happened in the past and acknowledge the harm done to Indigenous People. Many of the chapters in this book shed a light on the challenges faced by Indigenous persons in the criminal justice system and their resilience and vulnerability in the face of adversity. Only by learning about the experiences of Indigenous People in the criminal justice system in the past can we move forward.

Mahsi Cho.

    — *Chief Justice Shannon Smallwood*
      Supreme Court of the Northwest Territories, 2023

INTRODUCTION

MINDFUL OF CULTURE & TRADITION

Indigenous Justice, Book 10 in the Durvile True Cases series, is comprised of chapters written by the very legal and law enforcement professionals to whom we dedicated this book: judges, lawyers, police, and parole officers, both Indigenous and non-Indigenous, who have supported and continue to support First Nations, Métis, and Inuit Peoples through their trials and tribulations with the criminal justice system. We have chosen an image of Cree leader and peacemaker *Pîhtokahanapiwiyin* for the cover of this book because of the strong connection that many of the stories have to the province of Saskatchewan, and notably the Battleford area, Also known as Chief Poundmaker, *Pîhtokahanapiwiyin* was born around 1842 in Rupert's Land near the present day Battleford. He played a significant role in the events leading up to the North-West Resistance of 1885, an event mentioned by both Eleanore Sunchild KC and Brian Beresh KC in this book as a battle formerly known as "the Rebellion." The resisters were eventually defeated by federal troops, the result being the permanent enforcement of Canadian law in the West, the subjugation of Plains Indigenous Peoples, and the conviction and execution of Louis Riel.

After the resistance was suppressed by the fledgling Canadian government, Chief Poundmaker was arrested and charged with treason. He was later released, but died just months later, on July 4, 1886. He is remembered as a skilled diplomat and peacemaker who worked tirelessly to improve the lives of his People. In 2019, Prime Minister Justin Trudeau formally exonerated Chief Poundmaker of the treason charges, the exoneration being part of a broader effort to recognize and reconcile the historical injustices that Indigenous Peoples have suffered. Poundmaker's story serves as a reminder of the importance of recognizing the injustices of the past and working to build a more just and equitable future.

In recent years there has been a growing movement to return artifacts taken without permission from Indigenous communities. In 2023, artifacts dating from 1886 belonging to Poundmaker were returned to his descendants in a repatriation ceremony at the Royal Ontario Museum. The museum transferred his ceremonial pipe and a saddle bag back to his family members.

Other museums are also repatriating stolen artifacts. The Royal Alberta Museum recently returned artifacts from its collection to the Athabasca Chipewyan First Nation, and internationally, the UK-based Buxton Museum returned their entire collection of First Nations artifacts to the Haida and Blackfoot communities.

Returning sacred objects from museums to First Nations aligns with early steps of support from the Vatican to reflect on the dignity and rights of Indigenous Peoples. The Vatican's recent rejection of the *Doctrine of Discovery*, a legal concept that justified Europeans claiming Indigenous lands, shows that dispossession of land was not legal and calls into question the manner of colonization. (*Says Raymond),*

> The *Doctrine of Discovery* was like the thieves' bible. Sensible minds have moved in and called it for what it was, thievery and crimes against humanity. The land was ours and at first contact with whiteman, it was as if we were nothing. It was all about the resources and it's hard to sell the bones of your people.

• • •

Indigenous Justice is written by legal and law enforcement professionals who share stories that provide perspective into their belief in the principles of reconciliation. How might these same principles extend into other important professions such as education, urban planning, and cultural industries such as fashion and art?

From the perspective of librarians and information professionals, Métis Nation citizen Colette Poitras says that the priority is to make sure that all community members can access the Truth and Reconciliation Commission's (TRC) report and findings. In addition, she recommends that librarians purchase and provide books written by Indigenous authors and provide an inclusive space and programming opportunities that support Indigenous ways of knowing and being. Poitras facilitates Indigenous culture and history training and often hears that Canadians have missed out on learning the true history of Canada. Poitras says,

> Learning about the First Peoples of this country make all people richer by knowing more about the land on which we live and the Indigenous ways of knowing and being. It creates dialog and an ongoing relationship which includes respect and reciprocity. It makes individuals and society more tolerant, inclusive and empathetic. The sacred values of love, respect, honesty, humility, truth, wisdom, and courage are values that make society strong. These are values that everyone benefits from and that can lead to true reconciliation.

Dr. Frank Deer, Kanienkeha'ka from Kahnawake and professor of Indigenous Education at the University of Manitoba, believes that to be supportive, university faculty leaders should consider how Indigenous knowledge might be used in their own academic areas of endeavour and commit to change for the benefit of students and communities. For instance, what do they believe they are actually doing when making a land acknowledgement? What does reconciliation mean to them? When asked how people might benefit from understanding Indigenous ways, he comes to the conclusion by saying, "Indigenous Peoples are an important part of Canada's demographic, so coming to understand our experiences and identities will lend to the harmony within our social fabric." Dr. Deer believes that there is an important journey in formulating a new relationship between Indigenous and non-Indigenous people, and it must include a sense of our shared history.

Bob Montgomery, citizen of the Métis Nation, is the Indigenous Engagement Coordinator at the Beaver Hills Biosphere, a UNESCO Biosphere Reserve east of Edmonton. Montgomery says, "Only now in the ten-year wake of Idle No More and eight years after the TRC is western science starting to publish papers that acknowledge the brilliance of Indigenous environmental consciousness that exists in our worldviews and languages." When asked how the general public might benefit from his environmental work, he says, "It's quite simple really, Indigenous Peoples have lived on this land for millennia and it is in everyone's best interest to listen to them and follow their guidance on how to live harmoniously here." As an analogy we might all be able to relate to, he adds,

> You wouldn't spend an evening at a friend's house and immediately redesign the plumbing and the garden; there is knowledge already there of how things work in situ. Sometimes our communities are reluctant to share sacred or treasured information because of legacies of having their knowledge taken and sold for profit, never receiving any recognition or compensation. That is the legacy of colonialism. So if you are lucky enough to learn from Indigenous Peoples, follow their lead, make sure they are always included and compensate them and their communities fairly for the immense efforts they have made to keep that knowledge alive through all the violence they've endured.

Urban environments can also benefit by following the guidance of Indigenous Peoples. Crystal Many Fingers, Blackfoot academic and Indigenous landscape strategist for the City of Calgary, says, "When it comes to Indigenizing urban community space, there are levels of respect that must be addressed." Many Fingers describes the first level as,

> Engagement with all leadership of the Treaty Nations whose territorial land is under proposal. This engagement with leadership, Chief and Councils, may take time, but it is essential to work cooperatively with them to validate their support and respect their values. This must not be rushed, as is often the case under a colonial approach.

Secondly, she insists upon familiarity with the Assembly of First Nations (AFN) Principles of OCAP (ownership, control, access, and possession).

> This means that First Nations control data collection processes in their communities and own, protect, and control how their information is used. Access to First Nations data is important and First Nations determine, under appropriate mandates and protocols, how access to external researchers is facilitated and respected.[1]

When it comes to how the public can benefit from the implementation of Indigenous ways in city planning, Many Fingers expresses that, "The public needs to be given opportunities to learn about the rich history and ways of being of the land that they live and work on."

In the significant field of arts and culture, beading artist Trudy Wesley from the Stoney Nakoda First Nation says this regarding non-Indigenous people wearing Indigenous fashion:

1   The Assembly of First Nations (AFN) Principles of ownership, control, access, and possession (OCAP) can be found by scanning the QR code in the margin above.

If people wear Indigenous beading or other fashion elements without understanding, it could be considered cultural appropriation. On the other hand, many Indigenous artists create clothing and other cultural items that are meant to be shared and enjoyed by all people. Non-Indigenous people should strive to be respectful and mindful of Indigenous cultures and traditions, and should try to learn about the cultural significance of any items they wish to wear.

Dene artist and author Antoine Mountain summarizes with this recommendation:

Strive to be a cultural ally, become familiar with Indigenous rights and ways of being. Be enchanted with and spiritually uplifted by Indigenous cultural content in the Arts.

• • •

As an editorial team, we have a dedicated interest in the North. It has been a privilege to work with Chief Justice Shannon Smallwood of the Supreme Court of the Northwest Territories on the foreword for this book, and the lead chapter in this book, by the late Hon. Mr. Justice Thomas Berger, is about the sanctity of the lands of the North. Entitled "The Mackenzie Valley Pipeline Inquiry," this important speech from history reflects back on Justice Berger's decisions in the 1970s that prioritized the hunting, fishing, and trapping economy of the First Nations Peoples over pipeline construction, with its negative environmental implications. We are grateful to Beverley Berger, Erin Berger, and Drew Ann Wake for giving us permission to print the transcripts of this significant speech. It was presented by Justice Berger to the "World Conference of Faith, Science and the Future" at the Massachusetts Institute of Technology (MIT) in 1979.

The Honourable Nancy Morrison writes in the introduction to her three stories in this book,

> It was not until 1966 when I first read the *The Indian Act* that I began to realize the inequities and often-horrific abuses suffered by Indigenous Peoples and the need for society and our laws to make the necessary changes. Our society, laws, and justice system have shown they can and do evolve. The need and work must continue. I remain optimistic.

It is in the light of this optimism and the hope of rectification of wrongs that we gathered the stories of injustice and suffering for this book. Impacts of the Treaties and residential schools form a deep backstory to many of the heartbreaking chapters: Catherine Dunn's chapter about a family shattered by domestic violence; Judge John Reilly's chapter about adjudicating crimes committed as a result of traditional lands taken away; and Joseph Saulnier's defence of a boy who was born suffering from the effects of his mother's heavy drinking.

Also seen in the book, though, are vibrant stories of recovery and rehabilitation through the discovery and implementation of Indigenous Ways of Knowledge. Constable Val Hoglund's story "The Unwitting Criminal: Alone but Full of Hope" for example, about the recovery of a drug-addicted homeless teen, offers hope within the title itself, and Hon. John Z. Vertes' story, "The Case of Henry Innuksuk" is about a community in Nunavut that became an active participant in the justice system through Inuit healing techniques.

Some of the stories in this book, previously published in the Durvile True Cases anthologies, have been thoughtfully brought up to date by authors Hon. Kim Pate (The Story of S), Doug Heckbert (Getting FPS# Off Our Backs), and Hon. Nancy Morrison (Three Stories). The copyright page lists the stories that have appeared in previous books.

Our approach to decolonial scholarship with this book has been to follow the editorial principles and best practices of what has become known as "The Younging Style Guide."[2] Notwithstanding, we allowed the inclusion of colonial terminology when authors reflect on memories from years gone by, or when chapter text, or quotes from other texts, were written in earlier times.

If people were to ask us what we hope readers will come away with from *Indigenous Justice*, we might say:

> The belief that the legal professionals and law enforcement officers in this book truly give a care about reconciliation with Indigenous Peoples and that they'll spread this good work among their peers.

Taking action on Colette Poitras' advocacy earlier in this introduction, we as publishers and editors commit to the sacred values that make society strong: love, respect, honesty, humility, truth, wisdom, and courage. We truly give a care about reconciliation too.

— Dr. Lorene Shyba, co-editor &
Raymond Yakeleya, co-editor,
Calgary and Edmonton, Alberta, 2023

---

2   Gregory Younging, *Elements of Indigenous Style: A Guide for Writing By and About Indigenous Peoples*. (Edmonton, AB: Brush Education. 2018).

PART I

THE JUDGES
AND SENATOR

HON. THOMAS R. BERGER

HON. NANCY MORRISON

HON. JOHN REILLY

HON. KIM PATE

HON. JOHN Z. VERTES

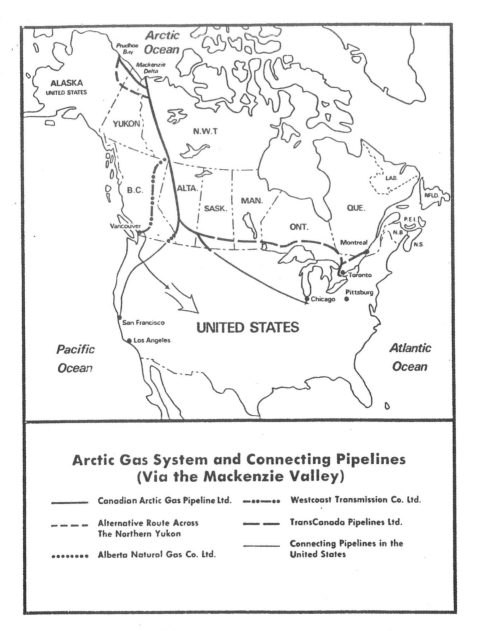

Arctic Gas System and Connecting Pipelines
(Via the Mackenzie Valley)

——————— Canadian Arctic Gas Pipeline Ltd.   —••—•• Westcoast Transmission Co. Ltd.

— — — — Alternative Route Across   — — — TransCanada Pipelines Ltd.
The Northern Yukon

••••••••• Alberta Natural Gas Co. Ltd.   ——————— Connecting Pipelines in the
United States

Map A. Original Arctic Gas pipeline plan, transporting gas from Prudhoe Bay across the north slope of Alaska and the Northern Yukon to the Mackenzie Delta, connecting with a pipeline transporting gas from the Delta and then run south along the Mackenzie Valley to the Alberta border and thence to cities in Canada and the US.

ONE

The Hon. Justice Thomas R. Berger

THE MACKENZIE VALLEY PIPELINE INQUIRY[1]

ے۔

SCIENCE AND TECHNOLOGY confront us with choices whose consequences are not easy to foresee. We know that science and technology can change our world. We used to think that the changes wrought by science and technology would be altogether benign, but in recent years another view has begun to take hold: that the advance of science and technology—especially large-scale technology—may entail social, economic, and environmental costs that must be reckoned with.

So, when the oil and gas industry proposed that a gas pipeline be built from the Arctic to the mid-continent, along a route from Alaska through Canada—along the Mackenzie Valley to the Lower 48—the Government of Canada appointed a Commission of Inquiry to examine the social, economic, and environmental impact of the proposed pipeline.

The Mackenzie Valley Pipeline Inquiry[2] may well be unique in Canadian experience, because for the first time we sought

---

1   This paper entitled "Science and Technology as Power" was presented by The Honourable Mr. Justice Thomas R. Berger of The Supreme Court of British Columbia, Commissioner, Mackenzie Valley Pipeline Inquiry 1974 to1977, to the "World Conference of Faith, Science and the Future" at the Massachusetts Institute of Technology (MIT), Cambridge, Massachusetts, on July 20, 1979.

2   The Inquiry was established on March 21, 1974. Hearings began on March 3, 1975, and were completed on November 19, 1976. The report of the Inquiry was handed in to the Government of Canada on May 9, 1977.

to determine the impact of a large-scale frontier project before and not after the fact.

The pipeline was to be built by Arctic Gas, a consortium of Canadian and American companies. They wanted to build a pipeline to transport gas from Prudhoe Bay across the north slope of Alaska and the Northern Yukon to the Mackenzie Delta, where it would connect with a pipeline transporting gas from the Delta and then run south along the Mackenzie Valley to the Alberta border and thence to metropolitan centres in Canada and the United States *(see Map A on page 8)*.

The Arctic Gas pipeline project would be the greatest project, in terms of capital expenditure, ever undertaken by private enterprise, anywhere. The Arctic Gas project would entail much more than a right-of-way. It would be a major construction project across our northern territories, across a land that is cold and dark in winter, a land largely inaccessible by rail or road, where it would be necessary to construct wharves, warehouses, storage sites, airstrips—a huge infrastructure—just to build the pipeline. There would have to be a network of hundreds of miles of roads built over the snow and ice.

The capacity of the fleet of tugs and barges on the Mackenzie River would have to be doubled. There would be 6,000 construction workers required North of 60° to build the pipeline, and 1,200 more to build the gas plants and gathering systems in the Mackenzie Delta. There would be 130 gravel mining operations. There would be 600 river and stream crossings. There would be pipe, trucks, heavy equipment, tractors, and aircraft. We were told that if a gas pipeline were built, it would result in enhanced oil and gas exploration activity all along the route of the pipeline throughout the Mackenzie Valley and the Western Arctic.

The Government of Canada decided that the gas pipeline, though it would be a vast project, should not be considered in isolation. The Government made it clear that the Inquiry was to consider what the impact would be if the gas pipeline were built and were followed by an oil pipeline.

What I have said will give you some notion of the magnitude of the Inquiry. I was to examine the social, economic, and environmental impact on the North of the proposed pipeline and energy corridor. The merit in such a comprehensive mandate is plain: the consequences of a large-scale frontier project inevitably combine social, economic, and environmental factors.

So, there was to be a public inquiry. The issues were to be canvassed in public. But how could the public participate effectively in the work of the Inquiry? After all, the Mackenzie Valley and the Western Arctic constitute a region as large as Western Europe. Though it is sparsely settled (only 30,000 people live in the region), it is inhabited by four Peoples: White, Indian, Inuit, and Métis, speaking six languages: English, Slavey, Loucheux, Dogrib, Chipewyan, and Eskimo. They were all entitled to be heard. *(Editors' note: The Northwest Territories [NWT] recognizes 11 official languages. Languages referred to in this chapter are now known as North Slavey Dene, South Slavey Dene, Gwich'in, Tlicho, Chipewyan, and Inuktitut).*

Governments have lots of money. So does the oil and gas industry. So do the pipeline companies. But how were the Native people going to be able to participate? How was the environmental interest to be represented? If the Inquiry was to be fair and complete, all of these interests had to be represented. A funding program was established for those groups which had an interest that ought to be represented, but whose means would not allow it. On my recommendation, funding was provided by the Government of Canada to the Native organizations, the environmental groups, northern municipalities, and northern businesses, to enable them to participate in the hearings on an equal footing (so far as that might be possible) with the pipeline companies—to enable them to support, challenge, or seek to modify the project. These groups received $1,773,918. The cost of the Inquiry altogether came to $5.3 million.

In funding these groups, I took the view that there was no substitute for letting them have the money and decide for themselves how to spend it, independently of the Government and of the Inquiry. If they were to be independent, to make their own decisions, and present the evidence that they thought vital, they had to be provided with the funds, and there could be no strings attached. They had, however, to account to the Inquiry for the money spent. All this they did.

Let me illustrate the rationale for this by referring to the environment. It is true that Arctic Gas carried out extensive environmental studies, which cost a great deal of money. But they had an interest: they wanted to build the pipeline. This was a perfectly legitimate interest, but not one that could necessarily be reconciled with the environmental interest. It was felt there should be representation by a group with a special interest in the northern environment, a group without any other interest that might deflect it from the presentation of the case for the environment.

Funds were provided to an umbrella organization, "The Northern Assessment Group" that was established by the environmental groups to enable them to carry out their own research and hire staff and to ensure that they could participate in the Inquiry as advocates on behalf of the environment. In this way, the environmental interest was made a part of the whole hearing process. The same applied to the other interests that were represented at the hearings. The result was that witnesses were examined and then cross-examined not simply to determine whether the pipeline project was feasible from an engineering point of view but to make sure that such things as the impact of an influx of construction workers on communities, the impact of pipeline construction and corridor development on the hunting, trapping, and fishing economy of the

Native people, and the impact on northern municipalities and northern business, were all taken into account.

The usefulness of the funding that was provided was amply demonstrated. All concerned showed an awareness of the magnitude of the task. The funds supplied to the interventors, although substantial, should be considered in the light of the estimated cost of the project itself, and of the amount expended, approximately $50 million by the pipeline companies, in assembling their own evidence.

The Inquiry held two types of hearings: formal hearings and community hearings. The hearings went on for 21 months.

The formal hearings were held at Yellowknife, the capital of the Northwest Territories. At these formal hearings, expert witnesses for all parties could be heard and cross examined. The proceedings resembled, in many ways, a trial in a courtroom. It was at Yellowknife that we heard the evidence of the experts: the scientists, the engineers, the biologists, the anthropologists, the economists—people from a multitude of disciplines, who have studied the northern environment, northern conditions, and northern peoples. Three hundred expert witnesses testified at the formal hearings.

At the formal hearings, all the parties were represented: the pipeline companies, the oil and gas industry, the Native organizations, the environmental groups, the Northwest Territories Association of Municipalities, and the Northwest Territories Chamber of Commerce. All were given a chance to question and challenge the things that the experts said, and all were entitled, of course, to call expert witnesses of their own.

In recent years the Government of Canada has carried out a multitude of studies on the North. These studies cost $15 million. The oil and gas industry carried out studies on the pipeline that we were told cost something like $50 million. Our universities have been carrying on constant research on northern problems and northern conditions. It would have been no good to let all these studies and reports just sit on the shelves. Where

these reports contained evidence that was vital to the work of
the Inquiry, they were examined in public so that any conflicts
could be disclosed, and where parties at the Inquiry wished to
challenge them, they had an opportunity to do so. It meant that
opinions could be challenged and tested in public.

At the same time, community hearings were held in each
city and town, settlement, and village in the Mackenzie Valley
and the Western Arctic. There is a tendency for visitors to the
Mackenzie Valley and the Western Arctic to call at Yellowknife,
the centre of government, and at Inuvik, the centre of the oil
and gas play in the 1970s. They see very little else. But there
are 35 communities in the region. And the majority of these
communities are Native communities. In fact, the Native people constitute the majority of the permanent residents. I held
hearings at all of these communities. At these hearings, the
people living in the communities were given the opportunity
to tell the Inquiry in their own languages—and in their own
way—what their lives and their experience led them to believe
the impact of a pipeline and an energy corridor would be.

In this way, we tried to have the best of the experience of
both worlds: at the community hearings, the world of every
day, where most witnesses spend their lives, and at the formal
hearings, which was the world of the professionals, the specialists and the academics.

In order to give people— not just the spokesmen for Native
organizations and for the white community, but all people—
an opportunity to speak their minds, the Inquiry remained in
each community as long as was necessary for every person who
wanted to speak to do so. In many villages, a large proportion
of the adult population addressed the Inquiry. Not that par-
ticipation was limited to adults. Some of the most perceptive
presentations were given by young people, concerned no less
than their parents about their land and their future.

I found that ordinary people, with the experience of life
in the North, had a great deal to contribute. I heard from

almost one thousand witnesses at the community hearings: in English (and occasionally in French), in Loucheux *(Gwich'in)*, Slavey *(North Slavey Dene and South Slavey Dene)*, Dogrib *(Tlicho)*, Chipewyan, and in the Inuit *(Inuktitut)* language of the Western Arctic. They used direct speech. They seldom had written briefs. Their thoughts were not filtered through a screen of jargon. They were talking about their innermost concerns and fears.

You may say, what can ordinary people tell the planners and the policy-makers in government and in industry? The conventional wisdom is that a decision like this should only be made by the people in government and industry: they have the knowledge, they have the facts and they have the experience. Well, the hearings showed that the conventional wisdom is wrong. I found that ordinary people who lived in the region had a great deal that was worthwhile to say. We discovered what should have been obvious all along: that the judgment of the planners and policymakers at their desks in Ottawa and Yellowknife might not always be right.

The contributions of ordinary people were important in the assessment of even the most technical subjects. For example, I based my findings on the biological vulnerability of the Beaufort Sea not only on the evidence of the biologists who testified at the formal hearings but also on the views of the Inuit hunters who spoke at the community hearings. The same is true of seabed ice scour and of oil spills: they are complex, technical subjects but our understanding of them was nonetheless enriched by testimony from people who live in the region.

Let me give another example: when North America's most renowned caribou biologists testified at the Inquiry, they described the life cycle, habitat dependencies, and migrations of the Porcupine caribou herd. Expert evidence from anthropologists, sociologists, and geographers described the Native peoples' dependency on caribou from a number of different perspectives.

Doctors testified about the nutritional value of country food such as caribou, and about the consequences of a change in diet. Then the Native people spoke for themselves at the community hearings about the caribou herd as a link with their past, as a present-day source of food and as security for the future. Only in this way could the whole picture be put together.

The testimony of the people at the community hearings was of even greater importance in connection with the assessment of social and economic impact. The issue of Native claims was linked to all of these subjects. At the formal hearings, land use and occupancy evidence was presented in support of Native claims through prepared testimony and map exhibits. There the evidence was scrutinized and witnesses for the Native organization were cross-examined by counsel for the other participants. By contrast, at the community hearings, people spoke spontaneously and at length about both their traditional and their present-day use of the land and its resources. Their testimony was often painstakingly detailed and richly illustrated with anecdotes.

The most important contribution of the community hearings was, I think, the insight it gave us into the true nature of Native claims. No academic treatise or discussion, no formal presentation of the claims of Native people by the Native organizations and their leaders, could offer as compelling and vivid a picture of the goals and aspirations of Native people as their own testimony did. In no other way could we have discovered the depth of feeling regarding past wrongs and future hopes, and the determination of Native people to assert their collective identity today and in years to come.

The Inquiry faced, at an early stage, the problem of enabling the people in the far-flung settlements of the Mackenzie Valley and the Western Arctic to participate in the work of the Inquiry. When you are consulting local people, the consultation should not be perfunctory. But when you have such a vast area, when you have four different peoples speaking six languages, how do you enable them to participate? How do you keep them informed? We wished to create an Inquiry without walls. We sought, therefore, to use technology to make the Inquiry truly public, to extend the walls of the hearing room to encompass the entire North. We tried to bring the Inquiry to the people. This meant that it was the Inquiry, and the representatives of the media accompanying it—not the people of the North— that were obliged to travel.

The Northern Service of the Canadian Broadcasting Corporation (CBC) played an especially important part in the Inquiry process. The Northern Service provided a crew of broadcasters who broadcast across the North highlights of each day's testimony at the Inquiry. Every day that there were hearings, they broadcast both in English and in the Native languages from wherever the Inquiry was sitting. In this way, the people in communities throughout the North were given a daily report, in their own languages, on the evidence that had been given at both the formal hearings and the community hearings. The broadcasts meant that when we went into the communities, the people living there understood something of what had been said by the experts at the formal hearings, and by people in the communities that we had already visited. The broadcasters were, of course, entirely independent of the Inquiry.

The media, in a way, served as the eyes and ears of all Northerners, indeed of all Canadians, especially when the Inquiry visited places that few Northerners had ever seen, and few of their countrymen had even heard of. The Inquiry had a high profile in the media. As a result, there was public interest and concern in the work of the Inquiry throughout Canada.

When the Inquiry's report, entitled *Northern Frontier, Northern Homeland*, was made public on May 9th, 1977, it was a bestseller, and remained on the Canadian bestseller list for six months.

The pipeline issue confronted us in Canada with the necessity of weighing fundamental values: industrial, social, and environmental, in a way that we had not had to face before. The Northern Native people, along with many witnesses at the Inquiry, insisted that the land they have long depended upon would be injured by the construction of a pipeline and the establishment of an energy corridor. Environmentalists pointed out that the North, the last great wilderness area of Canada, is slow to recover from environmental degradation: its protection is, therefore, of vital importance to all Canadians.

It is not easy to measure that concern against the more precisely calculated interests of industry. You cannot measure environmental values in dollars and cents. But still, we had to try and face the questions that are posed in the North of today: Should we open up the North as we opened up the West? Should the values that conditioned our attitudes toward the environment in the past prevail in the North today and tomorrow?

The North is immense. But within this vast area are tracts of land and water that are vital to the survival of whole populations of certain species of mammals, birds, and fish at certain times of the year. This concern with critical habitat lay at the heart of my consideration of environmental issues. I urged that the Northern Yukon, north of the Porcupine River, be designated a national wilderness park.

Let me tell you why. The Northern Yukon is an arctic and subarctic wilderness of incredible beauty, a rich and varied ecosystem: nine million acres of land in its natural state, inhabited by thriving populations of plants and animals. This wilderness has come down through the ages, and it is a heritage that future generations, living in an industrial world even more complex than ours, will surely cherish.

If you were to build a pipeline from Alaska along the Arctic coast of the Yukon, you would be opening up the calving grounds of the Porcupine caribou herd. This is one of the last great herds of caribou, 110,000 animals, in North America. Every spring they journey from the mountains in the interior of the Yukon to the calving grounds on the Arctic coast. There, they are able to leave the wolves behind, they can forage on cotton grass, and they can bear their young before the onset of summer mosquitoes and bot flies.

In late August, as many as 500,000 snow geese gather on the Arctic Coastal Plain to feed on the tundra grasses, sedges, and berries, before embarking on the flight to their wintering grounds.

They must build up an energy surplus to sustain them for their long, southward migration to California, the Gulf Coast, or Central and South America. The peregrine falcon, golden eagle and other birds of prey nest in the Northern Yukon. These species are dwindling in numbers because of the loss of their former ranges on the North American continent and because of toxic materials in the environment. Here, in these remote mountains, they still nest and rear their young, undisturbed by humanity.

The proposal by Arctic Gas to build a pipeline across the Northern Yukon confronted us with a fundamental choice. It was a choice that depended not simply upon the impact of a pipeline across the Northern Yukon but upon the impact of the establishment of an energy corridor across it. This ecosystem, with its magnificent wilderness and scenic beauty, has always been protected by its inaccessibility. With pipeline construction, the development of supply and service roads, the intensification of the search for oil and gas, the establishment of an energy corridor, and the increasing occupation of the region, it would no longer be inaccessible to man and his machines.

The wilderness does not stop, of course, at the boundary between Alaska and the Yukon. The Arctic National Wildlife Range in northeastern Alaska, contiguous to the northern Yukon, is a part of the same wilderness. In fact, the calving grounds of the Porcupine Caribou herd extend well into

Alaska, along the coastal plain as far as Camden Bay, a hundred miles to the west of the international boundary; the area of concentrated use by staging snow geese, by nesting and moulting waterfowl and by seabirds, also extends far into Alaska. So, the future of the caribou, of the birds— of the whole of this unique wilderness region—was a matter of concern to both Canada and the United States.

Let me refer to another international resource, the white whales of the Beaufort Sea. I recommended that a whale sanctuary be established in Mackenzie Bay. In summer the white whales of the Beaufort Sea converge on the Mackenzie Delta to calve. Why? Because the Mackenzie River rises in Alberta and BC and carries warm water to the Arctic. So, the whales, some five thousand animals, remain in the vicinity of the Delta throughout the summer, then leave for the open sea. For these animals, the warm waters around the Mackenzie Delta, especially Mackenzie Bay, are a critical habitat, for here they have their young. Here in these warm waters, the whales stay until the calves acquire enough blubber to survive in the cold oceanic water. Nowhere else, so far as we know, can they go for this essential part of their life cycle. Dr. David Sergeant of the Department of the Environment, Canada's leading authority on white whales, summarizing his evidence to the Inquiry stated:

> ...the population of white whales which calves in the Mackenzie is virtually the whole of the population of the Beaufort Sea. I postulate that simultaneous oil and gas activities throughout the whole Delta in July each year could so disturb the whale herd that they would be unable to reproduce successfully. In time, the herd would die out. If we wish to maintain the herd, we must initiate measures now which we can be certain will allow its successful reproduction annually.

Is a whale sanctuary in west Mackenzie Bay a practical proposition? What will its effect be on future oil and gas exploration? Will it impose an unacceptable check on oil and gas exploration and development in the Mackenzie Delta and the Beaufort Sea? We are fortunate in that the areas of intense petroleum exploration, to date, lie east of the proposed whale sanctuary, both offshore and onshore. A whale sanctuary can be set aside, and oil and gas activity can be forbidden there without impairing industry's ability to tap the principal sources of petroleum beneath the Beaufort Sea.

We in Canada have looked upon the North as our last frontier. It is natural for us to think of developing the North, of subduing the land, populating it with people from the metropolitan centres, and extracting its resources to fuel our industry and heat our homes. Our whole inclination is to think in terms of expanding our industrial machine to the limit of our country's frontiers. We have never had to consider the uses of restraint, to determine what is the most intelligent use to make of our resources.

The question that we and many other countries face is: Are we serious people, willing and able to make up our own minds, or are we simply driven, by technology and egregious pattern of consumption, to deplete our resources wherever and whenever we find them?

I do not want to be misunderstood about this. I did not propose that we shut up the North as a kind of living folk museum and zoological gardens. I proceeded on the assumption that, in due course, we will require the gas and oil of the Western Arctic, and that they will have to be transported along the Mackenzie Valley to markets in the metropolitan centres of North America. I also proceeded on the assumption that we intend to protect and preserve Canada's northern environment and that, above all else, we intend to honour the legitimate claims and aspirations of the Native people. All of these assumptions were embedded in the Government of Canada's expressed Northern policy for the 1970s.

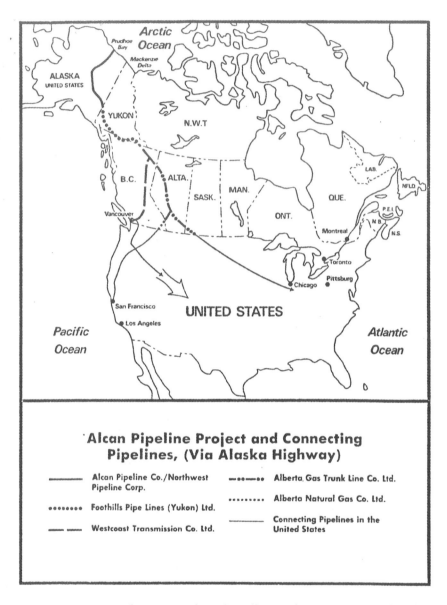

Alcan Pipeline Project and Connecting Pipelines, (Via Alaska Highway)

——— Alcan Pipeline Co./Northwest Pipeline Corp.	—••—•• Alberta, Gas Trunk Line Co. Ltd.
•••••••• Foothills Pipe Lines (Yukon) Ltd.	•••••••• Alberta Natural Gas Co. Ltd.
— —— Westcoast Transmission Co. Ltd.	——— Connecting Pipelines in the United States

Map B. Alternate pipeline plan, allowing for an international wilderness park in the Northern Yukon and Northeastern Alaska. Construction of this pipeline, along the Alaska Highway, would not threaten major populations of any species.

I sought to reconcile these goals: industrial, social, and environmental. I proposed an international wilderness park in the Northern Yukon and Northeastern Alaska and urged that no pipeline cross it, but at the same time, I indicated that the Alaska Highway route, as a corridor for the transportation of Alaskan gas to the Lower 48, was preferable from an environmental point of view. This route lies hundreds of miles to the south and to the west of the critical habitat for caribou, whales, and wildlife which I sought to preserve. Construction of a pipeline along the Alaska Highway route would not threaten major populations of any species. If a pipeline has to be built, then it ought to be along this route *(see Map B on page 22)*. I proposed a whale sanctuary in Mackenzie Bay, but I limited its boundaries to waters where no discoveries of gas or oil have yet been made *(see Map C on page 24)*.

I recommended the establishment of bird sanctuaries in the Mackenzie Delta and the Mackenzie Valley. Oil and gas exploration and development would not be forbidden within these sanctuaries, but it would be subject to the jurisdiction of the Canadian Wildlife Service.

I advised the Government of Canada that a pipeline corridor is feasible, from an environmental point of view, to transport gas and oil from the Mackenzie Delta along the Mackenzie Valley to the Alberta border. At the same time, however, I recommended that we should postpone the construction of such a pipeline for 10 years, in order to strengthen Native society, the Native economy—indeed, the whole renewable resource sector—and to enable Native claims to be settled.

This recommendation was based on the evidence of the Native people. Virtually all of the Native people who spoke to the Inquiry said that their claims had to be settled before any pipeline could be built. It should not be thought that Native people had an irrational fear of pipelines. They realized, however, that construction of the pipeline and establishment of the energy corridor would mean an influx of tens of thousands of

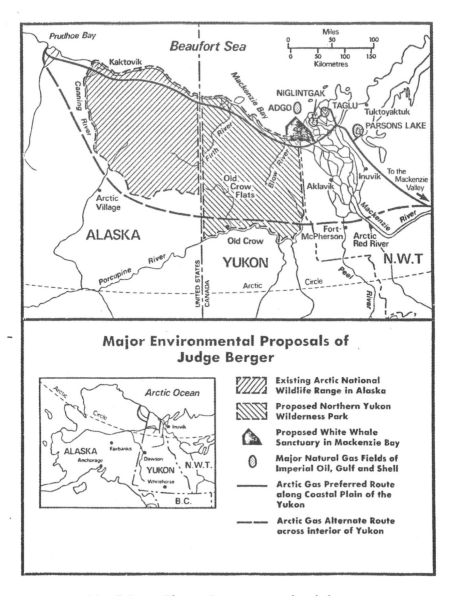

Map C. Justice Thomas Berger proposed a whale sanctuary
in Mackenzie Bay, limiting its boundaries to waters where no
discoveries of gas or oil had yet been made.

white people from all over Canada seeking jobs and opportunities. They believed that they would be overwhelmed, that their Native villages would become white towns, and they would be relegated to the fringes of northern life.

They realized that the pipeline and all that it would bring in its wake would lead to an irreversible shift in social, economic, and political power in the North. They took the position that no pipeline should be built until their claims had been settled.

They believed that the building of the pipeline would bring with it complete dependence on the industrial system, and that would entail a future which would have no place for the values they cherish. Native people insist that their culture is still a vital force in their lives.

The culture of Native people amounts to more than crafts and carvings. Their tradition of decision-making by consensus, their respect for the wisdom of their Elders, their concept of the extended family, their belief in a special relationship with the land, their regard for the environment, and their willingness to share—all of these values persist in one form or another within their own culture, even though they have been under unremitting pressure to abandon them. Their claims are the means by which they seek to preserve their culture, their values, and their identity.

The emergence of Native claims should not surprise us. After years of poor achievement in our schools, after years of living on the fringes of an economy that has no place for them as workers or consumers, and without the political power to change these things, the Native people have now decided that they want to substitute self-determination for enforced dependency.

Settlement of their claims ought to offer the Native people a whole range of opportunities: the strengthening of the hunting, fishing, and trapping economy where that is appropriate; the development of the local logging and lumbering industry;

development of the fishing industry; and of recreation and conservation. I urged in my report that in the North, priority be given to local renewable resource activities—not because I feel that such activities are universally desirable, but because they are on a scale appropriate to many Native communities. They are activities that local people can undertake, that are amenable to local management and control, and that are related to traditional values. But that need not exclude access to the larger economy—where large-scale technology predominates.

It will take time to learn these claims, especially as regards their implications for Native people entering urban life. Nevertheless, some elements are clear enough: for instance, Native people say they want schools where children can learn Native languages, Native history, Native lore, and Native rights. At the same time, they want their children to learn to speak English or French, as the case may be, and to study mathematics, science, and all the subjects that they need to know in order to function in the dominant society. These proposals are not limited to a frontier or rural context.

It is not only we in Canada who must face the challenge that the presence of Native peoples with their own languages and their own cultures presents. There are all the countries of the Western Hemisphere with their Indigenous minorities— peoples who will not be assimilated, and whose fierce wish to retain their own common identity is intensifying as industry, technology, and communications forge a larger and larger mass culture, extruding diversity.

The judgments that we had to make about these questions were not merely scientific and technical. They were at the end of the day value judgments. It is impossible—indeed, it is undesirable—to try to lift scientific and technological decisions out of their social and environmental context, to disentangle them from the web of moral and ethical considerations which provide the means of truly understanding the impact they will have.

What I have said will give you some idea of the magnitude of our task. The Inquiry had to weigh a whole series of matters, some tangible, some intangible. But in the end, no matter how many experts there may be, no matter how many pages of computer printouts may have been assembled, there is the ineluctable necessity of bringing human judgment to bear on the main issues. Indeed, when the main issue cuts across a range of questions, spanning the physical and social sciences, the only way to come to grips with it and to resolve it is by the exercise of human judgment.

The Government of Canada rejected the Arctic Gas pipeline proposal and decided that, if a pipeline were to be built, it should be along the Alaska Highway route, that is, along the alternate route that I urged be considered. Now the Government of Canada and the Government of the United States have agreed on the construction of a gas pipeline along the Alaska Highway route.

I think a fuller understanding of the northern environment emerged during the course of the Inquiry. The proposals made for the creation of an international wilderness park in the Yukon and Alaska, for a whale sanctuary in Mackenzie Bay, and for bird sanctuaries in the Mackenzie Delta and the Mackenzie Valley have attracted widespread support in Canada and the United States. There is a felt need and a perceived responsibility to preserve critical habitat for caribou, whales, wildlife, and wilderness, and there is an understanding of the special vulnerability of migratory species in the North to industrial advance. The foundations have been laid for the development of a firm policy designed to protect the northern environment. In fact, the goal lies within our reach.

The Government of Canada announced in July last year *(eds.—1978)* that it was withdrawing the Northern Yukon, north of the Porcupine River, an area of 9.6 million acres, or 38,700 km. (15,000 square miles) from new industrial development with a view to establishing the area as Canada's first

wilderness park, subject to traditional Native hunting, fishing, and trapping activities in the area. The Carter administration has proposed that the Arctic National Wildlife Range
on the United States' side of the International Boundary
should be designated wilderness. Canada has established a
scientific committee on whales. The committee is examining
the proposal I made for the establishment of a whale sanctuary in Mackenzie Bay.

As to Native claims, the decision not to build the Arctic
Gas pipeline gives us and the Native people, the time to
achieve a fair settlement of Native claims in the Mackenzie
Valley and the Western Arctic—an opportunity to meet what
I believe is Canada's greatest challenge in the North.

It will take time to settle these claims They constitute the
foundation upon which future development of renewable
and nonrenewable resources in the North can take place.
Settlement will not be easy to achieve. There is a quite natural tendency for governments to look upon Native claims
as something which can be settled swiftly around the table
by men and women of good will—to regard Native claims as
a problem to be solved, as a clearing of the decks to enable
large-scale industrial development to proceed. But here, perceptions differ. For Native people, their claims constitute the
means of working out the institutional relationships between
themselves and the dominant white society. For them, it is
not a problem to be solved but the means to the preservation
of their culture, their languages, and their economic mode—
the means by which they can continue to assert their distinct
identity in our midst and still have access to the social, economic, and political institutions of the dominant society.

The settlement of Native claims ought to provide the
means to enable Native people to thrive and Native culture
to develop in ways denied to them in the past; the means
to ensure that they know who they are and where they
came from. They can become hunters, trappers, fishermen,

lawyers, loggers, doctors, nurses, teachers, or workers in the oil and gas fields. But most important of all, the collective fabric of Native life will be affirmed and strengthened. The sense of identity of individual Native people—indeed, their very well-being—depends on it.

This is an unusual, perhaps unprecedented outcome—a recognition that industrial goals do not at all times and in all places take precedence over environmental values and Native rights. The pipeline debate is, in one sense, over. But it has precipitated another debate, a debate about some fundamental issues which were thrown into relief by the pipeline proposals: the need of the metropolis for energy, the implications of the advance of the industrial system to the frontier, the protection of the northern environment, and, above all, the rights of the Native people. Canadians perceived in these questions something that was basic to them all: a broad moral and ethical dimension.

Since the Industrial Revolution, we have thought of industrialization as the means to prosperity and wellbeing. And so, it has been to many people and to many parts of the world. But the rise of the industrial system has been accompanied by a belief in an ever-expanding cycle of growth and consumption. We should now be asking whether it is a goal that will suffice. Ought we and our children continue to aspire to the idea of unlimited growth? And, equally important, ought the Third World to aspire to this goal?

Our belief in an ever-expanding cycle of growth and consumption conditions our capacity and our willingness to reconsider or even contemplate, the true goals of the industrial system. There is a feeling that we cannot pause to consider where we are headed for fear of what we shall find out about ourselves. Yet events are pressing hard upon us.

Until 1875, the principal source of energy on this continent was wood. From 1875 until 1950, it was coal. Since then, our principal source of energy has been oil and gas. In the last 15 years *(ed. 1962 to 1977)*, world use of energy has doubled. North America now uses about five times as much energy as is consumed in the whole of Asia, and per capita consumption is about 24 times higher. The United States each year wastes more fossil fuel than is used by two-thirds of the world's population. According to the Energy Research Project at Harvard Business School, the United States uses a third of all the oil used in the world every day. A seventh of the oil used in the world every day is used on U.S. highways.

Certainly, if anything is plain, it must be plain that we on this continent shall have to get along with a smaller proportion of the world's energy and resources. This entails a reconsideration of conventional wisdom. I am not urging that we dismantle the industrial system. It has been the means to the material wellbeing of millions and an engine of prosperity for many countries. But I do say that we must pause and consider to what extent our national objectives are determined by the need for the care and feeding of the industrial machine.

To a large extent, we have conditioned ourselves to believe that the onward march of industry and technology cannot and must not be impeded or diverted. Our notions of progress have acquired a technological and industrial definition. Even our terminology has become eccentric. Those who seek to conserve the environment are described as radicals, and those who are undertaking radical interventions in the natural world think of themselves as conservatives.

Thus, the debate about the future often tends to become a barren exchange of epithets.

The issues are, in fact, profound ones, going beyond the ideological conflicts that have occupied the world for so long; conflicts over who was going to run the industrial machine and who was going to get the benefits. Now we are being asked: How much energy does it take to run the industrial machine, where does the energy come from, where is the machine going, and what happens to the people who live in the path of the machine?

I have said that we believe in an ever-expanding cycle of growth and consumption. This is the secular religion of our time.

The great agency of change throughout the world is industrial man. He and his technology, armed with immense political and administrative power and prepared to transform the social and natural landscape in the interest of a particular kind of society and economy, have a way of soon becoming pervasive. Industrial man is equally the creature of East and West. And of the Third World too. Many of the governments of the Third World share our commitment to endless growth, even though they may have no real prospect of achieving it. And this is so, whether they purport to share the ideology of the West or call themselves Marxist.

Our ideas are still the ideas of the mid-19th century: the era of the triumph of liberal capitalism and the challenge of Marxism, the era of Adam Smith, and the Communist Manifesto. Both of these creeds are the offspring of the Industrial Revolution. Capitalism (and I include under this heading all the regimes of the industrialized democracies as variants on the capitalist economic model) and communism constitute two forms of materialism competing for the allegiance of people in the world today. Neither has yet come to grips with the necessity for rethinking the goals of the industrial system. Yet the consequences of large-scale technology, out of control, can be seen around the world: tankers cracking up on the beaches; the ongoing destruction of the tropical rain forests of the Amazon; infant formula being sold indiscriminately in the Third World; the mining of soils in many countries.

Can the nations of the Third World achieve the levels of growth and consumption that have been achieved by industrialized countries? If they cannot—if the consumption of natural resources at a rate necessary to enable them to do so (not to mention the concomitant increase in pollution) is not possible in a practical sense—then what? We have been unwilling to face up to the moral and ethical questions that this would raise for all of us.

Thomas Rodney Berger QC OC OBC was a Canadian politician and jurist. He was briefly a member of the House of Commons of Canada in the early 1960s and was a justice of the Supreme Court of British Columbia from 1971 to 1983. In 1974, he became the royal commissioner of the Mackenzie Valley Pipeline Inquiry, which released its findings in 1977. He was a member of the Order of Canada and the Order of British Columbia. Justice Berger died on April 28, 2021.

TWO

The Hon. Nancy Morrison

THREE STORIES

A S AN ARDENT MEMBER of the law profession and judicial
system for over 50 years, it is difficult for me to relate stories in our courts and in our laws of willful blindness, discrimination, abuses, and lack of respect. But the need for awareness
of the problems precedes necessary law reform.

In 1958, as a first-year law student, I began to understand
the lack of rights, respect, and remedies accorded females in
society and the law. It was not until 1966, when I first read the
Indian Act that I began to realize the inequities and often-hor-
rific abuses suffered by Indigenous Peoples and the need for
society and our laws to make the necessary changes. Our society, laws, and justice system have shown they can and do evolve.
The need and work must continue. I remain optimistic.

KAMSACK, THURSDAY, 10 A.M.
1966. KAMSACK, SASKATCHEWAN

It was Thursday, an autumn day, and I was headed for Kamsack.
The poplars had turned yellow, and the harvest was almost finished. I knew my case, an impaired driving, would not be called
until later in the morning, so I could listen to Bruno Gerussi's
radio program until 10:00 a.m., then go into the courtroom.
The building also housed the local RCMP detachment and cells.

Kamsack is a picturesque prairie town in Saskatchewan where the Whitesand River joins the larger Assiniboine River, the aboriginal and early trappers' highway through the prairies. I had just begun practising law in Saskatchewan after three and a half years in Ontario, and although I was comfortable doing criminal and civil litigation, I felt I was the new kid in town who had to establish her own credentials.

The courtroom was filled. Thursday was court day in Kamsack. Mostly Indigenous people and RCMP officers filled the small courtroom. North of Kamsack are First Nation reserves, the Cote First Nation, the Keeseekoose First Nation and the Key First Nation.

The judge was a younger man, bright, and with a good sense of humour. I took out my yellow pad to start a letter while I waited for my case to come up. It would be a while, from the look of the court docket. A couple of quick matters were dealt with, which I tuned out, and then his case was called—an older Indigenous man from one of the reserves, who had been in the RCMP detachment cells overnight. The RCMP officer who was serving as clerk of the court called out his name.

The man stood up on shaky feet and was brusquely told to come forward. The man looked unwell, and confused. A woman got up from the courtroom and came toward the front of the court with great hesitation, saying, "He is my father. He does not speak English or understand much. Can I help him?"

Everyone was quiet in the courtroom. There was a nod of assent from the judge. The woman stayed beside her parent, very still. Where was the interpreter? You cannot conduct a case unless the accused understands every word that is spoken in the courtroom. That was so basic it never occurred to me that there were courts conducted otherwise. There was no court interpreter here.

No longer tuning out, I began to watch. The clerk/officer picked up the information and bellowed out the charges against the old man in a rapid singsong fashion, words so familiar to the officer they had achieved a rhythm. Being drunk in a public place and drinking off the reserve seemed to be the charges, but I missed the exact words, they were spoken so quickly.

The man looked bewildered. His daughter murmured briefly to him, but she did not look as if she had caught all that had been read out so quickly.

"Do you understand the charges?" Silence. The old man's eyes were downcast, and he looked ill.

"Do you understand the charges?" More insistent this time. The daughter tried to murmur to her father, but he still looked bewildered, humiliated.

"How do you plead? Guilty or not guilty?" The confusion seemed to increase for the old man. The audience sat very still. They could not help their neighbour. Some of them were next. The miserable couple standing were on their own.

Irritation and impatience were beginning to show on the judge, and the police. It would be a long morning if this kept up.

"Note that as a 'not guilty' plea and present your case," instructed the judge. A police officer was called to the witness stand, sworn in, and gave his evidence in a quick and professional manner to the court. He related when and where the previous night he had apprehended the accused, related how very drunk he had found him to be, and how he had placed him in the cells for the night.

The man and his daughter were still standing. They had not been invited to take a seat. There was no effort to ensure that the old man had understood the testimony of the officer or that it was fully interpreted; there were no pauses for any translation. The daughter murmured to her father, but not enough to match the words of the policemen.

"Do you want to ask the policeman any questions?" The look of confusion increased. A shrug from the judge, along with a look on the man's face that showed he begged to be left alone, in a place far from the courtroom.

"All right, step down," the judge said, dismissing the police officer who had given the evidence. That was the evidence for the Crown. The Crown's case was closed. I sat stunned. The accused had not followed everything, as far as I could see. Worse, I had failed to jump up and intervene as a 'friend of the court'.

"Do you wish to present any evidence on your own behalf?" Why were they yelling every time the clerk or the judge spoke to him?

"Do you want to testify?" A shrug to the daughter, then some murmuring between the two, both looking confused. The impatience of the court was becoming more obvious.

"All right, come forward. Come and take the stand. Come forward." This from the judge, motioning for the accused to come ahead into the witness box.

The daughter gently pushed her father forward and he was waved into the witness box. The daughter stayed behind, still standing, unsure of where she should go, but no longer at her father's side, no longer talking to him quietly. The judge did not invite her to come closer so she could interpret for her father.

A Bible was thrust into the old man's hands, and the clerk officer bellowed to him, "Do-you-promise-to-tell-the-truth-the-whole-truth-and-nothing-but-the-truth-so-help-you-God?" It was run off like a round from an M-16, all one long word. The old man's downcast eyes looked up briefly. The officer yelled out the oath once again, even faster this time, if that were possible.

Silence from the man and his daughter.

A questioning look was exchanged between the officer who was prosecuting the case and the judge. A wry shrug from this judge, whose sense of humour I had once admired. This was also a judge who enjoyed a close personal relationship with most of the police officers, a difficult position for any judge, in any community.

The accused stood there, seemingly unable to understand

what he was supposed to do in the witness stand, still clutch-
ing the Bible that had been put in his hands.

Then the judge said it.

"Give him a mickey to swear on. He'll understand that."

The policemen all laughed, and so did the judge. No one
else in the courtroom did. I was appalled.

The man gave no evidence. He was convicted. The judge
said to him, "I've told you, every time you are convicted of one
of these offences, the fine goes up another five dollars. This
time it is $65. In default of payment, five days in jail. Do you
have the money to pay the fine?" The daughter told the court
that her father did not, so the old man was taken back to jail.

Kamsack, Thursday, 10:00 a.m., where there was an absence
of respect, fairness, due process, and justice in a courtroom by
those entrusted with the law.

What was this about? Indians not being allowed to drink?
This was 1966. I knew nothing about the *Indian Act*, a statute
never mentioned at law school. On returning to Yorkton after
my case finished, I stopped by our office and picked up a copy
of the *Indian Act* to take home and read that evening. It was an
epiphany. As fine a piece of apartheid legislation as one could
hope to find in the world. One law for whites, another for subjugated Indians.

It was the beginning of my understanding that minority
rights extended far beyond women's rights. I became aware
of the *Indian Act*, but not the residential schools. Residential
schools were virtually unknown then to all but government
officials, administrators of the *Indian Act*, the churches
involved and the Indigenous communities themselves. The
enforced enrollments in those schools were still being man-
dated when I began practising in Yorkton. I knew nothing
about them. The last residential school to close in Canada was
in Saskatchewan in 1996, the Gordon Residential School.

My aboriginal clients never spoke of their time or treatment in those schools. The schools were never mentioned

in Pre-sentence Reports ordered by the courts. The existence, mistreatments and cruel legacy of those schools did not become public knowledge or understood until decades later. That belated understanding continues.

AN UNUSUAL JURY TRIAL

THE 12 PERSONS who serve on criminal juries come from all walks of life. There are 12 brains and 12 life experiences. Most accused persons facing serious criminal charges choose trial by jury. Jurors bring the street and common sense into the courtroom, and sense of justice. And once in a while, they give a surprising, even perverse, verdict, because to do otherwise would not be fair, or conform to justice as they see it.

Anyone who has served on a jury will tell you it was challenging—usually unforgettable.

This was an unusual attempt murder case before a jury in Yorkton, Saskatchewan, in February 1961. The accused, Sterling Brass, was a young man from the Key Indian Reserve, now the Key First Nation, north of Kamsack.

The charge against Sterling Brass was that on August 19, 1960, he attempted to murder Dennis K. by shooting him with a 30-30 Winchester rifle.

Dennis K. was another young Indigenous man from the same reserve, who had been disenfranchised and banned from the reserve for violent behaviour. Bernice Cote, who was living with Sterling Brass at his parents' home at the time of the offence, had previously lived with Dennis K. Her testimony in a previous court case was that Dennis K. had beat her and slashed her face because she had been getting letters from Brass. Dennis K. had told Bernice Cote he was going to get Brass "sooner or later." She passed the threats on to Sterling Brass.

On finding out that Dennis K. had returned to the reserve, Brass went home to borrow his father's 30-30 Winchester and drove to the house on the reserve where Dennis K. was said to be. He confronted Dennis K., demanding several times he come outside. Dennis K. refused and taunted Brass to go ahead and shoot. Brass shot him.

At the preliminary hearing on October 4, 1960, a friend of Brass testified that immediately after the shooting, "I just heard him say if I get hung, plant flowers on my grave." Sterling Brass handed the rifle to his friend, asking it be returned to his father, then drove away.

The next day at 6:45 a.m., Sterling Brass knocked on the door of the building in Kamsack where the RCMP cells were located. A civilian matron was on duty, with a female prisoner in the cells. Brass told the matron he had murdered Dennis K. and that he wanted to give himself up. He said he wasn't running away from the law. The matron did not believe him at first and told him to come back when the police were there. He refused to go and said he would wait. Brass insisted he wanted to give himself up to the police, as "Honest to God, I murdered Dennis K., and I don't know if he is dead or alive." So he sat on the steps, to wait. The matron called one of the officers who came over shortly and found Brass, still waiting, on the steps.

When RCMP Constable D. B. MacDonald arrived, Sterling Brass told him he felt he had killed Dennis K. He said he had no idea where or by what means or how he had got himself into Kamsack. He wanted to go down into the cells. MacDonald testified that the accused seemed to be very tired, sighing, and there was a slight smell of liquor.

Dennis K. did not die from the single shot. The bullet entered and exited his body. He spent over three weeks in hospital but made a full recovery.

Sterling Brass was committed for trial at the preliminary hearing and remained in custody for six months until the jury trial took place in Yorkton. The trial, before Mr. Justice C.S. Davis of the Court of Queen's Bench, took three and a half days. The jury came in with a surprising verdict of not guilty of attempted murder, but guilty of common assault, the lowest possible included offence under the *Criminal Code of Canada*. In 1961, that jury would have been all male and all white.

On February 16, 1961, Mr. Justice Davis imposed a sentence of two years less a day.

From the Provincial Jail for Men in Prince Albert, Saskatchewan, Sterling Brass gave notice of his appeal against sentence. Acting on his own behalf, he set out his grounds for appeal:

> I served six months on remand in Regina jail before I was sentenced. I was given the maximum sentence for common assault charge and the six months were not considered, which I had already served. If I should serve my complete jail term I will be released in October 1962, which is a bad time for me to find any work as I have no profession or trade. I am a labourer. If the six months were to be considered I would be out in the spring of 1962 which would give me enough time to be prepared for the winter.

Brass, 22 at the time, had a grade 6 education and worked as a labourer, often on nearby farms.

When there was an appeal from sentence, the Court of Appeal Registrar would write the presiding judge, as he did in this case on March 22, 1961. The Registrar wrote to advise Judge Davis of the appeal against sentence, adding the usual, "I shall be obliged if you will forward to me for the Court of Appeal such comment on this case as you may see fit to make." Not all judges saw fit to comment, but Judge Davis did in this instance.

Part of his letter to the Registrar, dated March 28, 1961, follows:

> This young man is certainly living up to his name. If justice had been done he would now be serving a term in the penitentiary of considerable duration. The

decision of the jury was manifestly perverse as Brass should have been found guilty of attempted murder, with which he was charged. I am satisfied that two things brought about the verdict of common assault; firstly, before I could stop him counsel for the accused had read to the jury the section of the Code which sets out the penalty is life imprisonment for the offence charged, and secondly, the man who was shot was a useless rogue. The jury evidently figured they would not take a chance on having the accused (a very presentable young man) go to the penitentiary for having taken a pot-shot at a rogue. In fact, after the jury had been out for quite a time they came back and asked what the maximum penalty was for common assault. I told them (namely two years) although this is not usually done. They returned and promptly came back and found him guilty of common assault.

It was admitted by the accused's counsel at the trial and fully substantiated by the evidence that at the time of the shooting the accused was neither drunk, insane nor in a state of blackout. The defence was that of "diminished responsibility" and based on the English case *R v Bastian*. However, that case was founded on the *Homicide Act* 1957, section 2, which has no counterpart in Canada. In other words, the accused offered no defence known to law in this country and accordingly, I have no hesitation in saying that the verdict was perverse.

I might add that when I asked the accused if he had anything to say why sentence of the court should not be pronounced on him his counsel replied quite frankly that he had expected his client to have been convicted as charged and had intended to call as a witness in mitigation of sentence the Rev. Taylor who was to have told the court that the accused was considered by him as a candidate for the Ministry—the Anglican Ministry. However, in view of the verdict he did not call any character evidence. Incidentally, the accused had two previous convictions against him of some less serious offences. On May 1, 1957, he was found guilty of breaking and entering and sentenced to one year in jail. He appealed the sentence and the Court of Appeal on the 9th of September of that year reduced the sentence to six months.

The accused is an extremely good-looking young Indian and conducted himself at court with great decorum which obviously impressed the jury. On the other hand, his victim was a hard-looking customer with a bad reputation whose liquidation would scarcely cause a ripple. So it would seem that the verdict was based not on the law or the evidence but on some sort of abstruse natural justice.

I gave the accused the maximum (less one day) for the offence with which he was found guilty because I could not conceive a more drastic case of "common assault." I feel satisfied that the jury in all its compassion intended that Brass should receive the maximum.

Following that letter from Judge Davis, the sentence appeal of Sterling Brass was denied by the Saskatchewan Court of Appeal. One might feel Davis should have given Brass credit for the six months served in pretrial custody. But perhaps Davis was balancing that decision with a decision he made near the end of the trial, a decision that favoured Brass.

When Brass's lawyer was giving his summation to the jury at the end of all the evidence, the lawyer read out the section of the *Criminal Code* for attempt murder, including the penalty "liable to imprisonment for life." It is a serious breach of rules governing criminal jury trials that jurors not be informed of the penalties of the charges before them. Jurors are to rule on the evidence before them, not decide on sentencing. That breach by the lawyer for Brass would normally have triggered an immediate declaration by the judge of a mistrial. Davis, an experienced trial judge, obviously chose not to make such a ruling. Had he done so, it would have meant a significant delay for a new trial, and more pretrial time in custody for Sterling Brass.

What became of Sterling Brass?

Inquiries indicated that Sterling Brass became a respected leader in his community. *The Saskatoon Star Phoenix* provided further information.

Sterling Brass died January 1, 2009, in his 71st year. His obituary of January 5, 2009, tells the life story of a man of dignity, integrity, and humour—a leader, a musician and a warm family patriarch. He was survived by his wife, Edna, 2 daughters, 2 sons, 14 grandchildren and 4 great grandchildren. Another son had predeceased him. Sterling had been a storyteller, with a passion for music, especially old time fiddling, going nowhere without his violin.

Born on the Key Indian Reserve, Sterling Brass was one of the countless Indigenous children sent to a residential school by the local Indian agent. He tried to run away to escape the abuses, only to be returned. It was a harsh beginning, as with so many.

The life Sterling Brass carved after the trial was one of service and leadership: Chief of the Key First Nation, time with the Department of Indian Affairs, Tribal Representative of the Yorkton Tribal Council, a Vice-Chief of the Federation of Saskatchewan Indian Nations, Chair of the National Aboriginal Trappers Association, and Chair of the Waneskewin Heritage Park. He worked for the New Democrats, was Liaison Officer for Saskatchewan Environment, and finally, was Director of the Saulteux Healing and Wellness Lodge on the Cote First Nation.

Sterling Brass left a proud and lasting legacy with his large and loving family, his triumph over adversities, and his example and service to his First Nations and country.

And long ago, a jury brought their best instincts and sense of justice into a courtroom.

THE SUBLIME BLANCHE MACDONALD

My appointment as a judge to the BC Provincial Court in 1972 had demonstrated, suddenly, there were slots for females in the law profession. But just one at a time. It was also a time when strong women were working together to bring attention and reform to the inequities plaguing women and all minorities. In Vancouver, Blanche MacDonald was one of those strong women.

The sublime Blanche MacDonald, with the gift of making everyone she encountered feel special, was beautiful, loving, smart, and a born entrepreneur. She was a Cree Métis woman, proud of her identity and heritage. By age 29, Blanche had established her eponymous modelling and fashion agency in Vancouver in 1960. That business has continued in various forms long after her early death in 1985, from cancer.

Blanche was committed to women's rights and the rights of Indigenous Peoples, particularly women. On March 7, 1978, Blanche and Pauline Jewett, a former Member of Parliament and then President of Simon Fraser University, appeared before the Royal Commission on the Incarceration of Female Offenders. The Commission was set up by the BC Government following serious allegations of sexual misconduct, fraud and other complaints occurring at the Women's Prison at Oakalla.

Blanche and Pauline were presenting a brief on behalf of an ad hoc Citizens Advisory Group. Their stated concerns were "The needs of women in prison with special emphasis on the Native Indian women." Their objective was to facilitate the integration of these women into society and their communities after incarceration. Their brief suggested, "the majority of women's offences can be categorized as either lifestyle-related or self-destructive offences, e.g. prostitution, alcohol and drugs."

They were seeking more community involvement to assist these women, including re-entry homes where needed. Their brief stated: "It is a truism in Canada that native Indian people are vastly over-represented in our prisons, far out of proportion to their numbers in the general population. The question of why this discrepancy exists has never been a subject of enquiry..."

This was 1978, 45 years ago.

Their recommendations included "a community based residential facility staffed by native Indian women," and that native Indian women be encouraged to apply for such positions. Also that there be an affirmative action program for all staff with ongoing in-service training and job upgrading skills. It was the stated hope that the objectives would develop positive feelings about being native and being female by encouraging identification with native culture, and contact with other women who could serve as positive role models. There was a recognition that these women needed to increase their knowledge of health, nutrition, parenting, financial matters, education, job training, and access to other services.

The recommendation continued, "We focused our attention on the problems of native women in prison because we felt that inadequate attention was being paid to their condition." There were 11 women in this ad hoc group that Blanche MacDonald, Pauline Jewett, and others spoke for. The group included three social workers, two lawyers, and a sociologist. Four of the eleven were Indigenous, including Blanche.

I was having dinner with Blanche and Pauline the day the *Royal Commission on the Incarceration of Female Offenders Report* came out in June 1978. In spite of Pauline's famous shepherd's pie, it was a grim evening. Still sitting as a judge on the Provincial Court, I was not involved, but very interested. I was one of those tasked with sending people to our prisons. The Commission wrote:

> This Commission is not convinced that there is a problem of great magnitude regarding native women in the prison system.... The Commission does not see any special problem presently surrounding the incarceration of native women.

For Blanche, those findings were particularly galling. She had worked with women in the prisons and in her community; she knew the problems. She knew these women at a deep and personal level; these were her sisters, her aunties, her grandmothers.

A few days later, in the British Columbia Legislature, commenting on the *Commission Report*, Rosemary Brown, who was the first black woman elected to a provincial legislature in Canada, rose to point out the problems faced by Indigenous women in prison. Her list included cultural isolation, discrimination against natives, the misleading statistics on who is identified as native, and the disproportionate number of native women in our prisons.

When Rosemary spoke to the Legislature on June 8, 1978, she said, "The whole impact of the justice system on Native Indians of both sexes is one that's always been a disgrace in this country." My friends were tilting against unforgiving and overwhelming windmills.

Later in June of that year, I accompanied Blanche on a trip to Haida Gwaii, home of the Haida Nation, then called the Queen Charlotte Islands. We flew into Skidegate for the historic raising of Bill Reid's carved totem pole, "Tribute to the Living Haida." It had taken Reid, the renowned Haida artist and carver and his assistants two years to carve the gigantic pole. We all watched in awe as dozens of men manually raised the totem pole before the longhouse in the Village of Skidegate. A potlatch followed that evening. It was an unforgettable experience.

It was a Friday, May 11, sunny and warm. It was Blanche's birthday. I called to wish her a happy birthday. "Is anyone taking you out for lunch? No? Let's go to Umberto's Il Giardino. My treat."

I called Rosemary Brown to join us. Back in practice at this point, I cancelled my Friday afternoon at the office. It was going to be one of those Vancouver Lotusland Friday lunches. Then Blanche called to ask if her older brother, Wylie Brillon, could join us. Wylie, a successful fisherman out of Haida Gwaii, was in town. Blanche adored him, and it was easy to see why.

It was a splendid lunch. We were almost the last to leave the restaurant. As we sat in the near-empty restaurant, it suddenly occurred to me: "I'm the only white person at this table."

"That's right, Nancy. How does it feel?" asked the wicked Rosemary, leaning forward with a now-you-know smile.

A lawyer, arbitrator, and judge, as well as a political activist and feminist, Nancy Morrison practiced law and adjudicated in Ontario, Saskatchewan, British Columbia, Yukon, and Northwest Territories. As a judge, she served for nine years on the British Columbia Provincial Court and 15 years on the Supreme Court of British Columbia. Raised in Yorkton, Saskatchewan, she now lives in Vancouver, BC. Her memoir Benched: Passion for Law Reform *was published in 2018 in the Durvile Reflections series.*

THREE

The Hon. John Reilly

BARET LABELLE AND RESTORATIVE JUSTICE

O NE OF THE MOST AMAZING EVENTS of my judicial career occurred in the course of an Indigenous sentencing circle. By the time I wrote the judgment in this case, I had been the judge primarily responsible for justice on the Stoney Nakoda First Nation, near Canmore, Alberta, for almost 10 years. In this case, the victim of a savage assault asked to say something. "My anger is gone," he said, forgiving his assailant, then added, "Just let him go." In my view, the change in victim John Anderson's attitude towards his assailant and his declaration that he had let go of his anger was miraculous. Anderson will never recover from the physical injuries he sustained that night, but by choosing forgiveness over anger his quality of life may be significantly enhanced.

Circumstances and details

On May 17, 1997, Baret Labelle, his cousin Sherman Labelle, and Marty Ear went out to the Seebe Campground to "shake some trailers." The campground is on land that was once part of the Stoney Nakoda First Nation but was taken back to allow for the construction of the Seebe Dam, Seebe Lake, and Trans Alta hydro-electric generating facilities. There has been resentment among Stoney People that the land had been taken from them. It was not unusual for Stoney youth to shake the trailers of people camping there. Perhaps it was to express their resentment, or it may have been just an excuse to harass the campers.

The background to the day is that Sherman Labelle had been out drinking with Marty Ear. They dropped by cousin Baret Labelle's house and invited him to go drinking with them. Baret joined them, and later in the evening, they decided to go and shake some trailers at the campground. The occupant of one of those trailers, John Anderson confronted them. In the ensuing violence, Mr. Anderson was severely injured and left with permanent brain damage. The impairment of his motor skills rendered him unable to work for the rest of his life.

I presided at the Preliminary Hearing in which Baret Labelle was charged with endangerment of life by committing an aggravated assault. Baret was the only one of the three charged in Provincial Court of Alberta. Even though Marty Ear was the main instigator in the matter, he did not actually strike the victim and the Crown needed him as a witness because neither the victim, nor his partner could identify Sherman or Baret. Sherman was not yet 18 when the assault was committed and so he was charged in youth court. Sadly, he hanged himself a few weeks before he was scheduled to appear on his Youth Court Charge.

It had been Ear who had suggested harassing the campers and Ear who had provided the socket wrench handles as weapons to Sherman and Baret. However, by giving evidence against Sherman and Baret, Ear was saved from being charged as a party to the offence. His evidence at Preliminary was that Sherman hit Anderson with his fist and knocked him down, then Baret Labelle hit John Anderson once with the socket wrench.

This appeared to be an understatement in both cases. The injuries to Anderson would indicate a much more severe beating. However, it was sufficient to order Baret to stand trial, which I did. Barct subsequently re-elected for a trial in provincial court and entered the plea of guilty before me. A pre-sentence report was ordered, and the matter was adjourned for sentence to September 7, 1999. It was then further adjourned to October 1 because the victim was unable to attend on September 7, 1999. Sentence was then passed at the hearing on October 1, 1999.

Accepting the plea

When I accepted the plea on June 29, 1999, I suggested, and counsel agreed, that pursuant to the Supreme Court of Canada decision in *R v Gladue, [1999] 1 S.C.R. 688,* it was an appropriate case to determine sentence by the use of a form of Aboriginal Healing Circle or Sentencing Circle. Rather than use the courtroom for the sentencing hearing in this matter, I arranged to use the boardroom located in the Provincial Building in the town of Cochrane, Alberta. This was a large bright room with large windows and generous floor space. The chairs were arranged in an open circle with no tables or other furniture separating those in the circle. There were two microphones from a GYR recording system located on the floor in the middle of the circle, and the court clerk was seated at a table outside the circle where she was able to monitor and log the recordings of the proceedings.

The victim, Mr. John Anderson, was seated on one side of the circle, with the investigating officer, Corporal Andrew Johnson, on his left. Mrs. Grace Auger, a member of the Crown prosecutor's office, sat to his right and the prosecuting lawyer, Mr. Lloyd Robinson, to her right. Mrs. Auger had attended for the purpose of observing only, but I asked her to sit next to Mr. Anderson. Mrs. Auger is Cree; Mr. Anderson is Ojibway. I expected that he would feel some support from her. It is recommended that there be a balance of power in the circle. I had requested the attendance of Mr Anderson's wife, but she declined to attend.

The victim, John Anderson, and his support group were already seated when the accused and his group were invited to enter the room. This is recommended procedure, designed to contribute to the comfort of the victim. Baret Labelle was then invited to enter the room with his support group. This consisted of his lawyer, Mr. Alain Hepner QC, Labelle's grandparents, Elders George Labelle and Sheila Labelle, and Baret's common-law wife, Tammy Scalplock. I sat with Mr. Kloster on my right, then Mr. Hepner, the accused Baret Labelle, his grandparents Sheila Labelle, George Labelle, and Tammy Scalplock. To my left were Lloyd Robertson, Grace Auger, John Anderson, and Corporal Andrew Johnson. The arrangement was deliberately set up so that the victim and the accused were across the circle from each other and facing each other.

I began by introducing myself and each of the participants. I said that I was acting as a facilitator with a view to generate conversation that would result in an agreement the accused was willing to accept and that would also satisfy the victim. Using the recommended script from the conferencing method, I indicated that the important thing was to focus on the incident, how the behaviour had affected the people involved, and to attempt to reach a consensus as to what the disposition should be.

Continuing with the script, I asked Baret to tell us how he came to be involved, what happened, what he was thinking at the time, and what he has thought about since. He told us that he had been at home when friends came by, and he went with them to Morley school. Marty Ear and Sherman Labelle joined them and they went drinking. Later they went by 'the park', (the campground at Seebe). The others decided to 'shake some trailers'. He said he protested, but he was given a weapon that he put in his pocket (the steel handle of a socket wrench). Mr. Anderson came out and asked what was going on. He told them he was native too, but Sherman said he was a white man and trespassing. Sherman hit him and knocked him down. Baret said Sherman shouldn't have done that. Then Anderson got a stick, and Baret ran away, throwing the wrench behind him and not knowing whether he hit anyone with it or not.

Baret said he was sorry and didn't mean for it to happen. He said he was scared, and threatened, and had just wanted to go home. When asked what he had thought about since, he said he wished that day had never happened and wished those guys had never come by to pick him up. He spoke about his cousin Sherman, saying that Sherman didn't want to go to court, and so he hanged himself.

The victim, John Anderson, said he couldn't remember much of the incident because of his brain injury. He said that he had been unable to work since the incident and that he had enjoyed his work. He said that his wife now has to work to support them and that they would've had their house paid off if he had been able to keep working.

Elder George Labelle, Baret's grandfather, said Baret was a gentle person and that in their culture, his cousin Sherman was his brother. Baret had no transportation, but he got picked up by Marty Ear. They did something they would not have done without the liquor. George said that Sherman, his other grandson, was afraid of going to court and perhaps that had led to his suicide.

Elder Sheila Labelle said she was very sorry that her grandson Beret had been involved because she had always found him to be a good boy. She spoke of losing her other grandson, Sherman, and that she was glad that she still had Baret. She said Baret's mom and dad were disabled and that he had been neglected a lot as a child.

At this stage, John Anderson said that he didn't want 'sorry', that he did not accept the apologies that were offered, and that he thought a year in jail might straighten Baret out. Mr. Robertson then indicated that he was not content with the admissions and that he wanted further details on the record regarding the injury to Mr. Anderson's neck. Mr. Anderson informed us that all of his back teeth were loosened in the beating and had to be removed by a dentist.

Smudging and prayer

I said from a legal point of view, I accepted the guilty plea on the basis that Baret admitted he was involved in the harassment of the campers that resulted in the beating and the injuries. At this point, Mrs. Auger said that it might have been appropriate to begin the meeting with a smudge, an Indigenous custom in which sweetgrass is burned and those present waft the smoke over themselves. It is a form of cleansing, and the smoke is said to attract good spirits. After some discussion, it was decided to interrupt the proceedings to do this. George and Sheila Labelle burned sweetgrass and went around the circle with it so that each of us could cleanse with the smoke, then Elder George Labelle prayed in Stoney. He briefly explained that he had asked the Creator to bless us, to thank Him for everyone in attendance, to ask Him to help us be gentle with each other, and to protect us on our way home.

After the smudging and prayer ceremonies, we continued with Mr. Robertson's formal presentation of injuries. He read two letters into the record. The first was by neurologist Dr. Suchowersky, dated January 26, 1988, which described Anderson having been beaten about the head and neck, causing dissection of the right carotid artery and damaging the right side of his brain, resulting in weakness to the left side of his body. It further asserted that he was suffering from depression and permanent disability and that he subsequently suffered a seizure to his left side that would require anti-seizure medication for the rest of his life.

The second letter was from Dr. Ghanji, which described spastic left hemiparesis, cognitive and neuro-behavioural impairment, deficits in self-care, and a right facial nerve palsy. These conditions resulted in disabilities such as impaired gait, limited balance, and impaired visual skills. Dr. Ghanji added that Anderson will remain incapable of ever doing gainful employment.

Asked to comment on these diagnoses, Mr. Anderson said

he is doing a lot of walking but his balance is not very good, and he often feels like taking a gun and putting it to his head. Hearing this, Mr. Robertson then stated that Baret should go to jail for a year to two years and afterwards should get counselling. He said that he did not think that a sentence served conditionally would be appropriate.

Mr. Hepner, Baret's defence lawyer, elicited information from Sheila Labelle. Baret's mother had a problem with alcohol and was drinking when she was pregnant with Baret. Baret was often left alone, and his grandmother Sheila would take care of him. Baret always had a speech problem, which was clearly evident when he spoke. At one point they had him in a special school to deal with the impediment, but his mother came and took him away and it was not continued. Baret's dad had a drinking problem and left when Baret was 2 or 3 years old. He overdosed on pills and became disabled. Baret had a grade 7 education and was not going to school when this incident happened, but was supposed to go to Viscount Bennett in Calgary. Mr. Hepner spoke of the lifestyle endured by Baret. He said Baret admitted his responsibility but he wondered if jail would solve anything. He pointed out that Baret was taking the responsibility alone because Marty Ear was not charged, and Sherman Labelle was dead.

Corporal Johnson confirmed that Marty Ear was not charged. Mrs. Anderson had confirmed that only two of the boys were involved in the assault while the other stood back. Mrs. Anderson was not able to identify the assailants. Marty Ear was not charged because he was needed to identify Baret and Sherman.

Elder George Labelle said that he would like to see treatment for alcohol as this seemed to be 'the main obstacle' for Baret, and he would like to see him upgrade his education.

At that point, I said I would like to see some good come out of this incident and asked if there were any suggestions as to how they there might be some way of repairing the harm done.

Repairing harm done

Suggestions came firstly from Mrs. Auger, who asked Baret if he understood the importance of Mr. Anderson attending and how difficult it was for him. She also acknowledged the difficulty for Baret to have to face what he had done. Then she suggested that perhaps supplying Mr. Anderson with wild game such as elk or deer might be something he could do. Mr. Anderson said this was not necessary. Mr. Kloster then spoke about how difficult this process was for everyone concerned and how angry Mr. Anderson was. Mr. Anderson confirmed his anger. I then raised the issue of Mr. Anderson being told that he was trespassing and asked about the element of racial hatred in this regard. George Labelle said there was some discontent over the transfer of land to the utility company, because only a few in the community benefitted from the transfer.

I suggested that if there was some element of Stoney discontent over the loss of this land that led to the beating, it might in some way help Mr. Anderson to understand why this had happened to him. We engaged in some conversation about Mr. Anderson's Ojibway mother and the battles between the Ojibway and the Sioux that had likely contributed to the Stoney, (a Nakoda Sioux people) coming to the eastern slopes of the Rockies.

Corporal Anderson said that there seemed to be an attitude among young Stoney People, when they were drinking, that they can harass people on the reserve and it is somehow justified, but he added it was more of a way of exercising power. He did not believe that it had to do with racial hatred.

Mr. Anderson repeated his suggestion of a year in jail. I confirmed that I was satisfied that he had suffered a vicious brutal beating. He said he wondered why the charge had not been attempted murder. Mr. Robertson referred to the case of *R v Bunes (D.H.) (1999) 232 A.R. 152*, in which the Court of Appeal approved an 18-month sentence, but not the conditional serving thereof because of the message it would give to the rest of the community. He also offered the theory that going to jail might be therapeutic for Baret because he could come back with the feeling he had paid for his wrongdoing.

I then asked Baret where he was living from day to day. He described that he and his wife and children lived in Calgary with his mother, except when his mother, as he described, "gets drinking," they go to his aunt Charlene's. I asked how he supports himself, and he told of doing jobs fencing and painting for old people. I tried to explain to Baret that the purpose of the justice system is to reduce, perhaps to eliminate crime and that I would rather see him spending the rest of his life doing good things for Mr. Anderson than spending a few years in jail. At this point, Mrs. Auger said there was something else Mr. Anderson wanted to say. I asked him what it was, and he said, "I would like to really say, let him go free."

I explained to him that as a judge I couldn't do that, that I had to impose some sanction that would convince Baret and others not to commit similar acts. Anderson said he didn't feel any hatred for him anymore, that by seeing him and his family, his hatred was gone. So, I suspended sentence for two years with a probation order that contained the following terms:

- Be of good behaviour and keep the peace,
- Report as required,
- Attend for assessment, treatment, and counselling as required by the probation authority,
- Attend for educational upgrading, job training as recommended by the probation authority, and then seek and maintain employment,
- Perform 50 hours of community service work, to consist of meeting with teachers at the Morley school to discuss speaking to classes, and to speak to classes about the results of alcohol abuse and the harm done to the victim and the community, and
- Abstain absolutely from alcohol.

After the conference, the participants, including myself, spoke to each other informally. I heard Anderson say to Tammy Scalplock that he hoped she would get a better husband out of this. Mr. Anderson spoke to me and said that he had started a lawsuit against Baret and wanted it withdrawn.

Appeal from the Crown, critical of my conduct
The Crown appealed. The Alberta Court of Appeal said the suspended sentence I had imposed was demonstrably unfit, but went on to say,

> In view of the tragic personal circumstances that surround this offender, his age, his family obligations, his role and, most importantly, the fact that the suspended sentence has now been served without any breach of the imposed terms, and his personal progress, we are not prepared to revisit the sentence to insist on a term of imprisonment at this time.

That said, they were critical of my conduct in every step of the proceedings. I had not allowed the Crown to establish the facts upon which the guilty plea was entered. This was a valid criticism. When Baret minimized his involvement and said he was an unwilling participant, the degree of his involvement became an issue that I had not anticipated. The circle is not for the purpose of establishing what had happened, and this created a problem.

The next point was that I had not invited the Crown and the defence to participate in the make-up of the circle. This was a somewhat valid criticism. I left it to the Crown and defence to select their supporters. I believe Mr. Hepner brought the Labelle grandparents. I had asked for the attendance of Mrs. Anderson, but she declined to come. In retrospect, I agreed that I should have included members of the community not associated with the matter. Makeup of the circle was a valid comment. However, when the matter was scheduled on September 7, I had other Elders present who were not able to come back when the matter proceeded on October 1. The offence was May 16, 1997, and we were now in October 1999, more than two years after the event. I did not wish to delay it further, so I proceeded with what I had.

The Court of Appeal said I misinterpreted the law in relation to the sentencing of Indigenous offenders. There is no question that I disagreed with the law and I believed that changes to the *Criminal Code of Canada* and the interpretation thereof by the Supreme Court of Canada had changed the law, but other courts and the higher provincial courts of appeal basically said it was business as usual.

In 1996, the *Criminal Code of Canada* was amended to include section 718.2(e) "All sanctions other than imprisonment that are reasonable in the circumstances shall be considered for all offenders with particular attention to the circumstances of aboriginal offenders." In the Gladue case, which said that lower courts should consider an Indigenous offender's background and make sentencing decisions accordingly, the Supreme Court of Canada said:

[48] The proposed enactment was directed, in particular, at reducing the use of imprisonment as a sanction, at expanding the use of restorative justice principles in sentencing, and at engaging in both of these objectives with a sensitivity to aboriginal community justice initiatives when sentencing aboriginal offenders.

[61] Not surprisingly, the excessive imprisonment of aboriginal people is only the tip of the iceberg in so far as the estrangement of the Aboriginal Peoples from the Canadian criminal justice system is concerned. Aboriginal people are over-represented in almost all aspects of the system. As this court recently noted in *R v Williams* there is widespread bias against aboriginal

people within Canada, and 'there is evidence that this widespread racism has translated into systemic discrimination in the criminal justice system.'

The Court of Appeal went on for 19 pages setting out my errors, and the reasons why a more restrictive sentence had been called for. In my early years as a judge, given the seriousness of the injuries to the victim, I would probably have sentenced Baret Labelle to three years without spending more than a few minutes in consideration. By the time I wrote the judgment in this case, I had been the judge primarily responsible for justice on Labelle's reserve for almost 10 years. I had spent many hours getting to know the people in the community and reading all the material I could find on Indigenous justice. The more I worked at it, the more I saw the recidivism in spite of lengthy terms of imprisonment I had imposed in my early years. Hence, the more merit I saw in the restorative justice of the Indigenous Peoples.

The intransigence of the Alberta courts was extremely frustrating for me. I wonder if they might look at it differently now, in view of developments in awareness of the circumstances of Indigenous Peoples? Why could the Court of Appeal not have looked at this with an open mind and said: "This worked?" This young man might have been destroyed by a year or more in prison. Instead, he spent two years doing the community service that was required on the probation order, and had been working and supporting his wife and children all the while. How can a period of imprisonment have been better than that? The court, of course, talked about denunciation and deterrence. I say that denunciation can be achieved without imprisonment, and in my view, our theory of deterrence is nothing more than a legal fiction.

I could have continued sitting as a supernumerary judge for 15 years longer than I did. But I became so disillusioned with what I saw as the stupidity and the racism of the justice system that I left it.

Healing and restoration

The Supreme Court of Canada in the Gladue case quoted the Royal Commission on Aboriginal Peoples: "The Canadian criminal justice system has failed the aboriginal people of Canada." In my view, it has failed everyone in Canada. This theory of deterrence goes back to the beginnings of the English system, which dates to William the Conqueror in 1066. Some think that because the system is a thousand years old, it's a really good system. I say that the system was created by primitive people who had no knowledge of psychology and the workings of the human brain. The only behavioural modification technique they knew was terrorism—making penalties so harsh that people would be afraid to commit offences. Yet, a thousand years later, criminal behaviour has not stopped.

My understanding of the Indigenous view of justice is that wrongdoing should be treated as ignorance in need of education, and sickness in need of healing. I believe this community conference was a powerful example of the good that can come within this process. We began the conference with the victim saying that the offender should go to prison for at least a year. Then, when he listened to the young man and his grandparents he said: "I just want to let him go free." He declared that after having met Baret and his family, his hatred was gone. He said he wanted to drop the law suit he had started against Baret.

In my view, this was a prime example of how the Indigenous restorative process works. When the Indigenous speak of restoration, they are primarily speaking of repairing relationships. This process changed Mr. Anderson's relationship with Baret that had been anger and hatred towards a faceless criminal. Instead, he observed and listened and now understood this young man, no longer seeking vengeance. Mr. Anderson actually partook in a healing process that gave him a sense of closure he would not have gotten from just hearing the court and sending Labelle to prison for a year or two.

Unfortunately, it was also a prime example of the 'white

justice system' not working for Indigenous People. The culture of most Indigenous Peoples is generally egalitarian, peaceful, caring, and gentle. The culture of northern Europeans at the time of settlement was hierarchical, cruel, authoritative, cold, and brutal. The culture of the European was Bible-based. It believed the creation story that God created everything and put man in charge of creation. That culture put man at the top. That concept also led to the concept of some men being higher than others.

My understanding of Indigenous beliefs is that water and soil were important things in creation because without them nothing grew. Next in order of importance and value were the plants because without plants, the animals could not exist. Next in importance were the animals, and the very least important part of creation were the human beings, because no other part of creation depends on us for its existence, whereas we depend on everything else for ours.

In his book *God is Red: A Native View of Religion*, Standing Rock Sioux lawyer, teacher and activist Vine Deloria Jr. asks:

Who will find peace with the lands? The future of humankind lies waiting for those who will come to understand their lives and take up responsibilities to all living things. Who will listen to the trees, the animals and birds, the voices of the places of the land? As the long-forgotten peoples of the respective continents rise and begin to reclaim their ancient heritage, they will discover the meaning of the lands of their ancestors.

Indigenous Peoples say that they don't own the land, the land owns them. This is a concept that European minds couldn't grasp. I believe it is an expression of deep spiritual belief. I believe that what we know of the first contact between Europeans and Indigenous Peoples is indicative of how they treated each other.

When Columbus landed in America, the Arawak people greeted him with fresh food, fresh water, and gifts. When the Pilgrims landed in what is now Massachusetts, the Wampanoag showed them how to grow corn and helped them through their first winter. When half of the men in Champlain's first settlement at Ile Ste.-Croix died from scurvy, the Mi'kmaq showed them the herbs that saved the rest of them. I believe this was the true nature of the Indigenous Peoples before European influence started changing them. I don't believe that people who treat strangers like this are in the habit of slaughtering each other.

Columbus came back in 1495 with 17 ships and a thousand men. They took the whole Arawak Nation prisoner and forced them to work as slaves. They treated them with such cruelty that within 150 years they were extinct. When the Wampanoag became concerned about the increasing number of pilgrims and the land they were taking they tried to stop them. There was war, and most of them were wiped out. The ones that remain are now on a few small reserves in Massachusetts. When Edward Cornwallis founded the city of Halifax, he issued the scalping proclamation of 1749, in which he paid a bounty for the scalps of Mi'kmaq people.

Final thoughts
Throughout my career as a judge, I have heard people tell me: "The Indians were killing each other off," and that "White settlement was good for them because it stopped them from killing each other." My own mother was not exempt from this conditioning. Her family immigrated from Belgium in 1914, and the likely reason for her misinformation was because that is what immigrants were being told so that they wouldn't have any scruples about buying the land that had been taken from First Nations Peoples.

I am satisfied that the Indigenous People were more peaceful, caring people than the Europeans, and I believe that the way they dealt with wrongdoing was a big part of, and a contribution to, their culture. The Indigenous tried to find the underlying causes and to repair the relationships that were harmed by wrongdoing. The Europeans were totally preoccupied with punishment, and I believe that mode of thinking contributed to the violence in their culture.

I believe the process I used in the Labelle case was a proper application of Indigenous principles of restorative justice. Unfortunately, the comments of the Court of Appeal were a proper application of 'The LAW' and a demonstration of its incompatibility with Indigenous culture.

Perhaps one day, the dominant society will make a serious effort at reconciliation and that will include admitting that our system doesn't work nearly as well as theirs.

For most of his 33 years on the bench Judge John Reilly was the circuit judge for the Stoney Nakoda First Nation at Mînî Thnî (Morley), Alberta. During his career he became interested in Indigenous justice and saw the failure of the 'white' legal system to do justice for Indigenous Peoples. He is author of Bad Medicine: A Judge's Struggle for Justice in a First Nations Community, Bad Judgement: the Myths of First Nations Equality, *and* Judicial Independence in Canada.

FOUR

The Hon. John Z. Vertes

THE CASE OF
HENRY INNUKSUK

ᓄᴺᵉ

Tᴏᴅᴀʏ it is common-place to speak of restorative justice as an alternative to standard criminal law practice in Canada's Indigenous societies. In Nunavut, where Rankin Inlet is now located, it is a regular practice of the court to have community representatives sit with the presiding judge to advise on the appropriate sentence for an offender. This practice leads to greater community involvement in the sentencing of Indigenous offenders. But in the 1970s, this type of community involvement was unheard of. Introducing it was a gamble I thought worth taking.

Yellowknife, Northwest Territories
In 1978, I was a young lawyer working in Yellowknife. I had moved to the Northwest Territories capital in the fall of 1977 from Toronto with my wife Louise. I had recently been called to the Ontario Bar, and we took an opportunity to go North for what we assumed would be a two-year adventure. Our plan was to return to Toronto after that, but our two-year adventure turned into a thirty-four-year career for both of us. We never did return to Toronto.

My legal experience in Toronto was with a civil litigation

firm specializing in insurance defence work and that was why I was hired by the Yellowknife firm of Searle, Richard & Kingsmill, as it was then known. And that was the work I got to do. But once I came North, I quickly developed a desire to do criminal defence work. I was drawn to the excitement of the Northern circuit—the Court party flying out from Yellowknife to hear cases in all the far-flung Northern communities.

My inexperience in criminal law notwithstanding, I put my name on the legal aid list and started taking on cases. I went on my first circuit in October 1977, a two-week trek around the Eastern Arctic in a DC-3 airplane that was older than I was, piloted by a former member of the Polish air wing of the RAF in World War II. But that is another story.

In April 1978, I received a call from the legal aid director asking me to go see a young man who was in custody at the Yellowknife Correctional Centre. The director did not call me because of my expertise; he called me because he knew I was keen to take on cases, and this one seemed somewhat problematic. The young man was Henry Suviserk Innuksuk, then eighteen years old, from Rankin Inlet. He had been arrested in Rankin Inlet on charges of breaking into various buildings in his community and setting fire to them. Essentially these were charges of arson. The buildings were all public buildings of importance to the community: the elementary school, the curling rink, the Hudson Bay Company store, the local Inuit Association office, the local housing association office, and a government office and public works shop. None of the buildings were completely destroyed, but they were all damaged and repairs were costly. All the offences occurred in a short time-frame in February and March 1978.

I was told that Henry could not communicate in English and there was some concern over his mental health. So when I first went to see him at the jail, I took with me a local Inuvialuit interpreter, Ms. Mikle Langenham, who was of great help in establishing ongoing communication with Henry. I made it a point to have Ms. Langenham with me whenever I met with Henry and at every court appearance.

It took several sessions with Henry to build up his confidence enough and his trust in me sufficiently so that he would communicate with me in anything more than the most simple utterances. These, of course, were in Inuktitut and would have to be translated for my benefit. But it quickly became apparent to me, as it did to Ms. Langenham, that Henry was illiterate. More significantly, it seemed that he was also suffering from some type of mental dysfunction. Henry did not evade the fact that he had committed these offences or that what he had done was wrong. Indeed, he confessed to the arresting police officer at the first opportunity. But I had reservations about his mental state and possibly his legal culpability.

As it turned out, I was not the first one to have such reservations. After my first meeting with Henry, I sat down with one of the Crown attorneys, who showed me the prosecution file. In the Northwest Territories, then and still today, all criminal prosecutions are handled by the federal Department of Justice. Their Crown attorneys had, for many years, the admirable policy of routinely giving full disclosure to defence counsel, usually by simply handing over their complete file for review. This was years before the Supreme Court of Canada formalized the disclosure obligations of prosecutors.

In the file was an assessment report written by a psychiatrist at the forensic services unit of the Alberta Hospital in Edmonton just a few days before I had seen Henry. Henry had been remanded at Alberta Hospital after his arrest in Rankin Inlet for observation and assessment. That report noted that Henry was not suffering from a mental illness but was 'mentally retarded'. More significantly, the report concluded that Henry suffered from psychopathic disorders and should be considered dangerous.

In those days, a court-ordered forensic psychiatric assessment was normally conducted at the Alberta Hospital. It is fair to say that in those days the doctors there had little, if any, familiarity with Inuit culture and certainly no knowledge of Henry's home community. The assessment seemed very superficial, even to my relatively untrained eyes. I was very concerned that if this report became the authoritative statement on Henry's psychological makeup, then his prospects on sentencing would be very grim indeed. Considering the nature of the charges, one could normally expect a relatively severe sentence, ordinarily one of several years of incarceration, even for a first offender such as Henry. So, if there was no alternative to pleading guilty, and I was hard-pressed to find one, I had to apply my resources to obtaining the best, or at least a less worse, sentence possible.

A second psychiatric assessment
I realized that I had to counter the Alberta Hospital report in some way. I, therefore, took steps to arrange a second psychiatric assessment, this time at the Clarke Institute of Psychiatry in Toronto. I knew that they had flying teams of mental health specialists who travelled periodically to communities in the Eastern Arctic. I hoped that at least they would have greater familiarity with Inuit communities and that they might have the resources to conduct a more in-depth investigation into Henry's circumstances.

In May 1978, I obtained an order for such a further assessment. The subsequent report from the Clarke Institute confirmed much of what I had been thinking. Henry was found to be fit to stand trial and was not suffering from a mental illness. He was intellectually disabled, likely due to several severe early childhood illnesses. But he was not considered to pose a danger to himself or to others. He did not exhibit signs of any significant psychological disorder. More important, his personality was described as meek, docile, and passive and not one exhibiting dangerousness or a propensity to setting fires. Finally, the report viewed long-term incarceration as definitely unhelpful, considering Henry's condition and background.

With this report now part of my arsenal, I started discussions with the Crown attorney handling Henry's case on what might be a suggested disposition should Henry plead guilty. And I concluded by then that there was no alternative if we were to have any chance at minimizing the severity of the potential sentence.

I never determined Henry's motives for setting these fires. The psychiatrists thought it was a form of attention-seeking. He may have been influenced or pushed into doing these things by others who supplied him with liquor—somebody's cruel way of having a laugh at Henry's expense. Henry was certainly impressionable and easily led and the fact that all the offences occurred within a short time span suggested to me that there may have been some sort of triggering event, perhaps a threat or some type of encouragement for him to act so out of character. But nothing definite ever came out of any of this, and all inquiries with respect to motive came to a dead-end. Hence my decision to concentrate on sentencing.

Two of the most significant factors in the eventual outcome of Henry's case were: firstly, the Crown attorney who prosecuted the case, and, secondly, the judge scheduled to preside at the sentencing hearing. The Crown attorney was John Bayly. John had come to Yellowknife in 1974 to work initially for several Indigenous groups appearing before the Inquiry conducted by Justice Thomas Berger into a proposed Mackenzie Valley gas pipeline project.

John Bayly went on to a varied and extremely successful career in the North, in both private practice and, from time to time, as a Crown attorney. By the time of his untimely death in 2004, he was rightfully considered a Dean of the Northern Bar, known for his integrity and professionalism. Henry's case was the first time I'd worked with John, but I am pleased to say it was only the first of many cases and projects over the years. I quickly developed great respect for both his abilities as a lawyer and his commitment to the interests of the people of the North.

John quickly recognized my concerns. Sentencing precedents called for a significant term of imprisonment for these offences, but Henry's personal characteristics were such that imprisonment would be devastating for him. John sympathized with his situation but there had to be sound arguments for deviating from precedent, especially since John was answerable to Department of Justice masters in Ottawa who did not necessarily share his empathy with people in the Northern communities.

On July 11, 1978, I appeared with Henry (who was still in custody on pre-trial detention) in court and entered guilty pleas to all charges. Sentencing was set for August 4 in Rankin Inlet. John had agreed with me that the case was sufficiently important to the community that the hearing should be held in Rankin Inlet.

I had decided to keep the case in the Territorial Court, which is the Northern equivalent of Provincial Court. I thought there would be an advantage in an early guilty plea without protracted proceedings. I was also betting on the presiding judge, Chief Judge Jim Slaven. The late Jim Slaven was originally from Nova Scotia and had worked as a counsel for the Northwest Territories government before his appointment as a judge in 1973. In my brief time before the Northern courts up to that time, I came to appreciate the many human and humane qualities Jim brought to the bench. No one would ever accuse Jim of intellectual arrogance, but he brought to his work, throughout his career, a sensitivity and appreciation for the situation of many of the people appearing before him. I thought that if there was a chance of convincing a judge to do something out of the ordinary, then Jim was my best opportunity.

Prior to the guilty pleas and in preparation for sentenc ing, I started contacting people in Rankin Inlet who might be able to provide information on Henry and his family. One of the people I spoke to was Ms. Jean Williamson, one of Henry's grade school teachers. She then put me in contact with her husband, Dr. Robert Williamson, who was a professor of anthropology at the University of Saskatchewan and the director of that university's Northern Research Centre. Of far more relevance was the fact that he had lived in Rankin Inlet for many years, spoke fluent Inuktitut, was familiar with the Inuit of that region, and was acquainted with Henry's family.

Dr. Williamson told me about the great interest in Henry's case amongst the Rankin Inlet community. Henry came from a very traditional family, a well-respected one but with difficulties since the death of Henry's mother several years earlier. Many people in the community, I was told, expressed regret over not being more attentive to Henry's situation. Dr. Williamson said that the case might be an opportunity for the people of Rankin Inlet to take a greater role in the criminal justice system and to show its strength as a community. In his opinion, they could draw upon Inuit tradition wherein the responsibility for sanctioning, correction and control of members of the community who commit deviant acts is placed in the hands of the community who would act as his surrogate family.

Rankin Inlet, Kangirliniq

Rankin Inlet, or as it is known by its Inuit name, Kangirliniq, meaning 'deep bay', is located on the northwestern coast of Hudson Bay, north of the tree line. Archaeological surveys revealed evidence of Thule hunting activities in that area since the 12th century; the Thule people being ancestors of all modern Inuit. The town itself was founded in 1957 by the owners of the Rankin Inlet Mine, an underground nickel and copper operation. Inuit from different regional groups came there to work in the mine until its closure in 1962. After the mine closed, the community stagnated until the mid-1970s when it was designated a government regional centre. This also drew Inuit from different regional groups to live there. Its population in 1978 was approximately 1,000 people; now, in 2023, it is nearly 3,000. The community is notable for its Inuit art and artisans as well as for its chilling winds and severe winter storms—the average high in January is -27 degrees C.

The important fact to draw from Rankin Inlet's history is that its Inuit population was made up of people from many different groups; people who had not lived together previously in any particular settlement. So, the community coming together to demonstrate a collective will was a ground-breaking event.

A few days prior to the date for sentencing, I was contacted by Dr. Williamson and told that the Rankin Inlet Hamlet Council wanted to meet with me prior to the hearing. Apparently the Council had decided to assume responsibility for Henry, together with his family. The Council members recognized that this was an opportunity to demonstrate their strength as a community and their collective responsibility for each other.

On August 4, the Court party assembled at the Yellowknife airport for the four-hour flight to Rankin Inlet. Besides myself, there was Chief Judge Jim Slaven, prosecutor John Bayly, my interpreter Ms. Langenham, a court clerk, a court reporter, and a court sheriff's officer. Henry had already been transported to Rankin Inlet by an RCMP aircraft. We arrived in Rankin Inlet at 10 in the morning and to nobody's surprise, it was a cool day with blustery winds. Court was scheduled to start at 11 a.m., but I had already told the judge and John about the request from the Hamlet Council to meet with me, so he agreed to delay proceedings until one in the afternoon.

Upon arrival, I immediately went to the Hamlet offices,

where I was greeted by a large throng of people, including the mayor and the Council members, all of whom were Inuk except for one. Also in attendance were Dr. and Mrs. Williamson; Henry's elderly father; two of his older brothers, as well as many community members. One by one, they spoke to me about Inuit traditional ways and about their concerns for Henry. The mayor said that he and every member of the Hamlet Council would be willing to act as surety and supervise Henry in the community if that would mean Henry's avoidance of a jail sentence. They felt sad that they had not paid more attention to Henry in the community, previously knowing his limitations. And now they wanted to take responsibility for his future conduct.

The meeting initially lasted well beyond 11:00 a.m., so I went to see Judge Slaven to request more time. He said that I could take as long as I need. I also took John Bayly, the Crown attorney, back with me to hear what these people were saying. John was far more familiar with Rankin Inlet than I was at that time, so he listened with great interest and empathy.

Court Proceedings
We finally started the Court proceeding at 4:00 in the afternoon. Public interest was so intense that the hearing was held in the largest facility in Rankin Inlet—the community hall. It was packed with people. Prior to commencing, John and I agreed that we would put forward a proposal that Henry not be given any more jail time, but instead be placed on probation under the supervision of a probation officer but with the active involvement of the community. John agreed to submit that, while jail was the norm in cases of this type, it would not necessarily be required in this case due to the special circumstances of Henry's condition and the willingness of the community to assume responsibility. We knew, however, that the final decision was strictly up to the judge.

The hearing lasted over seven hours. I called nine witnesses to testify as to Henry's situation, the strength of
the family, and the community response to the case. Dr.
Williamson testified as to how the action of the community
represented aspects of Inuit culture that should be fostered
and strengthened. All of the testimony was translated in
open court between Inuktitut and English. The psychiatric
reports were entered into evidence. After the witnesses were
heard, Jim adjourned court and asked to see John and me
outside the courtroom. What he really wanted was a smoke
break. We all wanted one because, at that time, all of us
smoked. So there we were, standing outside the community
hall, smoking in a bitterly cold wind, when Jim looked at us
and asked, in effect, "How can we justify a non-incarceration
sentence?" We said that would be the subject of our submissions. After we finished our smokes, we went back inside,
convened court again, and made our respective submissions.

Judge Jim Slaven suspended sentence on all charges and
placed Henry on probation for two years. The formal order
placed Henry under the supervision of a probation officer
but with the proviso that the officer be in a supportive role to
Henry's family and the community. In passing sentence, he
made the following remarks:

> It is so refreshing for me to come into a community
> and find a family and a community who are willing
> to take the responsibility to try and help one of their
> own instead of throwing up their hands and saying,
> 'Judge, you and the other fellows, you do it.' His only
> real chance to be rehabilitated and take a worthwhile
> role in society is the chance offered him here in
> Rankin Inlet in the hearts of his family and his com-
> munity. I have heard the nine witnesses, all residents
> of this community, who gave evidence today. I have
> seen them here today. From the evidence given here,

there was a meeting of the Hamlet Council today, I have seen the interest of the hundreds of people who have come to court today, and I am completely satisfied that the community and the family here afford the best chance for the long-term protection of society. I am satisfied that the family and the community can control this boy by supervising, directing, and supporting him.

I thank the family and the community for taking this course of action today. If you had not done so, if you had not offered to support this boy, I would have had to send him to jail for a lengthy period, and I am certain that would have ruined him forever. You will have to be supportive to him for as long as he lives here. You cannot let your enthusiasm of today die out in a couple of months' time, and my greatest wish for your success and Henry's success goes with you.

Henry was released, and the court party flew out of Rankin Inlet at midnight. Judge Slaven's willingness to delay proceedings until counsel were ready was nothing new. He recognized the need for flexibility considering the conditions in which the circuit court worked. He also recognized, in Henry's case, the importance of his disposition not just to Henry, but to the entire community. Jim was quoted in Jack Batten's book *Lawyers* (Penguin Canada, 1985) as saying, in reference to this case:

It was the first time such a thing had happened in Rankin, the first time the local people had ever sat down together. You see, coming from all various backgrounds the way they had, different strains of Eskimo *(sic)*, they'd never managed as a real community. There was a professor up there, fellow named Williamson from the University of Saskatchewan,

who'd been going to Rankin every summer for eighteen years, and he said this was the old traditional Inuit
way of doing things, meeting together and looking
after their own. Well, hell, under those circumstances
the court was pleased to stand aside for a few hours.
That might sound ridiculous to a judge in the south,
but northern justice is different.

Northern Justice
I wish I could say it was my advocacy that resulted in Henry
being able to go back to his family that night. But that result
had far more to do with the understanding displayed by the
prosecutor and the willingness of the judge to take a chance.
Most of all it was the result of a community coming together to
care for one of their own.

John Bayly's work on the case was not done, however. As I
understood it at the time, his superiors in Ottawa were not only
surprised by the sentence, calling it a miscarriage of justice, but
were insisting that he file an appeal. He kept up a steady argument against it, and in the end, he convinced his superiors to
drop the idea of an appeal.

I kept receiving information about Henry for some time
after the hearing. In a letter from his former grade-school
teacher Jean Williamson, in October 1979, she wrote that "he
was doing extremely well and appears to be happy and con-
tented." The last word I received about Henry was in February
1988 when the local director of community programs wrote
that Henry was working in the hamlet garage, living with and
under the care of one of his older brothers, and that "he gets
along well with people." The general sentiment in the community, 10 years after the fact, was that the court's decision was a
good one and things worked out very well.

Over the 35-plus years that I spent as a lawyer and a judge,
I often thought back to Henry Suviserk Innuksuk's case. It was

not only the first case that opened my eyes to a different way of doing things, it was also the first example in the North of a community becoming an active participant in the justice system. It made me realize that the community at large has a stake in how an individual offender is treated, how a particular case is disposed of, and, because of that, its collective views and wishes should be heard and respected. In this case, it was the community that was the victim. And it was that victim that extended mercy to Henry and a helping hand for his future.

John Z. Vertes arrived in Canada with his parents in 1957 as refugees from the Hungarian Revolution. A Judge of the Supreme Court of the Northwest Territories for 20 years, he retired as Chief Justice and is past president of the Canadian Superior Courts Judges Association. He was Commissioner for the Alberta Public Inquiry into Health Services Preferential Access. He pursues judicial and legal education initiatives. From 2012 to 2015, he served as President of the Commonwealth Magistrates & Judges Association.

FIVE

The Hon. Kim Pate

THE STORY OF S:
A STUDY IN DISCRIMINATION
AND INEQUALITY

A FEW WEEKS AFTER I was appointed to the Senate, Lisa Neve called me, as she has nearly every day for the last 25 years, asking me how 'senatoring' was going. Lisa is one of my dearest friends and an amazing Indigenous woman. She also urged me to do everything I can to free our friend S.[1]

S, also an Indigenous woman, is the longest-serving woman prisoner in Canada. S and I are the same age, but our opportunities and consequent life circumstances are not at all the same. After more than a decade of horrendous physical, sexual, and psychological abuse in residential school, she was rendered easy prey for a number of abusive men. Initially jailed as an accomplice to her abusive partner's drug trafficking, in prison, she accumulated many more convictions and has spent most of the past three decades in segregation in many different prisons, in torturous isolation that contributed to her now disabling mental health issues. By all accounts, when S first entered the prison system, she was a nervous, shy, and easily intimidated young woman.

1   Although I want everyone to know the injustices that this amazing woman has survived, and I want her exonerated, I am honouring her request to not be identified at this time.

On March 31, 1993, testifying before the Royal Commission on Aboriginal Peoples (RCAP), S described how, when she was young, she and her mother and siblings would flee her father, sometimes hiding for extended periods in the bush, as he roamed the reserve, sometimes on horseback, shotgun in hand, threatening to kill them all.

Family alcohol and drug abuse encompasses a large part of S's history—a part of her history that is responsible for some of the most traumatic events in her life, including the death of her two brothers: one who overdosed and one who was shot to death by a third brother, who was intoxicated. Her father's alcoholism was partially responsible for her falling behind in school. A list of S's family members indicates that almost all are current or past alcohol or drug addicts and that some were physically or sexually abusive.

From that start, S was jettisoned into 11 years of residential school. During her involuntary confinement in residential school, she suffered physical, sexual, and psychological abuse, as well as cultural and linguistic deprivation, all of which primed her for the abusive relationship that followed.

As the Truth and Reconciliation Commission (TRC) has documented in significant detail, the kinds of abuse that S suffered in residential school are major factors that contributed to her lack of knowledge and awareness of her language and culture. They also contributed to her mistrust of authority, physical and mental health issues, criminal justice involvement, and the virtual absence of what the Correctional Service of Canada (CSC) refers to as positive 'pro-social' role models or supports.

Most of S's early charges were drug related, and like many others who experience victimization from childhood on, there were no supports provided to S to address the trauma she had experienced or prevent abuse from continuing in the future. Instead, she was introduced to substances that might temporarily anaesthetize her to her circumstances but which ultimately heightened and exacerbated her life challenges. Her first criminal charges were intimately connected to this history and stemmed from her relationship with her abusive husband, whom she married at the age of 16. He introduced her to his drug-involved world.

Indigenous women now represent upward of 50 per cent of women in Canadian federal prisons. This rate is the result of an 85.7 per cent increase in the number of Indigenous women in prison over the past decade. This over-representation is an ongoing legacy of Canada's racist and colonial history that traces its roots back to the breaching of Treaties, the outlawing of cultural and spiritual laws, practices and ceremonies, forced removal from lands and communities, residential schools, the so-called Sixties Scoop, ongoing state-sanctioned forced removal of Indigenous children from their families and communities via child-welfare interventions, inadequate living conditions, and many other human rights violations, all of which have wreaked havoc in Indigenous communities and on Indigenous Peoples.

Ninety-one per cent of Indigenous women in federal prisons have experienced physical or sexual abuse, or both. Most are also poor, young, and have had access to extremely limited educational and employment opportunities.

On March 25, 2014, a psychological/psychiatric assessment summarized S's circumstances as follows:

> [S] has been continuously involved with the correctional system since age 16. She said her life "was a big shambles of nothing. ... I never had time to have a life," and after reviewing available information, her assessment seems accurate. While in the community, her life was dominated by alcohol and drugs, as well as petty and violent crime. While incarcerated, she was frequently involved in clashes with the system and/or clashes with other [prisoners], thus leading to volatility and deep isolation for long periods, and a resulting

lack of close, stable relationships. She stated that she is "tired of being incarcerated" and wants to move forward with the rest of her life.

The story of how and why S has been criminalized and institutionalized for approximately four decades is a testament to this country's ongoing failure to ensure safety and support for Indigenous Peoples and particularly Indigenous women, as well as its failure to confront the racist and misogynist biases in Canada's justice system that still too often mean that justice is not even attempted, much less done.

S and Lorna

S was imprisoned for second-degree murder resulting from the 1991 death by suicide of another prisoner, Lorna Jones, at the Prison for Women (P4W) in Kingston, Ontario. S pleaded guilty to this charge, as she did to far too many other charges while in prison. The lawyer who 'assisted' S to plead guilty to second-degree murder resigned, as he was in the process of being investigated for possible disciplinary disbarment due to allegations that he had sexually exploited women clients.

S's personal feeling of guilt for what might, at most, have amounted to an assisted suicide, was far too easily accepted by all involved. To this day, correctional staff and prisoners alike who knew Lorna and S at P4W reject that Lorna's death was anything but a suicide. By all accounts, Lorna was extremely palsied and prone to seizures, apparently as a result of a tainted dose of narcotics ingested at some point prior to her time at P4W. Yet, shockingly, Lorna was forced to rely on her fellow prisoners to help her perform the most basic functions, such as feeding, dressing, and cleaning. She and S were very close, and so S was often Lorna's helper.

The staff and women at P4W, as well as the evidence considered during the inquest into her death, revealed that Lorna often discussed her desire to die in the months leading up to her death. In addition to her physical condition, Lorna was concerned that the increased burden of care that she required from her sister prisoners might cause resentment and result in her being alienated from them. These factors, coupled with the recent death of her brother and the suicides of a number of her friends—all but one of whom were Indigenous women in prison, more than likely contributed to what CSC labelled "her suicidal ideation."

S and Lorna were very close and considered themselves to be sisters. They both spent a lot of time in segregation and they helped each other to survive the pain and isolation of imprisonment. S helped Lorna to light cigarettes, tie her shoes, use the washroom, and although she initially refused, she says that she eventually did agree to help Lorna commit suicide.

In 1993, S reportedly admitted to a counsellor that Lorna had asked her to help her commit suicide and that she had done so by helping to fashion a noose from a television cable. Sometimes, she says she helped to put the noose around Lorna's neck and tie the other end of the cable to the bars of Lorna's cell. These sorts of admissions were the primary basis for her conviction, even though police photos of the scene of Lorna's death did not match S's description. Notably, following the inquest into Lorna's death, the verdict was that the cause of death was unknown. It is nevertheless widely accepted as a suicide.

When he accepted S's plea of guilty to second-degree murder, the judge stated that,

> Lorna is dead. The authorities believed her death probably was a suicide. [S], because her conscience was bothering her, confessed to killing Lorna. If she had not done so, she would not have been charged.

Prior to her confession, S had not been charged because the evidence surrounding Lorna's death was inadequate to support her conviction. While there are inconsistencies between the accounts of the guards and S, none of the evidence points to S being responsible for Lorna's death. For instance, one guard testified that when she discovered Lorna hanging from the bars, she was unable to lift Lorna's body to relieve the pressure on her neck. S's slight frame makes it extremely unlikely that she could have hoisted Lorna's body up to hang her from the bars, particularly if Lorna was an unwilling participant being murdered.

In addition to the differences in description of the manner in which the noose was affixed to the bars, S's reproduction of the knot she claimed to have tied was inconsistent with that removed from the bars. In addition, timelines set out in CSC documents and S's own account were inconsistent. Finally, at no time since her sentencing on April 22, 1994, has the effectiveness of her legal representation been challenged. Regrettably, her lawyer has since suffered a permanently debilitating head injury.

The image that emerges is one of a criminal justice system that fails consistently to protect and treat with dignity or respect, marginalized, vulnerable and victimized Indigenous women such as Lorna and S, yet seems to spring vigorously into action to criminalize them at most opportunities. This phenomenon of under-protection and over-policing of Indigenous women, coupled with their tendency to take legal and criminal responsibility for actions that are not criminal, or which were not committed by them, has been described as the hyper-responsibilization[2] of Indigenous women and is part

---

2   "Women and the Canadian Legal System Examining Situations of Hyper-Responsibility" in *26 Canadian Woman Studies 94*. The line between moral and legal responsibility too often becomes blurred in cases involving Indigenous and other racialized women: "Canadian law is often built around expectations that individuals take responsibility for their actions and nowhere is this truer than in matters of criminal law. What we have noticed over the years is a number of situations where women (particularly when they are racialized, have a disability or a mental illness, are poor, or a sexual minority) are expected by the legal system to take more responsibility than others. This is the situation we are referring to as hyper-responsibility."

of what also contributes to the numbers of Indigenous women who are missing and murdered in this country.

S speaks of her confession as being made while she felt intense personal guilt and responsibility to confess to a death that had been accepted as suicide. CSC's own documentation underscores the reality that its ongoing and prolonged history of segregating S made it difficult for her to tolerate stress and stimulation. It may well have been S's conscience-manifested feelings of guilt that pushed her toward a confession. While S continues to feel guilty for her actions, she no longer believes she is a murderer. Mere feelings of guilt do not and should not equate to responsibility for death, and they should not have been permitted to form the basis of her conviction for second-degree murder.

S's history reveals a perilous propensity for hyper-responsibilization through resignation to the unfairness of State responses to her. She has consistently conceded and accepted the consequences of charges, convictions, and sentences without resistance. For instance, at the August 3, 1988 sentencing proceeding that commenced her current and continuing period of imprisonment, S did not heed the Saskatchewan Provincial Court judge's advice that she proceed with assistance from counsel. The judge undoubtedly recognized the minor part, if any, that S played in her husband's drug dealing, but was likely ignorant of the realistic lack of faith S and too many other Indigenous women have in a legal system that delivers racism but rarely justice. Like so many other women I know, S's response to that judge was,

> I just want to get it over with, that's all. I am going to plead guilty to the charges. I know it's very serious. I've been through the system. … I just want to get it over with you know, and cleared up, because last time I sat on remand for about eight months until I got sentenced.

She handled most other charges accumulated in prison in the same manner. Worse still, she initiated the process that resulted in the second-degree murder conviction.

S adamantly believed that she was responsible for Lorna's death. However, her personal feelings of culpability should not have resulted in a murder conviction. For S, her confession clearly alleviated her feelings of personal guilt. CSC staff recorded S's conversation with *Kingston Whig Standard* journalist Paulette Peirol, as follows: "This is very hard on me ... you know, saying I did it. But I have to get it out of my system, because if I don't, I'm a person that can't live with this for the rest of my life."

S also indicated that she thought Lorna's family could find peace if they learned that Lorna did not take her own life.

When S was informed that she may be given a life sentence for second-degree murder, she said, "I'm not even worried at this point in time, what I get, as long as I have a clear conscience and I could sleep good at night, and live with myself and love myself and like myself."

Many people, including her lawyer, agreed that she would not have been charged had she not confessed. Although, throughout its correctional files, CSC alleges that S does not take responsibility for her actions or emotions, her numerous guilty pleas to all manner of institutional and criminal charges emanating from within the multiple prison environments to which she has been subjected, including the most significant and devastating of these, her confession in relation to the death of Lorna, contradicts this assumption.

The travesty for S is not only that without evidence from her confession, she would likely not be serving a life sentence; it is also that she is serving a life sentence with a record that, without proper context, portrays S as violent. This record resulted in S being classified as a maximum-security prisoner for most of her multiple decades in prison. For federally sentenced women, a maximum-security classification results in confinement in segregated maximum-security units within a multi-security unit within each federal prison for women. As a result of her near-constant state of segregation, S and other women classified as maximum-security prisoners end up with limited to no access to programming, educational opportunities, or Indigenous ceremonies—all of which also render conditional release remote, as the lack of available opportunities to complete programs prejudices prisoners' abilities to reenter the community.[3]

Barriers to Reintegration

S's record was used again and again to maintain her security level as maximum and to segregate her and thereby deny her access to therapeutic and rehabilitative programs and services aimed at facilitating her eventual release from prison and integration into the community. Segregation created and then exacerbated S's mental health issues and impeded her ability to recover from the many traumas of her past.

For instance, during an October 1992 Case Conference, the Psychology and Psychiatry team members working with S expressed concern regarding the "effects of extended segregation on [S's] mental health." It was recommended that she be released from prison then, or at the very least, that a gradual release process be commenced post haste. I can only imagine that her life might have unfolded very differently had that recommendation been followed. Instead, S continued to serve most of her time in maximum security and to be segregated from the general prison population.

On April 22, 1994, the day that S pleaded guilty to second-degree murder, inexperienced staff at P4W intervened in a minor dispute between women in a manner that escalated the events to those which became the focus of the Commission

3   Office of the Correctional Investigator, *Spirit Matters: Aboriginal People and the Corrections and Conditional Release Act* (22 October 2012).

of Inquiry into Certain Events at the Prison for Women in Kingston (Arbour Inquiry). S and another Indigenous woman were already in the segregation unit at P4W when six other women were dragged in following a fracas on the range. All eight women, five of whom were Indigenous, were then subjected to what the Honourable Louise Arbour chronicled as evidence of the absence of the rule of law with respect to the treatment of federally sentenced women. The facts she documented included such unlawful actions as,

- Assaults by staff on women,
- Stripping by male staff, shackling and leaving women naked in stripped cells for days,
- Coercion to 'agree' to body cavity searches while shackled, in exchange for showers and cigarettes,
- Involuntary and unlawful transfers of women to the sex offender unit in Kingston Penitentiary for men,
- Denial of the right to counsel for more than a week,
- Unlawful segregation for ten to twelve months, and
- Coercion to enter guilty pleas to charges of attempted escape, assault and uttering threats, in order to be released from segregation.

When S eventually had access to a new, Indigenous lawyer, Don Worme, he requested that she be moved out of segregation and that her security level be reduced so that she might be held in a less-restrictive environment. However, the spurious legal basis underpinning S's murder charge unduly influenced CSC staff decisions regarding rehabilitative options for S. Worse still, the correctional officer who authored S's progress report at the time noted that her transfer would assist S in avoiding responsibility for the murder of Lorna. Until she was eventually transferred to Saskatchewan, in addition to the general experiences of all of the women outlined above, generic statements of claim filed against CSC on March 5, 1998, regarding the actions of the men in the Kingston Penitentiary Institutional Emergency Response Team (IERT) at P4W on April 26, 1994, asserted that each of the women was,

- Attacked without warning by eight masked, armed men,
- Stripped naked or required to disrobe completely by the team of men,
- Placed in chains,
- Forced, naked, into the common area of the segregation unit,
- Forced to kneel, naked, for long periods of time, and
- Left chained and naked in an empty and dirty cell, the effects of which remain with her.

What is not chronicled in the legal documents, but what S told me when I saw her in the segregation cell at P4W a few days later, was that she was forced to stand in the shower area naked while restraints and shackles were fastened to her. She indicated that a male member of the team pulled back her gown and laughed at her. She also indicated that while she was held with her face against the bathroom tiles, a baton was brought up between her legs. Other women described being assaulted, having their clothes cut and ripped off of them by male staff, having requests for heart medication and sanitary products ignored, having eyeglasses smashed, and having windows being opened while the women were left shackled and naked in their cells.

When S and the other women provided the detailed accounts of what had happened to them, they also advised me that officers had video cameras and that they appeared to be filming everything that they did to the women. Neither they, nor I knew whether the staff had actually videotaped everything they did, nor, if so, whether the videotapes still existed. When I eventually viewed the video recordings of the April 26 cell extractions, everything the women said had occurred was indeed captured on videotape, except for one important detail.

Although the video shows S being held by at least two fully armed and masked men, face to the bathroom tiles, who make odd hand motions to each other just before the tape skips ahead four minutes, neither CSC nor the video ever revealed what happened in those missing minutes. I will go to my grave believing that it was during those minutes that the baton was brought up between S's legs in the manner she described. There is no other similar skip in the tape, and everything else the women reported to me is recorded. There is no other logical explanation for the skip in the videotape timer.

In order to have the shackles removed, S and the other women were required to agree to a body cavity search. Worse still, as the evidence at the Arbour Inquiry revealed, a doctor colluded with CSC by bribing women to comply with body cavity searches in exchange for a shower and a security gown. The cavity searches were completed on a dirty blanket, in a dirty cell. Although women were then placed in the shower area, they were not given enough time in the shower to wash themselves fully and then had to walk naked back to their cells before they were given clean gowns. S remembered feeling dirty, disgusted, scared, and ashamed.

Despite the numerous breaches of the law and CSC policies documented in the video, S did not lodge any complaints, nor was any disciplinary action taken against the staff in relation to the 1993 or prior incidents. She was described as having chosen not to return to Kingston to participate in the inquiry in person, although, she was so heavily medicated and isolated at Regional Psychiatric Centre (RPC) in Saskatoon, it is difficult to consider her actions as voluntary and most certainly they were not based on full information and informed consent.

In January of 1996, even though construction of the regional prison was incomplete, in an effort to draw attention away from the Arbour Inquiry's documenting of the litany of horrors of the treatment of the women at P4W, CSC decided to transfer women to the Edmonton Institution for Women

(EIFW). All but one (a 17-year-old) of the Indigenous women transferred to Edmonton from the RPC unit were immediately segregated in the maximum-security unit, which was then euphemistically referred to as an 'enhanced unit'.

Parenthetically, during one of my visits to EIFW during that time, I happened to arrive at the prison at the same time as a new CSC employee. She was a social worker whom I knew from the community. She was extremely excited that she was going to be working with women in the enhanced unit. She thought it was so named because the women there had access to enhanced services and supports. She had no idea that the primary enhancements in the unit were static security in nature. In fact, that first enhanced and maximum-security unit set the stage for what continues to be an ongoing status of segregation experienced by women classified as maximum-security prisoners, the majority of whom are Indigenous.

The conditions of confinement were particularly egregious for the women in the enhanced unit, but the lack of visits and programming, near constant state of lockdown, excessive and unlawful strip searches, inexperienced staff and construction-zone nature of the environment took its toll on all. Within a few months, women were fleeing the prison. Although all were easily located, usually at their homes, and one returned herself to EIFW, after three of the maximum-security women fled 10 blocks before they were intercepted by police, CSC transferred all of the women to the Edmonton Remand Centre in August 1996.

A handful of women classified as minimum-security prisoners were eventually transferred back to EIFW, but all the women classified as medium and maximum security were transferred to the Saskatchewan Penitentiary (Sask Pen)—a prison for men. S and the other women would be temporarily placed at the men's penitentiary for much of the next decade, from December 1996 to February 2003.

Ineffective Grievances and Correctional Intransigence

While they were housed separately, the women's yard was visible from the men's living units and when men were moving throughout the prison yard. The men would yell obscenities at the women and unzip their pants and masturbate. When the women informed the guards, they were questioned about their behaviour and accused of enticing or otherwise provoking the men. In addition to being held responsible[4] for the men's behaviour, the women were frequently also punished by both the insinuations and by not being permitted to leave the yard until they had completed their full hour of recreation.

For most of the time the segregated maximum-security unit at Sask Pen was open, the 15 to 24 women imprisoned there were almost exclusively Indigenous. Although they were told they would only be held in the men's prison for a short time and that they would have full access to programs and services, as well as Elders and spiritual and culturally specific initiatives, they actually had little access to anything but self-study with the support of a part-time educational support staff for most of their time in the segregated maximum security units.

During the eight years they were held there, the women lived 2, 4, or 5 to a range in up to 7 different cell areas, with limited access to mix as a larger group. As they began to despair at never being moved out of Sask Pen, women began to self-harm at alarming rates, and one woman was found hanging in her cell. As the levels of hopelessness and desperation grew, the women were encouraged by some of the men at the prison to take hostages and make demands for the programs they sought. At first, they staged hostage-takings

---

4   The Canadian Association of Elizabeth Fry Societies (CAEFS) and the Native Women's Association of Canada (NWAC) have described this as the hyper-responsibilization of women, particularly Indigenous women. This is more fully discussed in the article, "Women and the Canadian Legal System: Examining Situations of Hyper-Responsibility" by CAEFS/NWAC, *Indigenous Women in Canada: The Voices of First Nations, Inuit and Metis Women*, Winter/Spring 2008, v. 26, n. 3,4, p. 94.

amongst themselves. When that didn't work, they started escalating their self-harming and hostage-taking.

On one visit to Sask Pen in 1999, I was called back into the prison by the acting warden, as S had barricaded herself on the unit and because there was another woman on the range with her, she was also accused of hostage-taking. The staff knew that S did not trust them and asked if I would intervene. With my then-infant daughter in a carrier, I went back in to speak with S. She was upset because staff had not followed through on their commitment to allow her to call her sister to check on the health of her father, so she refused to lock up until she could make the call. The warden allowed the call, and she locked up. Despite my pleas that she go to trial and my offers to testify on her behalf, she subsequently pleaded guilty to forcible confinement and threatening assault because of her actions that evening.

During another visit a few months later, women were increasingly anxious about the ongoing paucity of programs. After convincing 4 women who were segregated to file a group grievance, I proceeded to the rest of the 5 ranges and the hospital location to meet with 20 other women in the prison. When I was in the unit manager's office at the end of the visit, the head of security interrupted our meeting to advise that he was planning to bring in the emergency response team. I asked why. He advised that the women on the segregation tier, the first range I visited that day, were rioting—screaming, yelling threats, and banging the bars of their cells. I advised that I had been down there speaking with those women a few hours before, and they were upset about the lack of programming and spiritual support—they were all Indigenous—but that they were working on a group grievance to address their issues. What was striking to me was what the head of security said: "Why don't you take the baby down? I hear they like your baby." I wondered, How serious could the risk be that the women posed if the head of security believed a baby could calm the situation? Why would they risk the potential escalation and risk of harm that accompanies engaging the riot squad?

Massive Deterioration in Health and Mental Health

In 2005, following transfers back to EIFW from Sask Pen and then between EIFW and Philippe-Pinel Institute in Quebec, S was transferred back to RPC, which is dually designated a psychiatric hospital (pursuant to provincial health legislation) and a federal penitentiary for men. Most of her next decade would be spent there, punctuated by transfers to other prisons. In an incident on October 6, 2005, S was admitted to a hospital after being found unconscious in her RPC cell. Over-sedation was deemed to be the cause of her decreased level of consciousness. She was subsequently held in ICU for 84 consecutive days on mechanical ventilation for adult respiratory distress syndrome and aspiration pneumonia.

Despite being in a coma and initially assessed as unlikely to survive, S was placed in restraint chains and cuffed to her hospital bed. Against all odds, S survived and emerged from the coma with no memory of what had happened but was overjoyed to see her sisters, nieces, and nephews. I had never seen S as happy as when I entered her hospital room to see her propped up on the bed with four children cuddling, hugging, singing, and reading to her. Despite concerted efforts to argue for parole by exception for S, CSC refused to support the initiative. Instead, she was returned to RPC, re-designated as high-risk, and subjected to the 'Management Protocol' a super-maximum security designation more restrictive than that in the special handling units for men considered the most violent and dangerous in Canada.

When she was finally able to exit her RPC segregation cell, predictably, the devastating impact of chronic segregation became manifest again. S exhibited extreme anxiety and sensory overload, to the point that the laughter and mouth movements of other women were intolerably stimulating and inspired crippling anxiety and paranoia.

Following the inquest into the death of Ashley Smith, with whom S was segregated in 2007, and S's residential school claim, in addition to our attempts to secure a judicial review of S's sentence and conditions of confinement, CSC began to acknowledge that since much of S's behaviour was common for people placed in segregation for inordinate amounts of time, they would be best advised to start working to assist her to get out of prison.

In March of 2015, S was transferred to the Okimaw Ohci Healing Lodge, a minimum/medium-security prison for women. A 2014 Psychological/Psychiatric Assessment Report noted that because of her history of charges in prison, S's "static risk for future violence will always be rated high," and yet stated in its conclusions that, in practice, "currently [S] presents as a low risk to re-offend violently." This contradiction highlights both how S's conditions of confinement have largely been ignored and her criminal record has been used to portray her as a risk in ways at odds with her actual behaviour and interactions. The classification system has consistently discriminated against Indigenous women by over-classifying them in ways unrelated to the risk that they pose to public safety.[5]

The ongoing legacy of S's experiences at P4W are reflected today in the difficulties she faces in obtaining conditional release. Public safety is best served by supportive gradual releases, yet, in 2018, the struggle to get S out continued. She was 17 years past her earliest parole eligibility date. In October 2015, the Parole Board of Canada refused S's request to participate in a package of 15 cultural and personal development ETAs (Escorted Temporary Absences)

---

5   Canadian Human Rights Commission (2003), *Protecting Their Rights*. See also, *Ewert v. R (2015 FC 1093)*.

that would have allowed her supported, structured, and supervised access to ceremonies on the Nekaneet Cree Nation. They did so despite acknowledging assessments that S poses "a low risk to reoffend violently," that "global factors are assessed as low institutional adjustment, low escape risk, and low risk to the public," and importantly that her management team assessed her risk as manageable and recommended that the ETAs be authorized.

The Parole Board decision was overturned on appeal, but when they were consequently required to reassess their decision, they found as a fact that S is a violent individual and negated our attempts to obtain a royal prerogative of mercy to release her from her sentence. Rather, they labelled her a "repeat violent offender" and directed that she demonstrate a "further period of demonstrated change and compliance" just to secure an escorted pass into the community. S's 1994 guilty plea and consequent second-degree murder conviction with respect to Lorna's death continue to be relied on to support a view of S as violent, despite the reality that all who know the circumstances view the conviction as wrongful and Lorna's death as, at most, an assisted suicide. And, virtually all of the offences committed while in prison were directly connected to periods of mental health crises.

The story that S's criminal record and files tell about her, devoid of context and assessed with tools that systematically disadvantage women and Indigenous Peoples could not be more different than how S is viewed by those who know her well. For example, a February 9, 2015, correctional assessment carried out at RPC notes that staff who have known S many years note that,

> [s]he is polite and respectful toward staff and the
> other women. She will always step up to complete
> any task that is needed ... is successfully able to stay
> out of the drama that is a daily occurrence on the

women's unit. The other women look up to [her] as a model of what an individual can do when they are determined to change their lives.

Outrageously, S's ETA was also denied on the basis that she was not initially aware of the purpose of the ceremony, a giveaway dance, that she had been invited to attend. Her inability to articulate the purpose of the event could be accounted for by a multitude of factors: from her dislocation from her family, community and culture, as a result of residential school and more than three decades of imprisonment; her cognitive impairment and low verbal comprehension processing speed, as a result of the 2005 over-sedation while at RPC; to her discomfort, humility and nervousness during the hearing, given her lack of prior release history and extensive history of incarceration and residential school confinement.

Aside from indicating that S, "identify[ies] as an Aboriginal" and that, "[a]s a child [she] attended a residential school where [she] reportedly experienced sexual, mental, physical, and spiritual abuse, as well as starvation and neglect," the Parole Board failed to consider the implications of those circumstances for S as is required by Section 718(2) (e) of the *Criminal Code of Canada*.

Instead, Parole Board members disrespectfully derided S's ignorance and confusion. The Truth and Reconciliation Commission recognized cultural disconnection as contributing significantly to the victimization and criminalization of individuals like S. S's experiences, ones shared by too many Indigenous women, were approached not as needs that the criminal justice system must respond to, but as risks requiring caution, concern for safety, and punishment.

The Honourable Louise Arbour has called for the elimination of segregation for women, a call that has been echoed by the Canadian Association of Elizabeth Fry Societies, the

Native Women's Association of Canada, the Canadian and Ontario Human Rights Commissions, and the DisAbled Women's Network of Canada. This call reflects both the inherent harm of segregation, which the UN Special Rapporteur on Torture has declared can constitute torture, and the added discriminatory impact of segregation on women, particularly Indigenous women and those with mental health issues, both of whom are disproportionately and unjustly labelled as security risks, with no apparent regard for the impact of disabling mental health issues and past trauma resulting from abuse.

S has experienced the worst of our education, mental health, and prison systems. Her life has been a litany of the failures of Canada when it comes to Indigenous women. The abuse that she suffered at the hands of virtually every man, and later every state actor in her life, resulted in her continued marginalization, repeated victimization, and, until recently, incessant criminalization, and imprisonment.

After nearly two decades of trying to extricate S from prison, and despite fervent efforts by too many correctional service and psychiatric professionals to prevent it, in the spring of 2020, S was finally granted a day parole conditional release. She now lives with her sister and enjoys the support of her sister's children and others. Her health and mental health have improved in ways that are described by all who know her as nothing short of miraculous.

S describes how happy she is and how grateful she is to be in the community. In addition, after witnessing how well S is doing—in clear and direct opposition to the dire predictions of correctional authorities—her parole officer and other correctional service representatives are now in full support of her ongoing parole and describe her as no threat to the safety of the community.

Equally optimistically, in 2023, the court application is about to be filed. This commences the process in pursuit of the exoneration of S for the death of Lorna Jones.

We celebrate every step to ensure S may experience the dignity of her last few years with those who love and care for her.

The Honourable Kim Pate was formerly the executive director of the Canadian Association of Elizabeth Fry Societies. In 2014, she was named a Member of the Order of Canada for advocating on behalf of women who are marginalized, victimized, criminalized, or institutionalized, and for her research on women in the criminal justice system. She was appointed to the Senate of Canada on November 10, 2016. She is a member of the Independent Senators Group.

PART II

LAWYERS

ELEANORE SUNCHILD KC

JONATHAN RUDIN

CATHERINE DUNN

JOE SAULNIER

BRIAN BERESH KC

JENNIFER BRISCOE

JOHN L. HILL

SIX

Eleanore Sunchild KC

TREATY LESSONS
THE KILLING OF COLTEN BOUSHIE

IN BATTLEFORD, in 1885, in the province called Saskatchewan, the Indians from the surrounding reserves witnessed the hanging of eight Indigenous Warriors, who were part of the 'rebellion' and were told this is what happens when you stand up against the government.[1] The Warriors were defending their People and wanted the Treaty promises fulfilled. The settlers brought their religion to the territory and ultimately, they wanted the land. They promised if the Indians agreed to share the land, the Indians would also retain half the land with unfettered access to the lands. Such was the agreement that the ancestors wanted. On August 9, 2016, after Colten Boushie was shot, Leesa Stanley, the wife of Gerald Stanley said, "This is what happens when you trespass."[2] This was not the Treaty agreement for our Indigenous Peoples to be killed on our lands.

August 9, 2016, was a dusty, hot Saskatchewan day. Colten and his friends were driving around the back roads of Saskatchewan in an SUV, as young people sometimes do in the prairies. They had consumed alcohol and had been swimming in the Saskatchewan River. On the way back home to the Red

1   "Battleford Hangings," from *Saskatchewan Indian*. July 1972 v03 no7 p05.
2   From *R v Gerald Stanley*, Preliminary Inquiry Transcripts, 308.

Pheasant First Nation, they entered Gerald Stanley's property. The SUV they were driving had a flat tire and they were driving the vehicle on its rim. By all accounts, Colten was sleeping in the back seat of the SUV when it entered the property. He committed no crime. Moments later, Colten was shot in the back of the head. The Stanley family went into the house to have coffee while they waited for the police to arrive. Much has been written and said about what happened in between these moments when these young people drove into the Stanley yard and when Colten was killed. There is much to the story surrounding Colten's death and the systemic racism that was witnessed during this case.

First and foremost, I have great admiration for the Boushie/Baptiste family, who have had to endure five long, hard years since the trial of Gerald Stanley, waiting for some kind of justice. I also have been waiting for justice, and I have spent my career waiting for a place in the justice system where I feel safe. The week after the Stanley trial, I walked into my local courthouse. Lawyers who I had been practicing with for over 15 years at that point refused to acknowledge me for, I can only assume, my support of the Boushie family. Only my one lawyer friend, Robert, said hello to me. The rest avoided direct eye contact or gave me an icy stare before looking away. Perhaps I said too much publicly about racism in the Battlefords and in the criminal justice system for their comfort. Maybe they didn't know what to say or were processing the events, as many were. I am not done yet because I speak out for my People as a whole, and I comment about the system that does not serve Indigenous People well.

Notwithstanding what happened immediately following the trial, I do have some strong and gracious lawyers who are staunch allies and defenders of Colten Boushie and his family, to whom I am very grateful. I won't mention names for fear of missing someone, but they know who they are, both Indigenous and non-Indigenous, and they put their names and faces forward through messages, phone calls, writings and workshops, legal seminars, interviews and articles. They will not be forgotten, and their support meant so much when we were launching the battle for meaning for Colten—for Colten to be seen as a human being. Period. And not a racial stereotype of a drunken, thieving Indian. He was Colten, Debbie Baptiste's son and could have been any Indigenous loved one.

My role in the case

My role during the trial was not as a lawyer for the Boushie/Baptiste family. During the trial, I was support, trying my best to provide the family hope and explain to them what was occurring during the proceedings. The Boushie/Baptiste family had entered into a formal relationship with lawyer Chris Murphy at the time. The family had been left on their own to navigate a racially charged trial and were not familiar with the Court process. Had it not been for the Federation of Sovereign Indigenous Nations assisting them, they would not have had the assistance of Mr. Murphy, an experienced and educated criminal lawyer, to explain the criminal proceedings of the day.

As a Cree individual, I was provided instructions from my grandfather and other Elders who taught me that my role as a Cree woman with a law degree would also include advising, and, according to traditional teachings, to support. Thus, when Alvin Baptiste—Colten's uncle who is also a traditional knowledge keeper—asked me to assist, it was done in the way that Cree law demands, that is, to assist and to support. I did not come on as a formal family lawyer until the civil suits were commenced. I was a family friend, and I was front line in the media, a role that I did not choose. However, I was able to talk to media at that point during the trial when I was trying to alleviate the burden on the Boushie/Baptiste family, while also trying to come to terms with what was happening in the trial.

I have studied and have seen the colonial justice machine in action. The colonial system stole our land and stole our children through the Indian Residential School system. The first-hand and inter-generational effects suffered by Indigenous Peoples has resulted in over-incarceration in the criminal justice system. The justice system treats Indigenous People differently than non-Indigenous People. Moments after Colten Boushie was killed by white settler Gerald Stanley,[3] the RCMP issued a press release that RCMP were investigating a theft-related crime.

Alvin Baptiste called me the next day advising me that his nephew Colten was killed after he and his friends entered the yard to seek help for car trouble and that Colten had been blamed for stealing. I knew there had to be more to the story and perhaps this was another case of systemic racism that characterizes so many Indigenous Peoples' experience in the justice system. This was the first inkling of what was going to come.

I have practiced law since 2000, mainly as a criminal lawyer. Since the Stanley trial, I have not found the joy in criminal law that I once felt in the courtroom. In fact, I often feel apprehensive in those spaces, perhaps because I spoke out loudly and frequently about the systemic racism that I felt in the courtroom on those days in January and February 2018 during the matter of *R v Stanley*. I now am more attuned to the explicit and biased racism that I see in the courts. I see it when the system proceeds against Indigenous women who are victims of abuse. I continue to witness differential treatment of Indigenous People and people of colour. I see it when the Boushie/Baptiste family was only provided one-and-a-half hour's notice of the media conference regarding the appeal.

At that press conference, the Crown made an announcement of their decision not to appeal. One-and-a-half hours notification to the family was was not enough time for the family to organize any sort of response about the Crown's decision not to appeal. Despite a personal meeting with the Premier of Saskatchewan, Scott Moe and a meeting with the Minister of Justice at the time,

---

3   The term "white settler" needs to here be used to express the point that he was indeed a Caucasian man who was charged with the killing of a young Indigenous man.

Don Morgan, on February 10, 2018, the family was not advised that the Crown would not appeal the verdict.

The issue in this process is that the Crown ought to have a relationship with, or at least support, the family. Although there rests no obligation on the Crown to have a relationship with any of the families of the victims in the case, they do need to communicate. I have seen good Crown counsel do this in a good way in many cases. I have witnessed even caring relationships between the Crown and families. With Boushie/Baptiste family, the family had to hire their own lawyer, Chris Murphy, to explain the process to them.

I am sad to say that I see too much racism in the province where I live and practice. The racism is harsh and strong, especially in the Battlefords. Surrounded by eight reserves, the Battlefords has a long and dark history of racism. Ironically the Battleford Court of Queen's Bench is the same court that sentenced the eight Indigenous Warriors to death in the so-called 'rebellion'. These warriors were defending their People when, after signing the Treaty, the women were abused, and the People starved. John A. MacDonald, the Prime Minister at the time wrote, "The executions of the Indians ... ought to convince the Red Man that the White Man governs." After the 'rebellion', the government went into full oppression tactics with the implementation of such racist policies as the pass system, the taking of Indigenous children through the Indian Residential School system, the Sixties Scoop program where Indigenous children were placed with non-Native families, amongst other racist attacks.

I was a part of the Sixties Scoop. I was adopted by a farming family of Scandinavian and Scottish descent in a Saskatchewan rural community. An entire book, not let alone one chapter in a book, could be written about my Sixties Scoop journey, as it was often painful and complicated. Yet I had a firsthand account of Saskatchewan rural mindset. I witnessed racist banter of small-town Saskatchewan in coffee row, in the schools and even in the church I attended. I caution that not all the white people of rural Saskatchewan and the surrounding area are racist. There are many open-minded and educated people, but like most of Saskatchewan, it is the rural people especially who lack full and comprehensive relationships or friendships with Indigenous Peoples. Not surprisingly, many settlers do not have a familiarity with Indigenous People of Saskatchewan, given the segregation policies that shaped this country, even with the establishment of reserves or their reliance on centuries-old stereotypes of the "wild, unpredictable, and thieving Indian" in justifying their fears and racism. Well, I did not fully understand my history as an Indigenous person in Treaty 6, nor did I know that I was part of the Sixties Scoop. I grew up hearing about "the Indians," not appreciating that I was one of "the Indians," though I was repeatedly reminded at school by racist bullies that I was a "dirty Indian." There were those who were my defenders, yet for the most part, I would encounter a racist slur and then would face a room full of stares, as my classmates were also trying to figure out my place. I bring this up not to talk about my story, only to state that I was not afraid of the white, rural supporters of Gerald Stanley who filled the courtroom, the parking lots, and social media, as I was once a part of their world, almost a hostage, a stolen child. My childhood as a Native child in a white rural town and school gave me an insight into Saskatchewan colonial racism that an outsider would not know and also helps me to articulate and deconstruct the racism that I witnessed in this case, on my lands known as Treaty 6, where I practice law.

Without compassion or decency
This is the hardest part to write because I witnessed the racism unfold and was helpless to stop it. I believed in the justice system to come to a just and fair outcome, and in verdict, my worst fears came true. With the utterances of the words, "Not Guilty," the RCMP issuance of a racist, victim-blaming press

release formed the basis of a false narrative about Colten and his friends committing a theft-related crime, when there was never a theft, nor a crime committed by Colten Boushie. I witnessed Colten's mom Debbie Baptiste cry when she recounted how she was treated the night that Colten was killed, how numerous RCMP officers invaded her trailer on the Red Pheasant First Nation and told her without any compassion that her baby boy was dead. She fell to the ground and was picked up by an officer to "smell her breath" after assuming that because she was a Native woman, she had been drinking. An even-worse insult was that they checked the microwave when she told the RCMP she had left Colten's dinner in there, as he had not come home for dinner yet. They searched her trailer, disturbing and traumatizing her grandchildren. The RCMP delivered a death notification without compassion or decency, just a harsh, "Your son is dead," or cold words to that effect, leaving Debbie a blubbering mess on the floor.

I make the assumption that the RCMP were looking for some kind of evidence to lay their racist views on that Colten and his friends were stealing. The communications and transcripts between the RCMP officers responding to the shooting on the day of August 9, 2016 have been since destroyed. The comments on social media and in general racist, rural discussion can be summarized as follows: How dare Colten and his friends steal from a hard-working white farmer; how dare they go onto a white farmer's land and disturb their property; and what else is a hard-working farmer like Gerry Stanley to do but to shoot? Arguably, defence of property or self-defence is not shooting an unarmed man in the back of the head. Interestingly, neither self-defence nor defence of property were put forth as a defence, although such language was used throughout the trial.

There were references by the defence that, "Your yard is your castle," seemingly a reference to castle law. "Put yourself in Gerry's boots," seems to be a reference to the hard-working Saskatchewan rural farmer. Also, there was much questioning about the Indigenous victims' alcohol consumption and activities on the day Colten was killed, to portray Colten and his friends as an alcohol-fuelled, thieving group of wild Indians, mirroring earlier colonial times of the hard-working settler versus the wild prairie Indians where the use of force was seen as a necessary means to an end of colonizing the west. When Gerald Stanley testified he was afraid for his life and was in terror, it made sense to rural folk. What else was he to do? He testified that he placed two bullets in the chamber of the Tokarev pistol and he fired two bullets, not knowing that he had another bullet in the gun. He testified the gun went off and the shooting of Colten in the back of the head was an accident, a hang fire. But he did not show appropriate emotion on the stand for someone who had taken a life. He did not seem troubled for this tragic accident, and he showed no remorse.

As witnesses will sometimes do, he did not spontaneously utter any apologies. Instead, Gerald Stanley and his family sat around the kitchen table having coffee for and hour and a half while they waited for the police to come. The gun somehow ended up placed back in its case. At no point when the police arrived did he say, "I am so sorry, the gun just went off!" He was tight-lipped, and in the video-recorded statement he gave to police, he was almost smug.

These questions were not put to Gerald Stanley, and more questions should have been asked of the Defendant. For some reason more questions were not asked of him. I know the courthouse held a handful of lawyers who were asking the same questions, "Ask him how the gun was put back in its case." "Ask him why he didn't tell the officers that it was an accident. "Ask him if he heard his wife Leesa Stanley tell the young Indigenous girls that this is what you get for trespassing." "Ask him if his wife, Leesa Stanley, who is a nurse, checked on young Colten Boushie, if she checked if Colten was alive or not." "Ask Gerald Stanley if he was remorseful for this terrible tragedy." "Ask him why they sat around drinking coffee with a dead body in their driveway." "Ask him about the missing bullet—the one that killed Colten...." No such questions were asked, and these questions remain unanswered.[4]

It seems that the majority of Saskatchewan agreed with the verdict. Sixty-three per cent agreed, according to a February 26, 2018 Angus Reid poll.[5] The majority of white rural farmers stood behind his hang fire story, a claim of a magic bullet that caused the death of Colten Boushie. It lined up with the admission that the first two shots were warning shots, even though the Indigenous male witnesses testified that a bullet went whizzing by their heads and that the other one ricocheted in front of them, not indicative of warning shots being shot up in the air as one would assume warning shots go.[6]

The fate of the case was sealed up by an all-white jury of Gerald Stanley 'peers'. Of course, the all-white jury was comprised of Saskatchewan residents in a province where racism is almost a part of the Saskatchewan experience. Racism and discrimination are the basis of opinions and stereotypes against Indigenous Peoples. Still the Boushie/Baptiste family held on to the slight glimmer of hope that the verdict would be manslaughter, yet I saw the writing on the colonial house of the justice that the verdict was going to be 'not guilty'.

I cannot write about the moment of the verdict quite yet as it is a vivid and traumatic experience that I am not yet ready to share. It is both personal and a shared trauma that I do not have permission to write about. I can say, however, that moment changed my life as my heart broke for the Boushie/ Baptiste family who had hope that the justice system would prevail and provide to them verification that Colten mattered; and at the same time, for that naïve and exciting enthusiasm that I once had for the law I devoted so much time and energy to. My faith in the justice system was shattered because I knew

4   *R v Gerald Stanley, Preliminary Inquiry Transcripts*, 29
5   https:angusreid.org/boushie-verdict
6   *R v Gerald Stanley*, Trial Transcripts, 354-355

that if that was my Indigenous child, uncle, brother, husband, or even myself, as an Indigenous woman in Saskatchewan in the same set of circumstances, *we* would be blamed for causing this white settler to take a life because *we* forgot our position in this racial hierarchy we call Saskatchewan, and I, as an Indigenous female lawyer cannot rely on the fragile veil of justice that I encountered in this case.

I do see Indigenous people attempting to make change, as am I. It is hard when the system does not understand our history or our struggles. I do see hope in our efforts, though, as there are many allies who stood up with us and more as we as a profession learn about the Indian Residential School System and the true meaning of reconciliation which is more than land acknowledgements or the Indigenization of colonial systems. It is about Indigenous People obtaining justice and in this case there was none.

I struggle to reconcile this case, this trial, as Colten and his family were left without justice, as were so many Indigenous people who came before Colten. I raise the injustice and systemic racism that I witnessed moments after Colten Boushie was shot and that was carried through to the moment of the lack of appeal. It still resonates today. I have many questions about how this case was handled. As an Indigenous lawyer, I go from feelings of sadness and disappointment in the current criminal justice system, to full-blown rage and anger because my children, our children, remain in danger in our territories. As I release that anger, I find hope when I realize that Colten Boushie lives on in every Indigenous person who stands up for themselves in the face of racism and discrimination. Colten Boushie stands for every proud child, and he lives on in every legal battle that we as Indigenous Peoples engage in to protect our People and ourselves.

For the rest of my life and for as long as I practice law, I will never let people forget the injustice that occurred in the name of Colten Boushie and the need for us as members of a legal system that still oppresses Indigenous Peoples to demand better. Finally, Colten represents all our children and the promise of the Treaty that we will walk around freely in our treaty territories.

In that moment, when we are safe in our territories and the Treaties honoured, only then will be have Justice for our People and finally, Justice for Colten.

Eleanore Sunchild, King's Counsel, is a Cree woman from the Thunderchild First Nation. Mother, wife, lawyer and activist, Eleanore carries many roles. She has been a practicing lawyer since 1999 and continues to speak out against the injustice that she witnessed following the killing of Colten Boushie in the criminal justice system. She currently centres her practice around civil law actions in Saskatoon, Saskatchewan.

SEVEN

Jonathan Rudin

THE DEATH OF REGGIE BUSHIE
AND THE EIGHT-YEAR INQUEST

O N Thursday, November 1, 2007, the body of Reggie Bushie was recovered from the McIntyre River by Ontario Provincial Police divers. Reggie, aged 15, had last been seen the previous Friday evening near the river by his older brother, Ricky Strang. Later that same Friday evening, Ricky had arrived alone back at the boarding home where they both resided, soaking wet. Reggie had only been living in Thunder Bay for about a month prior to his death.

Reggie and Ricky were born and raised in the Poplar Hill First Nation, a fly-in community approximately seven-hundred kilometres northwest of Thunder Bay, Ontario. The boys came to the city because there was no high school in or near the Poplar Hill First Nation. The best option available to First Nations' youth in Northern Ontario who want to further their education is to attend high school in Thunder Bay and live in boarding homes, away from friends and family.

Reggie attended the Dennis Franklin Cromarty High School (DFC). The school was operated by the Northern Nishnawbe Education Council (NNEC), a body set up in 1978 to provide educational opportunities for First Nations students in northwestern Ontario who did not have access to secondary school education in their communities.

At the time, Reggie's death was the fifth death since 2000 of a young person who had left their First Nation for high school in Thunder Bay. It would not be the last.

After Reggie's death, his mother, Rhoda King, and stepfather, Berenson King, wanted to know what had happened to their son, so they pressed for an inquest to be called into his death. Their campaign was supported by the Chief of their community as well as by the Deputy Chief of Nishnawbe Aski Nation (NAN), Alvin Fiddler. Their persistence paid off. An inquest was called into Reggie's death by the Ontario Coroner's Office, to be presided over by Dr. David Eden. The inquest was set to start in June 2009. It didn't happen then.

The Long Road and Huge Challenges

It took another five and half years for the inquest into Reggie's death to get underway, and by then, the inquest had expanded to look into the deaths of seven young people from fly-in First Nations, all of whom died while attending high school in Thunder Bay. The inquest took 9 months, involved 27 lawyers representing 12 parties, and 165 witnesses were called. The inquest jury made 145 recommendations.

Christa Big Canoe, my colleague at Aboriginal Legal Services, and I represented six of the seven families at the inquest. The seventh family chose not to participate. My direct involvement with the case began just after Labour Day in 2010.

The twists and turns in the story leading up to the inquest and of the inquest itself graphically illustrated the difficult and massively unequal relationships between Indigenous and non-Indigenous people in Canada, and particularly the precarious situation of those living in remote First Nation communities. This story shows there is reason for hope but also that there are huge challenges that the country must be willing to confront.

To understand why it took over five years for Reggie's inquest to begin, we have to look at another inquest into the deaths of two young First Nations men, Ricardo Wesley and Jamie Goodwin, who had lived in the Kasechewan First Nation, another remote fly-in community in northern Ontario. On the evening of January 8, 2006, both men were arrested in Kasechewan for being drunk and were placed in the jail on the reserve. Later that night, a fire started in Ricardo's cell. The jail had no smoke detectors, no sprinkler system, and no master key for the cell doors. Both Ricardo Wesley and Jamie Goodwin died of smoke inhalation.

Kim Murray, then of Aboriginal Legal Services (ALS), was one of the counsel for the Wesley family. One of her concerns was to have a jury composed of at least some individuals with knowledge of the realities of life on a remote First Nation in Northern Ontario. In order to see if this was possible, she asked about the presence of First Nations residents on the jury rolls in the Kenora District of Northern Ontario, the eastern counterpart to Thunder Bay. In September 2008, in response to her inquiries, an affidavit was prepared by Rolanda Peacock, the Acting Supervisor of Court Operations in Kenora. The information in the Peacock affidavit surprised Kim, threw the entire jury system in Ontario into turmoil for years, led to cases being argued at the Ontario Court of Appeal and the Supreme Court of Canada and the calling of a Commission of Inquiry, chaired by former Justice of the Supreme Court of Canada, Hon. Frank Iacoubucci.

The Peacock affidavit stated that it was problematic getting Northern Ontario First Nations on-reserve residents on the jury roll. Jury rolls in Ontario are constructed by using the names on municipal assessment rolls. Since First Nations are not municipalities, residents are not included on those rolls. The Juries Act explicitly allowed the province to obtain names of on-reserve First Nations residents through other sources, and until 2000, that had been done by writing

Indian and Northern Affairs Canada (INAC). The ministry has gone through many name changes over the years but it has returned to the INAC acronym, although it now stands for Indigenous rather than Indian. In 2000 INAC wrote the Province and said they would no longer provide lists of band members.

In the Kenora district, where on-reserve First Nations members make up approximately 30 per cent of the population, this caused a problem. The Peacock affidavit revealed that in 2007 less than 8 per cent of jury notices sent to on-reserve First Nations residents were completed and returned, as compared to 56 per cent in the rest of the district. The memo revealed that 2007 was not an anomalous year, but rather the continuation of a trend that had been observed since 2000.

Because Kim Murray was representing Reggie Bushie's family, the issue of on-reserve First Nations representation on juries in the western part of Northern Ontario was front and centre for her. At the same time, Mandy Wesley, another ALS lawyer, was preparing for a February 2009 inquest into the death of a young Indigenous man named Jacy Pierre, who had been found dead in the Thunder Bay District Jail.

Both Kim and Mandy wanted to know whether the problems in the Kenora district extended to Thunder Bay. Despite their many inquiries and requests for information from the Crown attorneys who were acting as counsel for the coroners, they were met with bland assertions that there were no problems, although no supporting documentation was provided. Kim and Mandy sometimes received no response from them at all. When they asked to examine Robert Gordon, the man responsible for court operations in both the Kenora and Thunder Bay Districts for the Ministry of the Attorney General, they were told by Mr. Gordon that they would have to obtain a subpoena from the coroner first. The coroners were not prepared to issue those subpoenas.

Concerned that a lack of a representative jury roll would impact the fairness of the inquest, in January 2009 Kim asked Dr. David Eden to postpone Reggie's inquest until guidance could be sought from the courts with respect to requiring Robert Gordon to testify. Dr. Eden agreed. Mandy made a similar request of Dr. Shelagh McRae, the coroner who was conducting the Jacy Pierre inquest, but she refused. The Pierre inquest began, the family walked out and the matter eventually made its way to the Ontario Court of Appeal.

The hearing of the appeal into both inquests was scheduled for September 14, 2010. By this time, Kim had left ALS to take a position with the Truth and Reconciliation Commission, as Executive Director, and so Mandy was set to argue the case. Sadly, on September 5, Mandy's mother, Coleen Tenona Beardy, a residential school survivor from Northern Ontario, passed away. Mandy asked me to fill in at the Court of Appeal, which is how I got involved in the case.

Evident Lack of Understanding
In a decision released in March 2011, the Court of Appeal accepted our arguments. We, along with counsel for Nishnawbe Aski Nation, contended that the concerns regarding First Nations residents on jury rolls in Northern Ontario was a legitimate issue, and that the coroners should allow questioning on those issues with the relevant witnesses being produced. Since the Pierre inquest had already been held, the Court took the unusual step of ordering a new inquest. Before Reggie's inquest could start, or Jacy Pierre's could restart, we had to determine what the situation was like in Thunder Bay. In the summer of 2011, I went up there to discover what was or was not happening.

The hearing on the Thunder Bay jury roll was conducted by Dr. David Eden as part of the now-resumed inquest into Reggie's death. On behalf of the Pierre family, who ALS also represented, we agreed that findings with respect to Reggie's case would also apply to Jacy's inquest, whenever that started. The evidence that came out over three days showed that low response rates from on-reserve First Nations residents to jury questionnaires was also the case in the Thunder Bay District, just as in Kenora. The evidence also revealed a deep lack of understanding of the basic realities of First Nations life. For example, witnesses called from the Ministry of the Attorney General's Court Services Division, people who were responsible for compiling the jury roll in the Thunder Bay area, did not even know what lists First Nations kept of their members.

For example, none of the staff was aware that the electoral list of First Nations Peoples included the names of members who did not live on the reserve. In 2000, the Supreme Court of Canada decided that First Nations electoral lists have to include all of their members, wherever located. Somehow the significance of that decision had not been understood by anyone in the Ministry of the Attorney General responsible for obtaining names of on-reserve First Nations members for inclusion on the jury roll.

It got worse. Robert Gordon, the man responsible for court operations for the Ministry of the Attorney General, testified under cross-examination by counsel for Nishnawbe Aski Nation that the position he had taken requiring a subpoena to have him testify, was dictated to him by senior staff at the Ministry, and went against his instincts. He went on to say that had he been able to decide this question on his own, he would have provided the information that we requested. When given the opportunity at the hearing, he apologized to Reggie and Jacy's family for the hardship and delay that his position had caused. While the Kings were unable to be present for the hearing, Marlene Pierre, Jacy's grandmother, was there to hear the apology.

Testimony at the hearing concluded on July 28, 2011, and Dr. Eden indicated he would release his decision in the autumn of that year. Whatever decision he arrived at, it was clear that the Ministry did not have a handle on on-reserve First Nations residents participating in the jury process in the province. On August 11, before Dr. Eden released his decision, the Ontario Attorney General announced that he had retained former Supreme Court Justice Frank Iacobucci to conduct an investigation into First Nations representation on Ontario juries. Justice Iacobucci's report would be made public and was due in August 2012 but, to no one's surprise, given the complexity of the issues, it was delayed.

Proper Representation Demanded

Dr. David Eden released his decision on the Thunder Bay jury roll on September 9, 2011. He found that the problems with the jury roll in Thunder Bay were similar to the problems in Kenora and felt that an inquest could not be called until First Nations on-reserve residents were properly represented on the jury rolls. While this was a victory in one sense, it also meant the inquest into Reggie's death was going to be delayed even further. Since the time of Reggie's death in 2007, two more students from remote First Nations had died while attending high school in Thunder Bay.

Following the release of Dr. Eden's decision, we participated in a press conference along with representatives from Nishnawbe Aski Nation urging that the province call a public inquiry into the deaths of the students. There were now two major hurdles with respect to Reggie's inquest. The first was that it was not clear when it would ever be held, given the problems with the jury roll. The second issue was that an inquest solely into Reggie's death would not necessarily get at the larger issues surrounding the deaths of the seven students. It was hoped that a public inquiry would be able to overcome those hurdles.

What followed was a period of discussion and negotiation that concluded with the Office of the Chief Coroner announcing, on May 31, 2012, that the inquest into Reggie's death would now be expanded to look at the deaths of the seven young people. The inquest would not actually get under way for another three and half years.

An inquest of this scope and size had not previously been undertaken in Ontario, and getting it off the ground took more work and time than anyone had anticipated. Because the Ontario Provincial Police had to provide a brief of evidence into all of the deaths, all files had to be examined, and witnesses had to be contacted and interviewed.

When the expanded inquest was announced, the families of the other students who were now part of the inquest process also needed the opportunity to obtain counsel. In the end, the families of five other students asked us to represent them along with Reggie. We were now representing the families of: Jethro Anderson, who died on November 11, 2000; Paul Panacheese, who died on November 11, 2006; Robyn Harper, who died on January 13, 2007; Kyle Morrisseau, who died on November 10, 2009; and Jordan Wabasse who died on May 10, 2011. The family of Curran Strang, who died September on 26, 2005, decided that they did not want to participate in the process.

A Report Worth the Wait

As this work proceeded, Justice Iacobucci was also conducting his inquiry that included a number of trips to Northern First Nations as well as consultations in the rest of the province. Justice Iacobucci's report, "First Nations Representation on Ontario's Juries" was finally released in February 2013.

The report was worth the wait. It made 17 wide-ranging and comprehensive recommendations. On the day it was released, Hon. John Gerretsen, then the Attorney General, promised that the province would implement all of the recommendations.

One of the first recommendations in the report was that

the province create a new position in the Attorney General's office—an Assistant Deputy Attorney General responsible for Indigenous Issues. The person hired for this position was Kim Murray.

Another recommendation was that the Province consider the idea of allowing on-reserve First Nations residents to volunteer to be on inquest juries. This, too, was implemented and was in place by the time the inquest into the deaths of the seven First Nations youths began in Thunder Bay on October 5, 2015. In fact, one of the five members on the inquest jury was selected through that process.

The jury had much to deal with. First, of course, were the circumstances of the deaths of the seven youths. Paul died in the kitchen of his home in Thunder Bay, and there was no immediate cause of death. Robyn, the only young woman of the seven, died of alcohol poisoning on the floor of the boarding home where she had been living for just a few days since her arrival from the Keewaywin First Nation. As in the case of Reggie; Jethro, Curran, Kyle, and Jordan were all found in the rivers of Thunder Bay and had gone missing between late September and February (although Jordan's body was not found until May, he went missing in early February and it is assumed that he died very soon after he was last seen).

In addition to looking at the deaths themselves, the jury also needed to learn about the state of education on First Nations; why students had to leave home if they wanted a high school education; the way DFC and the Matawa Learning Centre (MLC), the other high school for on-reserve students in Thunder Bay, were operated and funded; the police investigations surrounding the deaths; and, of course, the broader circumstances of the realities of First Nations People in the North, including the legacy of residential schools.

The number of issues that were to be canvassed also meant there were many parties who felt that they had a need for legal representation at the inquest. In addition to the families, standing to call and examine witnesses was given to Nishnawbe Aski Nation (NAN); Northern Nishnawbe Education Council (NNEC); Matawa Learning Centre (MLC); Keewaytinook Omikanak Council; Ontario First Nations Young Peoples Council of the Chiefs of Ontario; the City of Thunder Bay; The Thunder Bay Police Board; the Chief and Deputy Chief and the Thunder Bay Police Services; the Thunder Bay Police Association; the Office of the Provincial Advocate for Children and Youth; the Province of Ontario; and Canada. Dr. Eden had his own counsel as well who were responsible for calling witnesses, scheduling and trying to keep things on track.

What all of this meant was that there were many issues to cover at the inquest and a lot of lawyers as well. Funding had been secured to ensure all the families could attend the opening of the inquest, closing submissions, and the final recommendations of the jury. Funding was also available to bring families in when the deaths of their loved ones were examined.

Unfortunately, things did not go well when the inquest began. Although a brand new courthouse had just been constructed in Thunder Bay with a number of large court-rooms, the one that was chosen for the inquest was too small to accommodate the family members who wanted to be there. The hearing was delayed on the first day as peo-ple tried to find chairs and make room for family members. After that very rough beginning, a courtroom was found that was large enough to accommodate the lawyers and the families.

Falling Finally into a Rhythm

Once all the bugs were worked out, the proceedings fell into a rhythm that often belied the challenges faced by the families. While it had been 4 years since the last death had occurred, and 15 since the first, the families had generally not received much information regarding the deaths of their loved ones. For that reason alone, the process was very difficult for family members.

In Reggie's case, his family had never really heard about the circumstances surrounding his death; they just knew he had drowned. Making it all the more difficult, the last person to have seen him alive was his older brother Ricky. During the portion of the inquest focusing on Reggie's death, coroner's counsel called Ricky as a witness. As counsel for the family, I had to cross examine him. It was a very tough time for Ricky and his family.

The evidence was clear that on that Friday evening, the two brothers had been drinking by the river with a number of other students from Dennis Franklin Cromarty High School (DFC). Since alcohol consumption was not permitted by the school and could result in students being sent home, the students drank by the river because it was a concealed spot and they were out of sight of bystanders. The drinking that evening was, in part, to say goodbye to a student who was being sent home for consuming alcohol. Ricky and Reggie and the other students were too young to purchase alcohol and they relied on a runner—an older person—to go to the liquor store in the mall by the river to buy the booze. While the recollections of the people present that evening were clouded by the passage of time and the amount of alcohol consumed, it was clear that around 9:00 or 10:00 p.m., Reggie and Ricky were the last ones by the river. The witnesses testified that Reggie was very drunk.

Ricky testified that he remembered being with Reggie. He then thinks he passed out and when regained consciousness he was in the McIntyre River. He got out of the river and made it back to his boarding home, cold and soaking wet. He did not recall seeing Reggie when he left but he had fleeting memories of trying to pull something out of the water. He also thought he might have been pushed into the water, but again he had no precise memories of anything other than coming to consciousness in the water.

The other river deaths followed generally similar themes—there was alcohol consumption and there were other people present for some period of time, although precisely how any of the students ended up in the water was never clear because no one saw them go in. In the case of Jordan Wabasse, the last student to die, he was last seen exiting a Thunder Bay bus near his boarding home and was not near the water at all.

Five Possible Verdicts
One of the purposes of an inquest is to determine the cause of death. At an inquest, there are five possible verdicts with respect to cause of death: natural causes, accident, suicide, homicide, or undetermined. As there was no evidence that any of the deaths were self-inflicted, there was never any consideration of suicide as a cause of death. In the coroner's context, homicide has a wider definition than in criminal law and includes a death caused by the actions of another person whether criminal or not. In all of the seven deaths, cause of death was a live and disputed issue.

With respect to Paul, who died at home at the age of twenty-one, the medical evidence indicated that it was likely some sort of heart issue that caused his death, but no precise determination could be made. The jury concluded his death was undetermined.

With 18-year-old Robyn, there was no question she died in her boarding home of alcohol poisoning. She did not consume the alcohol in the home; instead, on a cold January night, she had been drinking in a wooded area. She was returned to her home by staff at DFC who left her in the hall. Her boarding parent, who also worked for DFC, was at work and testified she checked on her at about 2:00 a.m. but took no steps to seek medical attention for her. It was the contention of the family that her death was best seen as a homicide because had the people responsible for her care taken the necessary care with her, she might not have died. The jury returned a verdict of accident.

The river deaths were, in some ways, the most difficult to determine. There is no question that the five young men all drowned, but how did they get in the water? All of the deaths occurred between late September and February, and all five were clothed when they were taken out of the water. There were no witnesses who could explain how they entered the water. In addition, evidence was received by way of an agreed statement of fact from a former student at DFC who said that on October 28, 2008, almost exactly one year after Reggie went missing and a year before Kyle, he was walking by the McIntrye River on the way back towards DFC when he was confronted by three men. The three men threw him in the water and tried to prevent him from getting out, but he managed to get to the other bank and escape.

There was not any direct evidence to suggest that any of the five was murdered, yet there was little evidence to suggest that the deaths were accidents. The pathologist called by the coroner suggested all the deaths should be seen as accidental but allowed that Jordan's death could be undetermined. In his final submissions, coroner's counsel suggested that Jordan and Kyle's deaths were best seen as undetermined. On behalf of the families, we contended that all of the river deaths were undetermined, as troubling as that finding might be. In this position, we were joined by Nishnawbe Aski Nation (NAN).

Troubling Conclusions

In the end, the jury found that the deaths of Jethro, Kyle, and Jordan were of undetermined causes but that Curran and Reggie's deaths were accidents. The jury is not required to explain its verdict, indeed, that isn't permitted, so why some deaths were undetermined and others accidental is unclear.

It may have been that the evidence showed that the last sighting of both Curran and Reggie had them on the banks of a river, whereas Jethro, Kyle, and Jordan were not last seen close to water.

The findings that at least three of the river deaths were by undetermined causes leads to some troubling conclusions. If the deaths were not accidents, they certainly didn't arise from natural causes either. Since suicide was ruled out in all deaths, that means that if they were not accidents, then 'someone or ones' were responsible for the deaths.

There were many other aspects of the inquest that revealed very troubling and systemic issues. The one that stands out most for me is the reality of pervasive racism—racism makes the 'undetermined causes' ruling of the deaths conceptually easier for me to understand. Almost all of the witnesses who testified about their experience attending high school at DFC spoke about the racism—racism that sometimes took the form of name-calling but often included food and drinks being thrown at them on the street. These incidents happened day and night. They happened not only over the 16-year period that the inquest looked at in detail, that is, from 2000 to 2016, but extended back to the 1980s and 1990s.

Students who came to the city from First Nations communities where this sort of racism was foreign had to live with the knowledge that these assaults could occur at any time. None of these students ever went to the police, and most didn't even report it to school staff. It was—and is—the price First Nations students pay for high school education.

With the release of the final report of the Truth and Reconciliation Commission looking at the impact of residential schools in Canada, there has been a great deal of discussion regarding the need for reconciliation. Yes, there needs to be talk about reconciliation—and not merely talk but action. That is why the Commission issued Calls to

Action as opposed to recommendations. The Commission's Calls to Action engages not only governments but many institutions, particularly educational institutions, to take steps to ensure that they tell a complete and accurate story of Indigenous people in Canada.[1]

Reconciliation is important. I do worry, however, that the term reconciliation can mask the darker realities that are still present in Canada. Reconciliation suggests that the evils have been done and what is now required is to work to remove the residue and the stains of those evils. With respect to residential schools, this is undoubtedly needed. The schools have now all been closed but the residue of the schools is still with us, and we need to recognize and address those impacts. Racism experienced by Indigenous Peoples in this country is not entirely a residue from the residential school experience, but it comes from the same mindset that allowed the residential school system to be developed in the first place—a belief that Indigenous People are less important than other Canadians. It is this belief that has allowed governments to ignore treaties, to criminalize Indigenous cultural practices, to strip Indian status from First Nations women who married non-status Indian men, and to not treat the disappearance of Indigenous women and girls seriously, to name just a few examples. This racism is, sadly, still alive in Canada.

Of course, not everyone in Thunder Bay throws things at First Nations students just as not everyone in Canada holds racist attitudes toward Indigenous People. But enough people in that city hold these opinions and act on them so that throwing things at Indigenous kids has become a practice that has transferred across generations.

The only way these pernicious practices can be rooted out is for everyone to take a stand against such behaviour and

1   *The Truth and Reconciliation Commission: Calls to Action* report can be downloaded as a pdf by scanning the QR code in the margin alongside this footnote.

attitudes. While there are limits to what the legal system can accomplish in this regard, there are no limits to what society as a whole can accomplish if it puts its mind to it. For me, the legacy of the inquest into the death of Reggie Bushie and the other six students will be found in the way that Canada moves away from the racism that marks its past and present toward a better and more inclusive future. It is possible, it is essential, and it cannot wait.

Jonathan Rudin received his LL.B. and LL.M. from Osgoode Hall Law School. In 1990 he was hired to establish Aboriginal Legal Services and is currently ALS Program Director. He has appeared before all levels of court, including the Supreme Court of Canada including representing ALS before the Supreme Court in R. v. Ipeelee (among other cases). At ALS, he helped establish the Community Council—the first urban Aboriginal justice program in Canada in 1992, and in 2001 helped establish the Gladue (Aboriginal Persons) Court at the Old City Hall Courts in Toronto. Mr. Rudin also teaches on a part-time basis in the Department of Liberal Arts and Professional Studies at Osgoode Hall Law School at York University and also at Ryerson University.

EIGHT

Catherine Dunn

SILENT PARTNER

༄

W HEN I FIRST MEET ANNA (a pseudonym), she is extremely
withdrawn and reserved. I am a stranger to her as she
has had no previous contact with the justice system. Anna is
understandably wary of me. She does not look at me or speak to
me, and when asked, she provides only the briefest responses,
averting her gaze and often covering her mouth with her hand
as she speaks. I try to establish a rapport with her, sharing that
I, too, am the mother of a toddler; speaking to her as gently as I
can about her background. I explain the charge against her, the
court process, and the consequences of a conviction. The facts
are extremely serious. Anna is being prosecuted by indictable
offence, which carries a maximum of five years in the penitentiary. Here are the details as I saw them.

Anna's Story
It is 1987. The last Indian residential school will not close in
Canada until 1996. Battered Wife Syndrome has yet to be val-
idated by the Supreme Court of Canada. It will be decades
before domestic violence, child welfare, and criminal justice
will be judicially linked to historical and cultural oppression
created by the impact of settler colonialism.

Anna looks younger than she is, a prisoner's grey sweatshirt dwarfing her tiny frame. Blue nylon boots issued by the Winnipeg Remand Centre hang off her feet. Her straight, black hair falls over her face, her cheek and jaw are bruised and swelling like a snake bite, squeezing her eye shut while leaking blood and water. Anna has been charged with "fail to provide the necessaries of life" pursuant to *Section 215(1)* of the *Criminal Code*. She has failed to seek medical treatment for her 9-month-old daughter, now dead from complications as a result of a blunt trauma injury to the abdomen.

Anna has been flown to Winnipeg from Bloodvein, a Treaty 5 First Nation on the eastern shore of Lake Winnipeg and home to Ojibwa hunters, fishers, and gatherers. The reserve is surrounded by the largest untouched boreal forest in the world. Local rock art petroglyphs date back over a thousand years. Despite a rich and proud history, Bloodvein, like many reserves, is challenged by third-world poverty, poor housing, lack of infrastructure, and paralyzing unemployment. In order to 'kill the Indian in the child', residents of Bloodvein, like residents of many reserves across the country, were forced to attend Indian residential schools, a policy initiated by the Canadian Government in the 19th century. As has been well-documented through the Truth and Reconciliation Commission, these schools had devastating social and cultural consequences, which continue to have a direct impact on First Nations people today.

Anna and her domestic partner, Felix (also a pseudonym), originally met in Winnipeg, having come from separate reserves in northern Manitoba. Anna was born on a reserve but raised in Winnipeg, in foster care. Shortly after meeting, they returned to live on Felix's reserve in Bloodvein where they have 3 children, ages 3, 2, and 9-months on the date of the offence. Anna lacks a strong connection with Felix's community and has few formal or informal resources on which to rely. Through Felix, she is able to obtain housing and band assistance, but has limited social contact, relying primarily on the women in Felix's family. Anna does not drive, does not have easy access to transportation, is often without a phone, has no access to daycare, has no control over the family's finances, and does not have contact with her own family of origin, having been placed in foster care at an early age.

Her partner Felix has a significant alcohol problem. He has a criminal record, including assault, and has a reputation in the community for raging alcohol-fuelled encounters resulting in injuries to other people and damage to property. Anna's medical file shows a steady stream of contact with the local nursing station for injuries for which no cause is ever recorded. Her injuries include broken bones, smashed teeth, and black eyes. Nothing in the medical file suggests that her partner is responsible, and there are no complaints by Anna against him to the Band Constable or to the local RCMP. There is no therapist or mental health worker on the reserve, nor is there a domestic violence shelter. Anna has no safe space to go to, and in the time up to and including the birth of her daughter, Anna has lived in a world of complete isolation, combined with a daily fear of being physically assaulted. In the dangerous world created by her partner for herself and her children, her silence is the only way in which to survive.

Anna has an exemplary parenting history. Medical reports from the nursing station confirm that she has taken her infant daughter, as well as her other children, regularly for medical checkups. Her infant is up to date on her vaccinations and is meeting her milestones for height, weight, and development. Any small health concerns, such as colds or fevers, are attended to promptly. There is no concerning medical history with respect to her two older children. After the death of her infant daughter, an autopsy confirms that the infant presented as a healthy, nourished baby with no unusual unhealed and unreported fractures, bruising or other issues. Anna has no history of alcohol abuse, does not have a criminal record, and has no apparent mental health issues. Although rarely seen in the community, Anna is considered to be law abiding. She spends most of her time in the family home and is only seen in the community accompanied by her three children, all of whom are bonded with her. By contrast, Felix spends much of his time away from the home, is often intoxicated in public, and is either the perpetrator or recipient of many assaults. Bloodvein is a dry reserve.

After the death of their infant daughter, both Felix and Anna are charged with failing to provide the necessaries of life. Felix's charge is dropped after the preliminary hearing as he has a partial alibi. In the hours leading up to the injury to the infant daughter, Felix, who is in his early 30s, was at a teenage drinking party taking place on the shores of Lake Winnipeg.

None of the information with respect to the hours preceding the injury and death of her infant daughter is provided directly to me by Anna, who remains mostly silent throughout my interactions with her over the next 12 months. Confirming she was with her daughter at all relevant times, she does not explain what she knows or doesn't know about the injuries received by her daughter. She does not comment on her role or understanding of those injuries and never at any time does she suggest that Felix was involved or responsible in any way for her own facial injuries noted at the time of her arrest or for the injuries which resulted in the death of her daughter. Anna does not explain why she failed to obtain medical intervention for her daughter, despite clear forensic evidence that her daughter would have been in obvious distress from blunt force injury to her abdomen, and which may have been intentional.

What Happened?

Although Anna never reveals what happened on the night in question, she slowly, and over a period of a year, provides me with a glimpse of her domestic life with Felix. She shares that on one occasion after being assaulted by Felix, who was in an alcoholic rage, she ran barefoot in her nightdress to her mother-in-law's home approximately three kilometres away. It was a cool September night in northern Manitoba. Anna arrived at the home, and, despite the fact that she could both hear and see people laughing within the residence, no one answered her knock or her pleas for help. Afraid to go back home, Anna made the decision to spend the cold night on her mother-in-law's wooden stoop. On another occasion, prior to her baby's birth, Anna describes having been forced to flee from Felix's wrath by running into the bush and hiding there, silent and shivering, while her husband searched for her, rifle in hand.

None of these incidences of domestic violence was ever reported. It is never suggested by Anna to me, or to the police, that Felix was responsible for her facial injuries or for the injuries to her daughter in the hours preceding her daughter's death.

When Anna is released on bail, she is permitted to remain in Winnipeg, subject to a reporting condition. She does not return to Bloodvein, nor does she return to reside with her common-law partner. Her two children remain in foster care in Bloodvein, having been apprehended by Child and Family Services. On social assistance, and reporting regularly to her probation officer as a condition of her recognizance, Anna lives trouble free on bail in Winnipeg.

The preliminary hearing is held in Bloodvein at the local Band Office. The entire court staff flies in from Winnipeg for the hearing. The judge is a white male, the Crown attorney is a white male, the court clerk is a white male, the RCMP officers providing evidence are white males, the primary Crown witness, a forensic pathologist, is a white male. The court audience observing the preliminary hearing are predominantly male, and are either members or friends of Felix's family. As per court protocol, there was never any communication, conversation or direct contact between court staff and my client other than with respect to her election to seek a Queen's Bench trial. It is unnerving for Anna to participate in the judicial process. Other than this incident, she has never had contact with the police nor with the court system. Its customs are alien to her.

The evidence at the preliminary hearing confirms that Anna called frantically for a medical transportation vehicle in the early morning hours regarding her daughter, who was unresponsive and cold to the touch. The report states that she did not complain about her infant being in obvious distress at any time (which contrast to the medical examiner's evidence about the consequences of the injury). Her partner was not home, and the only other adult in the home was Anna. She is described as appropriately shocked and disturbed by the condition of her daughter as she attends with transportation personnel to the nursing station. Upon arrival, the infant is pronounced dead and in the beginning stages of rigor mortis. Anna is described as inconsolable with grief. RCMP officers who return with her to her home note that the condition of the home is neat and tidy, the cupboards are well stocked with food and baby supplies, and upon arrival, medical personnel note that the two other children are asleep and otherwise unharmed.

The primary Crown evidence is provided by the medical examiner, a forensic pathologist. His evidence confirms that the location of the infant's injuries is concerning. The medical examiner is emphatic that the injuries could not have resulted as a result of the infant being dropped or the result of an accidental fall. The force was applied directly to the abdomen. The infant would have been in considerable visible and audible distress for a number of hours preceding her death. The autopsy report prepared by the medical examiner concludes that as a result of blunt trauma to the child's abdomen, her bowel ruptured and the contents excreted into her blood system, eventually causing sepsis and death.

As a mother and as a lawyer

As a mother myself, it was difficult for me to understand why any mother would not seek medical treatment for their infant daughter in the circumstances. Given Anna's excellent parenting history, it did not make sense to me that she would make a conscious, or even an unconscious decision to allow her daughter to suffer in such an agonizing way.

Coming to Anna's story from a place of privilege made it difficult for me to appreciate Anna's circumstances. Her life experiences and mine were vastly different. On an intellectual level, I could recognize Anna's circumstances as difficult and often bizarre; emotionally I had no real understanding of her day-to-day challenges. As a mother, I was deeply aware of the strong instinct to protect one's children at all costs. It did not seem possible from Anna's strong parenting record that she would deliberately choose to fatally delay medical treatment for her baby.

As a lawyer, I was aware that difficult circumstances often produce difficult results. Fear, anger, even resentment can create complex psychological perceptions and conduct which subjectively seem inexplicable. As a woman living in financial, physical, and emotional security, it was impossible for me to comprehend, at a gut level, the daily challenges Anna lived and which I never experienced.

In the months and years leading up to this tragedy, Anna lived a life of complete physical and emotional isolation. Her day-to-day survival was dependent on the behaviour of a domestic partner who was at times withdrawn and, at other times, unpredictable and explosive. I have, over the course of my career, seen hundreds of women living with the effects of domestic violence. They come from all walks of life, all cultural groups, and all socio-economic groups. Without exception, they articulate a sense of powerlessness about their situations. They believe their partners have complete control over their lives and their bodies. Even when physically separated, they continue to be subjugated by the power they perceive their abusers have, notwithstanding that they no longer live together as a couple. They struggle to appreciate that their legal rights are to protect them and not to protect their partner. They perceive their partner's legal authority to be bigger, stronger, and more oppressive than their own. They often feel that their own conduct is directly related to the negative consequences from which they suffer. It can take months, or even years, to erase the effects of even short periods of a cohabitation that is marred by domestic violence.

The image of Anna hiding in the bush, prior to her infant's birth, as her partner hunted her methodically through the night, and the equally disturbing image of her then nine-month-old baby needlessly suffering for hours prior to her death, was distressing. Anna at no time made a connection of any kind between her own dangerous situation and what happened to her daughter. What happened that night in the early hours preceding her daughter's death, I will never know. While Anna's partner was absent for a significant portion of the preceding 24 hours in which her daughter was injured, Anna was in attendance and present in the home for the entire period preceding and subsequent to the injury and death of her daughter.

The Legal Issue

The *Criminal Code of Canada* provides that every parent, foster parent, and guardian, or head of the family is obligated to provide the necessaries of life for a child under the age of 16 years, including medical treatment. The section imposes a legal duty. The personal characteristics of the defendant, falling short of mental capacity to appreciate the risk, are not relevant. The *Criminal Code* imposes liability on an objective basis and considers what the accused ought to have known. The Court must consider the conduct of a reasonable parent in relation to the facts of the case.

Anna's case was resolved approximately 12 months after the offence by way of a guilty plea before a Winnipeg Court of Queen's Bench judge. Because of the serious nature of the case, the Crown was seeking a three-year penitentiary term. It was the defence's position that Anna was not a candidate for the penitentiary, based on her lack of record and difficult history. The Court accepted a three-year period of probation on condition that she successfully complete a counselling program to be completed at an Aboriginal Healing Centre located in Selkirk, Manitoba. To my knowledge, Anna has never returned to the criminal justice system either as a victim, or as a perpetrator.

Exactly how her infant daughter came to be injured and why obvious medical treatment was never sought was not resolved through the Court process. It is possible that Anna, frustrated with her life of isolation and resentful of her partner, did not pursue medical treatment out of fear for her own actions. It is possible that her partner was responsible for the injuries to her daughter and given his penchant for violence, he threatened Anna if she sought assistance. Perhaps both parents were responsible for the injuries but subjectively did not appreciate the urgency of the situation. The latter scenario is not a defence. The legal requirement to seek medical treatment is based on an objective test—what a reasonable parent would know and would do in the circumstances. Given the evidence of the forensic pathologist, Anna would have objectively known her daughter needed medical treatment.

The criminal justice system now recognizes domestic violence as a substantial and serious issue. The gravity, indeed, of the tragedy of domestic violence can hardly be overstated.

Greater media attention to this phenomenon in recent years has revealed both its prevalence and its horrific impact on women from all walks of life.

In 1991, Canada ratified Article 19(1) of the *Convention on the Rights of the Child* and imposed an obligation on participants to,

> ...take all appropriate legislative, administrative, social and educational measures to protect the child from all forms of physical or mental violence, injury or abuse, neglect or negligent treatment, maltreatment or exploitation, including sexual abuse, while in the care of parent(s), legal guardian(s) or any other person who has the care of the child.

The Province of Manitoba specifically endorses this declaration.

It is an understatement to say that children and vulnerable adults such as Anna need greater support in the justice system. Anna's failure to provide medical necessities for her daughter may well have been the result of a desperate situation commencing months or even years leading up to this tragic event. Had Anna had access to justice-based, federally funded community programming, this tragedy may have been averted.

The failure of an otherwise competent and loving mother to protect her daughter in a culture that honours children above all else must be viewed in part through the lens of history and the ramifications of Indian residential schools. Felix, the child of a residential school survivor, was not exposed as a child to appropriate parenting in his own childhood and experienced and witnessed domestic violence in his home. Lack of education, employment and family of origin issues played a part in his addiction to alcohol and his subsequent inability to care appropriately for his partner and his children.

Systemic Change

Not much has changed since Anna was charged. First Nations communities still have little or no funding or assistance in dealing with domestic violence on reserves. There are few communities that have mental health therapists, domestic abuse counsellors, designated safe spaces, or access to those services that protect women and children from domestic violence. Few reserves have access to alcohol treatment centres on site. Many communities have only a single NDAP (Native Drug and Alcohol Program) worker in the community to assist members with alcohol and drug addictions. Privacy and anonymity are difficult on the reserve, a key component of AA philosophy.

Waiting lists for treatment outside the reserves are significant and often after-care programming on reserves are scarce. Overcrowding and inadequate housing create an unhealthy environment for domestic conflict, which, over time, can become domestic abuse. Funding for early education and daycares which would permit parents some flexibility in childcare is inadequate. Many reserves cannot afford to provide prevention services through its child welfare agencies, thereby placing young families at risk. As a result of inequities in the federal funding model, child welfare cases attracting child protection issues are funded more robustly than prevention cases. Despite overwhelming evidence that prevention is the key to ending child welfare issues, the Federal Government has been reluctant to recognize the importance of child welfare prevention funding on First Nations. I strongly believe that the presence of some or all of these resources would have prevented the death of this innocent baby and the loss of her two siblings to child welfare.

There are more Indigenous children in foster care in Manitoba than were in residential schools in the province during any given year. On January 31, 2014, a three-volume Commission of Inquiry report entitled "The Legacy of Phoenix Sinclair: Achieving The Best For All Our Children" was released by the Honourable Commissioner Ted Hughes. At the time, I was acting as Intervener Counsel on behalf of a community-based Indigenous organization during two of the three phases of the Commission Hearing. The Inquiry resulted from the 2005 death of Phoenix Sinclair, a toddler in foster care who was systematically physically abused, starved, and eventually murdered by her mother and step-father after she was returned to them by child welfare.

The Commission of Inquiry commenced in March 2011 and was one of the longest and most expensive inquiries in Manitoba history, at a cost of $14 million. The Inquiry focused on the child welfare system in Manitoba. At its conclusion, Commissioner Hughes made 62 child welfare reform recommendations. Specifically, he recommended that long-term funding for community-based organizations be funded by the Federal and Provincial Government agencies to permit families to obtain support for community-based programming in their home communities that would address early child welfare prevention by including enriched early education programming for First Nations children. It is important to note that the Federal Government refused to participate in the Commission for Inquiry, notwithstanding that they are the legal and exclusive funders of Indigenous children on First Nations.

Future health

Anna is one of over a thousand Indigenous women I have encountered over my career, both as a lawyer and through my involvement with a local Indigenous women's shelter. They have shown me that in spite of often-grinding poverty, they have a singular courage, born of desperation, and the resilience to rise again. Despite being faced with so many systemic obstacles, Indigenous women such as MLA Nahanni Fontaine, and Knowledge Keeper Leslie Spillett are firmly entrenched as leaders in providing support to women dealing with domestic violence and child welfare. In addition, they are providing political direction and mentorship to upcoming generations of Indigenous women.

The future health of Indigenous communities in Manitoba and throughout Canada lies with the women in these communities as the slow process of decolonization helps them to reprise their traditional roles as cultural and political leaders, as organizers, and as caregivers. Sadly, however, over a forty-year career as a practicing lawyer, I am keenly aware that there are still many more Annas out there who are alone and silent, wrapped in bruises and bruised by history.

ـ૭ـ

Catherine Dunn received her LL.B from the University of Manitoba and practiced law for 40 years. She has served as co-chair of the Child Protection Defence Lawyers Association and is past Chair of Ikwe-Widdjiitiwin Inc., an Indigenous women's domestic abuse shelter in Manitoba. Catherine is an originating member of 'Jumping Through Hoops', a study that examined the experiences of Indigenous mothers involved with child welfare and the legal system.

NINE

Joseph Saulnier

JUSTICE IN HAZELTON
ONE FAMILY, TWO MURDER TRIALS,
A HUNDRED YEARS APART

A HUNDRED YEARS AGO, an Indigenous trapper went on
trial for the murder of two men near Hazelton, British
Columbia. He had been at a tavern when a burly packer named
Alex MacIntosh insulted him. The two drunk men fought, and
the trapper lost. He left the tavern, threatening to return and
"fix" MacIntosh. The next morning, MacIntosh and another
man, Max LeClair, were found dead, shot off their horses from
behind. When the police went to arrest the trapper, they found
he had already fled.

What followed was the longest manhunt in British
Columbia's history.

Thirteen years later, the trapper finally surrendered to
police. He was a Gitxsan man from the isolated Kispiox/
Hazelton area of northern BC. But he was put on trial at the
New Westminster courthouse, near busy Vancouver, over 1,200
kilometres to the south. The manhunt was well known and the
trial was front-page news. Witnesses testified about the trapper threatening MacIntosh. Others said that the trapper had
confessed.

The all-white jury deliberated for only 15 minutes.

Then they acquitted him.

If the verdict is surprising, the story behind it is astonishing. Those with a historical bent may know the legend of Simon Peter Gunanoot, the skilled trapper who was put on trial. He was a prosperous businessman who became British Columbia's most notorious outlaw. After the shootings, Gunanoot fled with his family into the forests and mountains near Kispiox, outrunning and outsmarting the police, posses and mercenaries who chased after him for 13 years.

But while Simon Gunanoot's story has some local notoriety, you won't know the story of his descendant 'Johnny', another Gitxsan man who was tried for a murder in Hazelton a hundred years later. (I have changed the names of Johnny and his immediate family, including the victim, to protect their identity.) Johnny's trial was also moved from Hazelton to Vancouver. It also took place many years after the event, but in obscurity with little news coverage. Like Simon Gunanoot, Johnny was acquitted. I defended him.

But whereas the story of Simon Gunanoot tells of a prosperous Gitxsan trapper and shopkeeper who became an outlaw, then a celebrity, Johnny's life and criminal trial tells a much different story of a plight of a young Indigenous man in modern times. Johnny's story illustrates the impacts of a century of residential schools, colonialism, addiction, and generations of a family that was separated by government intervention.

Sadly, and disturbingly, a hundred years later, it seems some of Gunanoot's descendants had it worse, not better.

Kispiox and Hazelton

Ancient Kispiox and newer Hazelton are small interior towns located in northwestern British Columbia, at the confluence of the Skeena and Bulkley rivers and next to the looming Rocher Déboulé mountain range, locally known as the Roche de Boule. This area is breathtakingly beautiful. For millennia, it has been home to the Gitxsan and Wet'suwet'en First Nations. Indigenous villages like Gitanmaax, Hagwilget and Kispiox have been there for many centuries. This was traditionally an important region on an ancient trade route, with 60-foot cedar canoes transporting goods to and from the coast.

Pre-contact, the First Nations in this region had well-established political, economic, social, and legal institutions. Non-Indigenous people came to the area in the mid- to late-1800s during the gold rush. They brought in new institutions. Settlers, traders, prospectors, and missionaries interacted with the long-established Indigenous communities. Emily Carr famously painted the totem poles of Kispiox.

Hazelton was founded in 1866 and would soon grow and prosper as a town of Indigenous and non-Indigenous alike. Soon it would become important on newer trade routes—on an intercontinental train line, and as the northern terminus for riverboats that brought supplies and people from the south. The Gitxsan continue to assert the right to self-government and ownership of their territories, a region of 33,000 square miles.

Simon Gunanoot was born in the land of his ancestors at a time of change in the region as more and more non-Indigenous people arrived by steam train, pack train, horse, and riverboat.

Simon Gunanoot: BC's most notorious outlaw
In 1874, Simon Peter Gunanoot was born in Kispiox, 15 kilometres from Hazelton. He was a member of the Gitxsan First Nation and the son of two hereditary chiefs. Gunanoot personified the co-existing Indigenous and non-Indigenous worlds of the Kispiox region at the time. His father taught him about the land, and Gunanoot became a skilled trapper and hunter, at home in the forests and mountains of the area, known for being a crack shot with a rifle. But he also received a Western education, at a residential school. Eventually as an adult, he wore suits and kept a moustache, "like a white man."

Gunanoot was a savvy businessman. If someone offered him a poor price for his furs, he would tell them to "shit in your hat" and would take his wares to the next town. Gunanoot had a successful store in Kispiox, reportedly with $3,000 worth of goods at the time of his flight following the murders. Gunanoot also had a ranch and shares in a lumber business. He was prosperous and respected by Indigenous and non-Indigenous alike.

The Murders of MacIntosh and LeClair

In the morning of June 19, 1906, the bodies of Alex MacIntosh and Max LeClair were found, separately, on different trails near the Two Mile House tavern. Both men had been ambushed and shot in the back.

The tavern served a mix of Indigenous and white people (even though Indigenous People were not meant to be permitted in taverns)—farmers, prospectors, packers. It was a rough place. The night before he was killed, MacIntosh, a local tough guy with a bad reputation, was drinking in the Two Mile House tavern. He had just been released from jail that day, and would have been heading out on a pack train the next morning.

Gunanoot had been out buying fish. He stopped at the tavern on his way home with his brother-in-law Peter Himadam. That night, Gunanoot and MacIntosh got in a fight, reportedly after MacIntosh claimed to have slept with the trapper's wife. Gunanoot cut MacIntosh's finger with a knife, but MacIntosh was a huge man and got the best of Gunanoot, leaving him bloodied. The two men shook hands after, but Gunanoot was still angry. He left the tavern, threatening to get a gun and "fix"MacIntosh.

Gunanoot was seen riding away from the tavern around four in the morning, then returning soon after. Later that morning, MacIntosh's body was found on a trail near the tavern. The one police constable, James Kirby, was called out. Not surprisingly, Gunanoot became the top suspect. Many years later at trial, Cst. Kirby admitted Gunanoot was the only suspect he considered.

Constable Kirby gathered a posse and headed for Gunanoot's

ranch. On the way, they found LeClair's body. Both men had been shot in the back. Now, Gunanoot was suspected of two murders. When they arrived at the ranch, Gunanoot was already gone, apparently killing four horses before he left. His wife Sarah said her husband and Himadam had come back in a hurry, angry and drunk, killed the horses, then fled. She also said her husband had confessed to killing multiple men, including Cst. Kirby and "two half-breeds." (MacIntosh and LeClair were, in fact, of mixed race.) But Cst. Kirby was very much alive, and only two men were dead. The confession was inaccurate, and at the time, a wife could not be compelled to testify against her husband. Nonetheless, the so-called confession confirmed the police suspicions.

Constable Kirby thought he saw Gunanoot on the other side of the river, but members of his own posse convinced him he was wrong. In fact, those members of the posse were helping Gunanoot escape. When they went looking elsewhere, Gunanoot and Himadam returned to the ranch, collected their families and supplies, and fled into the wilderness for good. This started both the longest manhunt in BC history, and the legend of Simon Gunanoot.

The Hunt for Simon Gunanoot

The stories about the search for Simon Gunanoot are straight out of a spaghetti western. It was the wild west in British Columbia: a time of gold prospectors, fur trading, horses, guns, and posses. After Gunanoot fled, rewards were issued and wanted posters were put up. Early on, police arrested Gunanoot's father, hoping that his son would try to rescue him, but Simon Gunanoot didn't come. Several days later, Gunanoot's father escaped through some loose boards in the jail's outhouse. It is rumoured the authorities let the father escape, hoping he would lead police to Simon, the fugitive. But this also failed.

For three years, the police continued to pursue the Gunanoots. Finally, the superintendent of provincial police hired the Pinkerton's Detective Agency in Seattle. Pinkerton's was a private police force, famous for tracking down train robbers and for having thwarted an assassination attempt on Abraham Lincoln. They sent two mercenaries, well-provisioned and well-armed, who disguised themselves as prospectors and pursued Simon Gunanoot for a year.[1]

The longer Gunanoot evaded capture, the more his legend grew. The truth is, the police and the mercenaries were never going to capture him. Firstly, Gunanoot was at large in the enormous Gitxsan territory, a land he knew well from hunting and trapping. He knew the area well. His pursuers did not. Secondly, Gunanoot was well-armed, he was a good shot, and he wasn't alone. It would have been dangerous to try to arrest him. Last and most importantly, he had support. Gunanoot was well-regarded by the local Indigenous and non-Indigenous communities alike. They helped him, may have hidden him, and certainly didn't turn him in. Many people had heard the story of MacIntosh and felt the murder was justified. The same could not be said for poor LeClair, who had not done anything.

Gunanoot was probably never far from Kispiox and Hazelton. He even went into these towns to sell furs, check on his business interests, and collect money. One time he went to Hazelton to see a silent film. He got a haircut, bought a new suit, and either wasn't recognized or, if he was, no one was going to turn him in. In some ways, he was hiding in plain sight.

Gunanoot was never captured, but after 13 years, he finally turned himself in. He was tired of being on the run, with his family not having a home. His lawyer Stuart Henderson arranged for his surrender. Gunanoot had been negotiating for a year, both about his surrender with police, and about his lawyer's retainer. They considered trying to collect the $1,000

---

1   The book *Pinkerton's and the Hunt for Simon Gunanoot*, by Geoff Mynett, Caitlin Press, 2021, tells this story in detail. I have relied on this book for much of the background in this chapter.

reward money to use for legal fees. Instead, they put off our render so that Gunanoot could trap for a further season to pay Henderson's retainer. Gunanoot might have been a fugitive for 13 years, but he was still a businessman, and in the end he managed to retain Henderson, then regarded as the best criminal lawyer in BC. Soon Henderson would prove that this reputation was well-founded.

Simon Gunanoot's Trial

Gunanoot was put on trial in 1919 for the murder of Alex MacIntosh. Henderson quickly arranged to transfer the trial from Hazelton to the New Westminster Courthouse, near Vancouver. Given the timing of the assize court, the Crown prosecutor would have little time to prepare. Further, in the newspapers of the big city, Gunanoot was portrayed as a romantic figure, a Robin Hood of the North.

There was huge public interest in the trial. The gallery was full, and the evidence was reported in the Vancouver papers daily. Witnesses testified about the fight with MacIntosh and Gunanoot's threats afterward. They described Gunanoot riding to or from the tavern. An old prospector told the jury that a Gitxsan hunter named 'Simon' confessed to killing a man. But many of the witnesses were either unprepared, or after 13 years, had forgotten details. In cross-examination, Stuart Henderson was able to challenge their stories and raise doubts.

At the close of the trial, the prosecutor asked the jury to ignore Gunanoot's celebrity status and focus on the evidence. For the defence, Henderson implored: "I ask for no mercy, only plain justice."

As noted, the all-white jury took only 15 minutes to find Gunanoot not guilty. The trapper returned to the North, to his ranch and business, and lived surrounded by his children and eventually grandchildren. A century later, one of Gunanoot's progeny was himself involved in a murder trial.

A Hundred Years Later: A Tragedy in the Family

On June 3, 2009, a distraught grandmother called 911. She claimed her 20-month-old grandson had fallen down an embankment. The paramedics rushed there, too late. He was dead. But the details didn't add up. Police suspected the grandmother had lied to protect her 15-year-old son 'Johnny', who was an angry young man with significant cognitive difficulties. He was the obvious suspect. He was also Simon Gunanoot's descendant. Eventually, I would represent Johnny at his murder trial.

I work at a Vancouver criminal law firm which has, for many years, represented 'wards' or 'children in care' of the province when they are charged with crimes. So I have defended many teenagers throughout the province—too often Indigenous—charged with serious crimes like murder .

The over-representation of Indigenous children in the province's 'care' is a legacy of residential schools. Indigenous children continue to be taken from their parents and raised in foster care or at group homes, away from their family and culture. My 'ward' clients have often been subjected to trauma and have significant cognitive and addiction problems. They may have been raised in poverty and had limited educational opportunities. Children in care are more likely to go to jail than to graduate high school. Many times the victims of the crimes are themselves Indigenous and have also experienced neglect and trauma.

So it was that my firm came to represent a 15-year-old Gitxsan boy in Hazelton, charged with murdering his 20-month-old nephew.

Johnny and Hercules

Johnny was born suffering from the effects of his mother's heavy drinking. He was soon given the same labels as many of my clients, things like: Fetal Alcohol Spectrum Disorder (FASD), an extremely low IQ, and 'mental retardation.' Johnny had difficulty controlling his impulses, got into trouble, and wasn't going to school. At 15, he was functionally illiterate and struggled to print his first name. He had been in and out of foster homes and the 'care' of the province his entire life, since he was a baby, usually when his mother was drinking too much to be able to care for him.

Johnny had a 20-month-old nephew, 'Hercules'. After Hercules' mother was charged with stabbing her boyfriend, he and his siblings were taken away from her and given to his grandmother Mary. So it was that, in the summer of 2009, Mary, her half-blind partner, her cognitively challenged son Johnny, and three grandchildren under the age of 5 were living in a small rundown house in Hazelton. Mary had her hands full.

Hercules was a bright and rambunctious young boy. He loved his grandmother. He loved cartoons. He loved to get into mischief. As his name portended, Hercules was big and strong for his age, and he was smart. His grandmother would try to keep him contained while she cooked or tended to the baby. But Hercules would climb out of his crib; he'd manage to open the front door; he'd explore.

In the weeks before his death, Mary brought Hercules to the hospital several times with minor injuries. She said he had fallen off a swing or down the front steps. At Johnny's trial, Crown would lead this evidence, arguing that it was Johnny who kept hurting his nephew.

On June 3, 2009, a panicked and sobbing Mary called 911, using a neighbour's phone since she did not own one. She told the operator that her grandson Hercules wasn't breathing. She had taken him for a walk in his stroller, she said. He had managed to unbuckle his seatbelt, crawled out, and fell down a steep embankment not far from their house. She climbed down and got him and returned to their house.

Paramedics arrived quickly. But Hercules's body was already cold and hard. He was dead and had been for a while.

The police were immediately suspicious. They asked the grandmother to show them the spot where he fell and had her re-enact what happened. Her story was not believable.

Police investigators believed Mary was lying about the fall down the embankment in order to cover up for Johnny. It was easy for the police to infer that the troubled teenager with FASD and 'mental retardation' had killed his nephew.

About a week after Hercules died, the police brought Mary to the police station. They told her she was a suspect in the murder, but they understood she might be covering for someone else. Undoubtedly scared, Mary told police that on the morning in question, she had seen Johnny walking out of a bedroom with a smirk on his face. Suspicious, she entered the room and found Hercules, lying beside his crib, dead. On the basis of this statement, Johnny was arrested and charged with second-degree murder. Youth trials are supposed to happen quickly, but this trial would not take place for five and a half years.

Before Trial: Johnny's Years in a Psychiatric Hospital
Brock Martland KC, my law partner, was retained by the BC Ministry of Children and Family Development to defend Johnny. Johnny would quickly be found unfit to stand trial. With his IQ and severe cognitive challenges, he could not understand the charges against him or hope to competently instruct counsel.

When an accused is found unfit to stand trial, the Review Board takes over from the court, holding regular fitness hearings to monitor the accused until they become fit and can be tried, or the charges are dropped. Rather than stay in jail, Johnny would stay at the high-security 'Crossroads' unit of the youth forensic hospital near Vancouver, to be monitored.

Prior to his trial, Simon Gunanoot had been a fugitive for 13 years, but at least he was with his family. In contrast, after his arrest, 15-year-old Johnny was very much alone. The

Crossroads was far from Hazelton. As far as I know, Johnny only ever had one visit from family, when the government paid for his grandparents to fly to Vancouver for a fitness hearing.

At Crossroads, youths got their own rooms and could put up posters. There were televisions and mismatched sofas all around. Johnny liked to wear his iPod and headphones, listening to rap music and pretending to be a gangster. When I visited Johnny, he was excited to see me—not as a lawyer, but as someone he knew. He invariably asked if I had brought him alcohol or pornography. (I had not.)

Then Johnny turned 18 and was immediately moved. Johnny had allegedly been violent with staff at Crossroads, and they said it wasn't safe for him to be there. So Johnny went to Colony Farm, the adult forensic hospital in Coquitlam, a suburb of Vancouver, not far from the infamous, now-shuttered Riverview Hospital. The grounds are actually quite serene, next to the Fraser River. But not for Johnny. Now an adult charged with murder, he was placed in the highest security unit, with other dangerous adults. The first time I visited, I was given an emergency button to press at any time for help. It was not a nice place to visit and was obviously a worse place to live. Johnny might have had a low IQ and many cognitive challenges, but he was a teenager, and he wasn't psychotic. I didn't think he belonged there.

As long as Johnny was unfit to stand trial, he might stay at the forensic hospital forever, at least as long as he was still charged with murder. But then, on June 3, 2013, four years to the day that Hercules had died, Mary died of heart failure. She was a grandmother, and had been in poor health from years of alcohol abuse, but she was only in her early 40s. One of the Crown's key witnesses was now dead, and their case was getting weaker. From my perspective, it was time for trial.

Staff at the hospital worked to make Johnny fit to stand trial. They tried to teach Johnny about court, using a sort of diorama of a courtroom with a judge, two lawyers, and an accused. Eventually Johnny was able to recite, in simple terms, the roles of the different people in court. He knew he was charged with killing his nephew. He knew his lawyer helped him and that the judge decided if he went to jail or not. And with that, the Review Board found Johnny, "fit but fragile", meaning he could stand trial, but he was too mentally fragile for jail. He would continue to stay at the forensic hospital, where he would be medicated and monitored.

As a result, as with Simon Gunanoot's trial a century before, I was able to move the trial from the BC Supreme Court in Smithers (near Hazelton) to Vancouver. This was to ensure that Johnny could stay at the psychiatric hospital and remain fit to stand trial. For me personally, it meant the trial was held mostly across the street from my office, in my back-yard instead of the Crown's.

Johnny is Abandoned by the Province

Before I turn to Johnny's trial, I must contrast Gunanoot's legal representation with Johnny's. Even as a fugitive, Gunanoot had been able to earn and save enough money to privately retain the best criminal defence lawyer in BC. On the other hand, Johnny had grown up in poverty, and there was no way his family could pay a private retainer for a murder trial.

When Johnny was first charged, as a ward of the prov-ince, the Ministry of Children and Family Development paid Johnny's legal fees. They were his legal guardian after all. But as soon as Johnny turned 19, around the time he was finally found fit to stand trial and really needed representation, the Ministry turned off the tap. Johnny had 'aged out of care', so he was no longer their problem and they would no longer pay his legal fees. Fortunately, because Johnny was a young person who had been charged under the Youth Criminal Justice Act, he qualified for legal aid, which would fund Johnny's defence for the next year. Then, just at the time Johnny most needed his lawyers, legal aid would also turn off the tap.

I was mistaken about the Crown's case getting weaker. Shortly after his arrest, Johnny had allegedly confessed to a jailhouse informant. I already knew this, but I didn't know of three additional confessions allegedly made by my client to staff at the Review Board and hospital. The Crown told me about these confessions and that they intended to lead them at trial. Further, the Crown was applying to lead the video-taped statement of my client's deceased mother Mary, implicating Johnny. If it was admitted, I wouldn't even be able to cross-examine.

My associate Jenny Dyck and I suddenly had a lot more work on our hands. A few months before the trial, we had to conduct several applications to challenge whether this evidence would be admissible at trial. We successfully excluded the three new confessions and Mary's statement. Our client's chances at trial were now much better, due to the weeks of court applications and preparation we had done.

Our reward was for the provincial Legal Services Society to cut off our legal aid funding, a month before the trial. They said the case had been funded to capacity. They would only pay for me to sit in court, but they would no longer pay for me or my associate to do any trial preparation. And there was much preparation left to do. They were willing to let an Indigenous, cognitively disabled young man go on trial for murder, seemingly indifferent to whether he was properly defended.

I considered adjourning the trial. If it had been to the client's benefit, I would have done so. But I was confident we could get Johnny acquitted. If we adjourned, Johnny could spend another six months or more in that terrible, maximum security unit at the adult forensic hospital. A lawyer's ethical duties do not allow us to do a half-hearted job. A criminal defence lawyer must defend their client fearlessly and to the best of their ability. So my associate and I marched on and continued to prepare for trial, unpaid.

Johnny's Trial

Johnny's Supreme Court trial started in November 2014, before the Honourable Mr. Justice A. Silverman. In the end, the trial was held in both Vancouver and Smithers, and the judge and lawyers flew back and forth.

The lead trial prosecutor was Declan Brennan, a long-time Crown lawyer in northern BC who specialized in prosecuting major crimes, like murders. Working with him was Nina Purewal, now Madam Justice Purewal of the BC Supreme Court. Both prosecutors were excellent, experienced lawyers. They did the most they could with the evidence they had left, but by trial, much of the important evidence had been excluded.

For the defence, it was me and Jenny Dyck. Dyck is now an experienced prosecutor in Vancouver, but at the time she was my junior associate, and she did yeoman's work on the case. Her work ethic was incredible and I could not have successfully defended Johnny without her.

Crown's case wasn't completely gutted. They still had evidence of motive, propensity, and opportunity. There was evidence that Johnny was jealous of his nephew, had previously assaulted him, and was in the house when Hercules died. The most important witness at trial was a young man who had briefly been in the youth jail with Johnny after his arrest. This witness claimed my client confessed, in detail, to killing his nephew. However, 'jailhouse informants' are treated with skepticism by the courts. They are inherently unreliable, often trying to barter confessions for leniency in their own case. It can be easy for informants to turn details about the case learned from the news, or from normal conversation, into the details of a supposed confession.

By trial, the informant was again in jail, this time as an adult. Prior to trial, I interviewed him, at the jail, with his lawyer's permission. I didn't need to ask about the confession; I just needed the informant to talk. In my research, I found that he had once been declared missing, so I asked him about it. He explained that drug dealers had kidnapped him, held him in a basement for days, and broken his leg. He managed to escape out a window, used a piece of the broken window frame as a splint for his leg, then ran a mile to escape his captors. He added additional outlandish details. I knew I had him.

At trial, I cross-examined the informant about the so-called confession and how he tried to reduce his sentence by cooperating with police. But the most effective part of cross-examination was simply having him re-tell his wild stories. Yes, he testified that Johnny made a chilling confession to him, in detail. But under oath, the informant told other detailed stories that were obviously false. He was a good storyteller, and he was a liar. In the end, the judge agreed that he could not accept anything this witness said, unless it was corroborated.

The most emotional part of the trial was when the mother of Hercules, my client's sister, testified. She and Johnny had not spoken since his arrest. Now she faced her cognitively disabled younger brother, who was accused of killing her son. After she testified, Mr. Justice Silverman, always compassionate, allowed their request to speak privately. Johnny and Hercules's mother could not speak alone, so I was left in the room. I won't divulge their conversation, but there were a lot of tears. It was one of the most emotional scenes I have ever witnessed.

Justice in Hazelton

Closing submissions in Johnny's trial took place in December 2014. I was not as rhetorical as Gunanoot's lawyer Stuart Henderson had been a hundred years earlier; nonetheless on January 9, 2015, Johnny was acquitted.

Unlike Simon Gunanoot, Johnny did not have a ranch and store to return to. And either his family didn't want him, or somebody thought it was a bad idea for him to return to Hazelton. A year after the trial, Johnny asked me to visit him at the care home where he now lived with several full-time caregivers, near Vancouver. They told me they couldn't leave

Johnny unattended and followed him everywhere. He proudly showed me his room, video games, and backyard. He seemed happy, but it all made me sad. Johnny had been through so much, but talking to him was still like talking to a child.

Simon Gunanoot had lived until his 60s. After his acquittal, he continued his business and was surrounded by family. A century later, many of his descendants were wrecked —from addiction, from residential schools, and from babies being taken from their parents. Johnny's mother drank herself to death. Hercules died at 20 months, possibly killed by a family member. And Johnny spent five and a half years in a mental institution and still lives in a care home.

Simon had a fair trial and was acquitted. Johnny had a fair trial and was acquitted. Arguably the legal system worked the way it is supposed to. But somehow this family did not get justice.

Joseph Saulnier studied law at the University of Victoria. He serves on the Advisory Committee to the British Columbia Judicial Council. He was a member and then president of the Advocates Club and served as a board member and chair of the Vancouver Criminal Justice Subsection of the Canadian Bar Association (BC). Along with Brock Martland KC, he is partner at Martland & Saulnier, a leading Vancouver criminal law firm.

TEN

Brian Beresh KC

A LIFE'S JOURNEY FOR

INDIGENOUS JUSTICE

I CONFESS that my career-long struggle to find justice for
Indigenous clients started as a naïve Saskatchewan farm boy
who'd had limited exposure to First Nations People of the area
and the systemic prejudice I now know existed back then, and
perhaps still today.

My hometown of Kipling, Saskatchewan had few, if any,
'Indians,' as we called Indigenous individuals back in the 1950s
and 60s. Kipling was not situated close to any First Nations and
my early exposure was practically non-existent. That changed
slightly when my father started to hire Bobby to assist us each
fall with harvest. He was from a reserve about 50 kilometres
from Kipling. Each year, Bobby would walk to our farm, unan-
nounced, and stay for about two weeks and then leave as quietly as he arrived. Bobby became a part of our family. Although
we ate together, I still recall that he never slept in our house but,
rather, in our barn. We worked together during the harvest. He
was very quiet and very hard working.

I recall that one year Bobby didn't make his fall harvest
appearance. I asked my dad about this. He reluctantly told us
that Bobby had, while drunk, killed his brother and that he

had been convicted of manslaughter and sentenced to a penitentiary term. I was in disbelief and frankly didn't understand what had occurred. It seemed very confusing and foreign at the time. The following year, Bobby reappeared and was embraced, again as a member of our family. His brother's death was never discussed. Life continued with Bobby as it had before that event. With hindsight, I am ashamed that throughout my contact with Bobby, I never asked him about his home, his culture, or even his family—including his brother.

My life's journey took me from the farm to Regina and then Saskatoon for my undergraduate and then my law degree. Although my classes included theoretical discussion about discrimination and First Nations, I was not realistically exposed to it until I volunteered as a second-year law student at the Legal Aid clinic in Saskatoon. Then reality struck hard. The cases I worked on revealed the difficulties that my Indian clients, as I knew them, faced with attempting to survive in an urban/uncaring environment. For the most part, the charges my clients faced were minor. In my view, they did not arise from 'real criminal conduct.' Most of the charges arose as a result of poverty, discrimination and attempts to survive in a hostile urban environment. They reflected conduct of people not accepted as true citizens—and I also had a feeling that they were treated like refugees or 'displaced people.'

At that time, I was aware of how victims of such thought might feel. My own Hungarian history was full of examples of how my people had been treated upon arrival in Canada as refugees. This was true throughout Canadian history and, in particular, the 1956 Hungarian revolution. It was well known that a true Hungarian patriot who settled in my hometown innocently decided to paint his picket fence in the proud colours of the Hungarian flag: red, white, and green. The White Anglo-Saxon Protestant town council ordered it to be repainted or removed.

The despair caused by the disparity my clients faced in Saskatoon was vividly brought home to me on a very memorable occasion. While at the Legal Aid clinic, I met with a First Nations client in his early 20s. He had been charged with a fairly minor criminal offence. When we met, he described his struggles in life, particularly in an urban setting where he had not been raised. I tried to offer him my best (amateurish then) counsel and advice. He still seemed very upset by having to face the criminal justice system.

A few days later, two burly Saskatoon detectives came to my office asking to see me. I confess I was scared, not knowing the purpose of their visit. They explained that they required my assistance as my Legal Aid business card had been found. They produced a dirty and water-stained card for my inspection. It was my card. They explained that it had been found on a body floating in the South Saskatchewan River the day before. They asked if I would assist by attending the morgue to identify the body. What raced through my frightened mind was, "Why me, Lord?" At that moment, I also recalled my client had told me he did not have a single relative living in the city. No one else was available for the identification of the body. I assisted with the sobering process at the morgue.

I have thought of this young man often, trying to fathom the despair he felt, compounded by what I thought was a bogus criminal charge. Despite my attempt to alleviate his fears, he was driven to take his own life. I still live with the thoughts that I did not do more or say more to him, and my understanding of his dilemma, with hindsight, was shallow.

Admitted to the bar
Upon being admitted to the Saskatchewan bar, I accepted an exciting job at the North Battleford Legal Aid clinic, my first real professional job. I enthusiastically researched the history of my new home, knowing that it had once been the capital of the Northwest Territories (Battleford) until 1905. My research

revealed that Stipendiary Magistrate Judge Charles Roleau, who was also a counsellor of the Northwest Territories, had presided over a trial and, on November 27, 1985, sentenced eight Indigenous men to be hanged. This involved six persons as a result of incidents at Frog Lake and two as a result of what was referred to at the time as the 'North-West Rebellion'.

I discovered that the death penalties followed a trial of 11 Indigenous men, some of whom spoke only Cree. Despite that, they did not have the assistance of translators at the trial. The complete unfairness of this trial has never escaped me, and I use it now in a course I teach at the Law School on wrongful convictions. Today, Section 14 of the *Charter of Rights and Freedoms* would never allow this to occur. Judge Roleau, after the trial, publicly threatened that, "Every Indian and halfbreed and rebel brought before him after the insurrection was suppressed would be sent to the gallows, if possible." Today, if a judge made such a public statement, he or she would clearly be removed by the Judicial Council and/or Parliament. As striking as this incredible piece of history revealed, the rampant colonialism approach took on greater significance later in my career and may have been a foreshadowing of events to follow.

Later in my career, I was fortunate to meet Rodney Soonias, a very gentle Indigenous soul, who was raised on the Red Pheasant Reserve near North Battleford. I met Rod after he had graduated and was practicing as a lawyer. In our discussions, we discussed this mass execution resulting from Judge Roleau's decision. He advised me that his great-grandmother was, at the time, a student at the Battleford Industrial school (clearly an Indian residential school). It was situated on the south bank of the North Saskatchewan River, about a half kilometre from where the hangings occurred on the north bank of the river. She described to Rod how her teacher nuns herded the female students down the riverbank to watch the hangings. They were told by the nuns, in no uncertain terms, "If you are bad and don't follow our rules, this could happen to you."

In today's world, it is hard to fathom such an event—a mass execution of eight citizens. Such a public display of society's anger and demonization of citizens is hard to grasp for an adult. I cannot imagine the traumatic and life-long terror caused to such young children—while cloaked in the name of justice. In my view, for these sins, we must atone.

A new job

In the summer of 1976, I packed my 1963 Chevy and travelled to my new job through the beautiful countryside, generally following the path of the beautiful North Saskatchewan River from Saskatoon to North Battleford. As I made the journey, I had clear hopes that things in North Battleford had changed over the ensuing 90 years since the Roleau rule.

I started my career as a staff lawyer at the Legal Aid clinic in North Battleford. On my first day on the job, the Director assigned me to conduct a trial that afternoon, my first real trial as a real lawyer. My client, an Indigenous man from the Poundmaker First Nation, was charged with driving without due care and attention. I wore my best wool suit for the occasion (frankly, the only suit I had). The thermometer that day hit 30 degrees Celsius.

The trial was held in the 'Box courthouse' (Provincial Court), and started in the afternoon with a young RCMP constable testifying about my client's inappropriate driving. I grilled him in cross-examination for about 20 minutes and thought I had scored several points. The young constable simply did not look reliable or believable. Without notice, the trial judge suddenly called an afternoon recess. The courthouse lacked air conditioning and, I confess, given the wool suit, I had been profusely sweating so I went outside with my client for some fresh air.

Ten minutes later, I returned to the small courtroom off which was a small anteroom serving as the Judge's chamber. As I entered the courtroom, I heard a raised, angry voice speaking in what sounded like a chastising manner. I approached the area of the Judge's chamber to hear words being shouted at someone, expressing criticism of the police investigation. My curiosity caused me to stick my head around the corner, only to see my trial judge in his office criticizing the young RCMP witness in my case and obtaining a promise from him to improve his future conduct.

I quickly realized that they were alone and discussing my case, in the middle of my cross-examination. I didn't like it, but it was only years later that I would learn of its significance. The trial judge quickly realized that he had been caught out, and an acquittal followed. The acquittal was, in my view, because I had witnessed a serious breach of our court rules—a judge interfering with the trial. Judges should not speak to witnesses privately or otherwise whilst they are in the midst of testifying.

Legal Aid lawyer experiences

This event was only the start of my experiences in a community that welcomed Indigenous shoppers from about seven area reserves—but who also felt plagued by the 'Indian problem'. At that time, there were over a thousand Indigenous citizens living within 90 kilometres of North Battleford. My North Battleford practice developed to being about 85 per cent Indigenous clients. It soon became clear to me that what I was seeing every day in my practice were not criminal justice issues, but rather socioeconomic/poverty issues. Outside of my office, very few citizens shared my view. What I witnessed for 4 years was the warehousing of the poor, the addicted, and the unfortunate. It was a disturbing revolving door. Some misguided colleague once suggested my clients wanted to be incarcerated in order to have a warm home during the winter months. I couldn't fathom that.

I recall representing a young Indigenous mother who had two children. Late one night, she left her home and walked two blocks to pick up a pizza. The children being safe and comfortably asleep, she left her home for a short trip expected to take no more than 10 minutes. Unfortunately, she encountered a problem with a person near the pizza outlet. An altercation resulted in a broken window whereby she was arrested and charged with public mischief under $50. Her actions were witnessed by others.

She pleaded guilty before Judge Joe Policha in North Battleford Provincial Court. I urged the court to show leniency and impose a short period of probation. She had no criminal record, and the value of the glass was about $25. Rather than emphasize rehabilitation, Judge Policha became fixated on her worst crime (in his mind) which was leaving the children unattended. I felt this fixation was related to her race and unrelated to the charge.

The sentence imposed by him on this mother was 14 days in jail. The irony of her crime of abandoning her children was the basis for preventing her from seeing her children for 14 days. The logic of the decision still escapes me. In imposing this sentence, he knew that she would serve her time before we could obtain her release pending an appeal.

Daily, in my work for four years in that community, I witnessed systemic racism in its most grotesque state and at all levels of the criminal justice system. I recall one afternoon, an Indigenous woman came to see me. But for her struggles with addictions, she would have been viewed as a wise First Nations Elder. To protect her identity, I will refer to her only as J.K. She hesitatingly and reluctantly revealed to me that years before she had been threatened by a social worker that her children would be removed from her care if she did not provide him with sexual services. She refused. He persisted to the point that he removed the children from her home. He left open the option of returning her kids if she was willing to perform.

I have often reflected on what courage and bravery she showed to pick me over him to assist her with this dilemma. My heart went out to her. I confess I didn't know the answer to her dilemma. I had no one else to consult with at that time with this unusual situation. I chose my only option. I called social services, spoke to the director and 'extorted' the immediate return of the children in exchange for not making public my client's complaints. Within 30 minutes a decision to return the kids was made and we had succeeded. The last thing my client wanted after that was for there to be any publicity of her plight.

Bureaucracy that can easily drown a young lawyer fought to protect its grossest sins within minutes. I continue to wonder how common J.K.'s experiences repeated themselves in a variety of circumstances at that time. J.K. was a very quiet soul and not vindictive at all. I often wonder what her response would be when, years later, that social worker was convicted and sentenced for numerous sexual assaults committed on Indigenous victims.

Christmas celebrations

It was a few days before Christmas in 1978. My Indigenous client and a co-accused had been charged with kidnapping. A Preliminary Inquiry was scheduled for peaceful-but-frozen Onion Lake, Saskatchewan Provincial Court. The temperature hovered around -35 degrees Celsius. Weather forecasters recommended staying indoors. I arrived at court by 11:00 a.m. The docket before Judge Joe Policha had moved very slowly. I sat in the court gallery, waiting for my case to be called. He was clearly in a foul mood, and I thought he might be anxious to get out of court to do some last-minute Christmas shopping. As I sat through the balance of the docket, the courtroom temperature dropped, and the Judge's mood noticeably became more solemn and angered. Like a trapped animal, he wanted out.

Co-counsel on my case, whose red-cherried nose suggested he had already imbibed in Christmas spirits, quickly announced that he would "in the spirit of the season" waive the Preliminary Inquiry even though his client sat in custody without bail. I was convinced my client was innocent, and I wanted to fight for a discharge after the Preliminary Inquiry. This would mean his likely release from jail.

At every turn during the Preliminary Inquiry, the Judge shut me down, scorning my advocacy and causing me to be concerned about how effective I was as counsel. "Need we go through this again?" was the refrain I repeatedly heard. Finally, at about 3:00 p.m., the Judge called a halt to the proceedings bellowing, "I have heard enough; your client is committed to stand trial." This announcement caught both the prosecution and me by surprise, as the prosecutor still had three witnesses to call. A committal in the case would mean that my client would remain in custody over the Christmas break and until trial.

Disappointed, I left Onion Lake on that bitterly cold day and in my two-hour travel home, I wondered what had caused this miscarriage of justice to occur. I questioned my own conduct and tactics. I was somewhat comforted by the fact that the prosecutor was as surprised as I was by the Court's outburst and sudden halt to the proceedings.

Police officers are not necessarily the best 'keepers of secrets'. Weeks later, word got back to me that I had singularly and disappointingly caused the Judge to be delayed in his arrival for a planned Christmas celebration at the Onion Lake RCMP detachment. I also learned that this was an annual event and invitations were sent well in advance. I learned that he and my defence co-counsel had been invited as guests for the afternoon Christmas celebration, and some young buck (me) had played the protagonist and unnecessarily caused the delay in the start of the celebration.

After years of what I saw as injustice, I met with a law school classmate who was also a prosecutor in the North Battleford community. He is now a celebrated Senator. We were concerned about the judicial conduct of one judge that we were witnessing, even though we were on opposite sides of the file. To a large extent, this was the conduct we witnessed in relation to Indigenous accused.

We rallied other local lawyers to join us and meet with the province's Chief Judge to voice our complaints about that judge.

All of our colleagues agreed to offer support and be present at the meeting. None disputed our concerns. The date for the meeting arrived, as did the Chief Judge from Regina. To our surprise, none of our legal colleagues appeared for the meeting.

Prior to our meeting, the Chief Judge had been told we had strong bar (legal) support for our concerns. The absence of our colleagues at the meeting betrayed our strength. I suppose our colleagues were afraid to challenge 'the institution'. The Chief Judge recognized our lack of support and, in the end, no formal action was taken against this judge. We were told he was warned but his subsequent court conduct suggested he didn't heed that warning. The word ungovernable struck home. Fortunately, years later, after I had left the community, the Judge was informally asked to retire.

Within a few years of arriving at the Legal Aid clinic, I was asked to become its Director. In that capacity, I was approached by other members of the legal community, court workers, social workers, and the police to join a committee to study the issue of whether a local jail ought to be established in the Battlefords. My good friend and defence lawyer colleague, Richard Gibbons, was on the Board. For some time, I resisted the invitation as I had come to believe that there was excessive reliance upon incarceration (particularly of Indigenous offenders) and my personal view that jails do not and have not ever satisfied the public's need for personal and general deterrence to come. I confess that I had reluctantly accepted that, for some of the most serious crimes, incarceration was probably society's only answer. My concern was with mid-level and low-level criminal activity and society's failure to realize that criminal activity was caused by social factors, not true criminal conduct. We failed to effectively search for other answers or solutions.

At the time, a particular problem existed in that offenders sentenced to 90 days or less could serve the sentence intermittently (generally weekends) and there was no facility in the community to accommodate such sentences. Offenders were being transported to Prince Albert, two-hundred kilometres from North Battleford, where they would serve the time non-intermittently with many of them losing their jobs and being disengaged from their families.

Despite that, I remained reluctant to join the committee.

Approximately four months later, I was convinced by a friend, Sharon Foreman, who worked as a probation/parole officer, that my voice was needed at the table. Thereafter, I recall, at meetings, voicing my concern about the excessive warehousing of Indigenous offenders. I was assured that building this jail would have the opposite effect. I was not convinced.

The institution was established on the Saskatchewan Psychiatric Hospital grounds in the southeast area of the city. It initially housed approximately 30 to 40 inmates and was located in the old nurses' residence. The institution was soon filled to capacity and remained at that level for years. In hindsight, I made a mistake joining the committee and thereby endorsing the concept. My observation was that some judges, who otherwise would have imposed non-custodial sentences, were now leaning toward imposing shorter periods of incarceration (non-intermittent— over 90 days).

I am reminded of the old expression, "If you build it they will come." Had the jail not been built, judges would have to have been more creative in sentencing. I also came to learn that we, as a society, seem to have an insatiable appetite to incarcerate offenders, even though many functionaries within the justice system have a strong inner belief that incarceration is not effective and does nothing more than show the vindictiveness of our society. Those who suffered most in that community were Indigenous citizens and their families and communities.

I left North Battleford in the summer of 1980. I regretted leaving good friends, good clients, and fond memories. In my travels during my four years in the community, I met wonderful people within the legal fraternity from court reporters, court clerks, probation officers to judges who I believed were trying to make a difference. People like lawyers Richard Gibbons, Dave Arnot, Judge Ray Blais, and probation officer Sharon Foreman fought hard to try to improve the system. Our collective problem was that we were trying to use a blunt criminal justice system to deal with what were actually social, socio-economic, and historic issues. Rolling a large stone up a steep hill has many limitations.

It was also during that time that I met and became friends with John Tootoosis, an Elder from the Poundmaker Reserve. I had called Mr. Tootoosis as an expert witness on a case. After the conclusion of the case, he gifted me with about a hundred rough, photocopied pages of original handwritten and typed transcript of Treaty negotiations conducted, involving Saskatchewan and Alberta Treaty rights

Unfortunately, many of my memories of the injustices I witnessed—and that I was a part of in the legal institution myself—still haunt my soul. It caused me to reflect on whether I had been co-opted into a system that still perpetuated systemic discrimination and that I had not done enough to stand up and confront it directly. The silver lining for me was to use this experience to dedicate my life's work to the prevention of injustice, whether it is caused by differences in race, culture, or socio-economic circumstances.

And in the end, I am very happy that I was not on the invitation list to the Onion Lake RCMP Christmas party.

Brian Beresh KC, founding partner of Beresh Law, Edmonton, has practiced criminal law for over 45 years. He is a past president of the Criminal Trial Lawyers Association and an original director of the Canadian Council of Criminal Defence Lawyers. A former Bencher of the Law Society of Alberta, he has taught Advanced Criminal Law and other courses at the University of Alberta Faculty of Law for over 30 years. He was also nominated in Canada for the "Best Lawyers" award in 2022.

ELEVEN

Jennifer Briscoe

FLY-IN JUSTICE IN THE NORTH

I STOOD THERE. The darkness was overwhelming; no cars, no lights, no sound. It was hard to believe we had flown several hours north from what seemed a very northerly point of our country. It was still dark at 8:30 a.m.

The silence was absolute, broken only by the crisp sounds of our footsteps on the snow as we slowly moved from the plane across the landing strip.

I will never forget the feeling that I had been transported to another world. I soon realized that, in many ways, I had. The Department of Justice Fly-In Squad had arrived at Old Crow in the Yukon Territory, north of the Arctic Circle. It was mid-October, yet winter had arrived. The silhouette of innumerable crows could be made out, perched atop the snow-covered roofs of the houses. As we approached, large flocks of them lifted off and scattered—the only other sound in what was a deafening silence. The town was still asleep.

As daylight began to emerge, I was struck with the beauty of Old Crow's log cabins, some of them with drying furs and caribou carcasses neatly hanging outside. The cabins and town were surrounded by trees and bush, a surprising and unexpected sight for me this far north.

"Go North!"

Back when I started at the Department of Justice, several senior counsel gave me the same advice about practicing criminal law. "Go North," they'd say, meaning that if I experienced criminal law in small remote communities, I would get a practical under-standing of criminal justice and its impact from an up-close and personal perspective. It would also test my creativity in applying the law, they suggested.

The Fly-In team, as it was called, was comprised of a judge, defence counsel, Crown counsel, court reporter, clerk and translator. It was, in essence, a travelling Criminal Justice Court serving Canada's remote Northern communities. As soon as I was offered the opportunity to assist in the North, I jumped at the chance.

My first trip was to Whitehorse in the Yukon. The city of Whitehorse is a spectacularly beautiful corner of this excep-tional country I call home. The courthouse was relatively new, and the lawyers' lounge looked out over a snow-peaked mountain range. It felt surreal that I could retreat to this place between court breaks. It was glorious and meditative. Up until that time, my practice had been confined to big city courthouses in Ottawa, Montreal, and Toronto. I was unfamiliar with either living in or practicing law in a small community. Moreover, the presence and influence, the art and lifestyle of the First Nations People was far more evident.

I made several trips to Whitehorse before I was asked to handle the circuit court in Old Crow, a community that could only be reached by plane, some eight-hundred kilometres north of there. The pilot re-arranged our seating and court bags to even out the weight in the plane. It occurred to me there was danger in what I had undertaken. Having just returned safely from a weekend hiking trip through Kluane National Park, with bear sightings but no incidents, I wondered if I was pushing my luck. As it turns out, this experience had an indelible impact on my life and career and changed the way I practiced law.

Being part of the Fly-In team, as I was on many occasions over the next 30 years, is a life-changing experience for every participant, most certainly for me as Crown counsel. I soon learned that preconceptions and big city procedures are best left on the airplane. So here I was in Old Crow.

Our first stop was the RCMP station, a small outpost nothing like the big city counterparts. As we entered the building, I observed a large plastic bin filled with empty alcohol bottles. I learned the town was a dry community, and these bottles represented the recent seizures from unregulated bootleggers. This prohibition was not uncommon in some communities in the North, often welcomed by them.

On the morning of trial, the RCMP travelled around the village rousing and ensuring attendance of participants in the criminal process. Court started when the police signalled that the majority had gathered. The octagonal-shaped community centre at the heart of the town was transformed into a courtroom with photos of the Elders lining the walls and gazing down upon us. The makeshift courtroom became a community theatre.

As court unfolded, many in the community were there to watch. One learns quickly to discard the city scripts. Measurement of time and distance are irrelevant in communities with no street signs, few points of reference, and a vast emptiness, often with little daylight as we know it.

One also learns to embrace common sense. In the first case I prosecuted in Old Crow, an accused had discharged a firearm at another. Identification of the perpetrator was in issue and I asked the victim witness, "Can you please indicate if you see the person you described present before the Court?" Once translated, the witness looked quizzically at me and responded, "Don't you?" The laughter was far from muted, and I cringed at how silly my question must have sounded.

The Court is important whether makeshift or not. Few are not affected by its presence in their town. Many in the community attend and put their everyday tasks on hold, but only to a degree.

A woman's husband had been charged with assault causing bodily harm. He had chopped her thumb off in a fit of rage during an argument. Despite the fact that she did not wish to testify against him, the charge was serious, and her injuries severe enough that she had to be flown to Whitehorse for surgery and treatment.

We began the case. It was very difficult with a reluctant witness who was torn between her wish to protect her husband and the fact that she was testifying before many in the community who knew the truth about their relationship. Suddenly, in the middle of the trial, someone burst into the makeshift courtroom. In the chaos, the Court learned that a canoe had tipped while crossing the Porcupine River and that a child had fallen into the water along with his grandfather. The trial was no longer relevant as the courtroom emptied. By chance, our Fly-In team's presence offered an opportunity for rescue. The pilot, standing by until court ended, was seconded to encircle the area to search for the lost child. Sadly the search was in vain, night fell early in this area of the world. The Court did not resume, the pilot returned, and we all took some time to recompose. We left at day's end, a docket unfinished, a community in shock and in mourning.

Nunavut

My next series of circuits to the Arctic Circle took me to various communities in Nunavut—all unique and different, yet somehow linked by a strong connection to the land. Igloolik is located on a small island in Foxe Basin off the northern tip of Melville Peninsula in Nunavut, another community served only by air. The population hovered at about 1,200 persons.

As the Fly-In team 'visited', life unfolded in another makeshift courtroom. Not unlike communities everywhere, one finds that mental illness, strained interpersonal relations, and occasional tragedy are not strangers to the experiences of cir cuit court members.

I was prosecuting a woman I will call Susie who was charged with several serious firearms offences. Her brother, concerned that she was armed and was going to hurt herself—as she had threatened to do and, in fact, had done in the past—called the RCMP detachment there to assist.

As they arrived, they were careful in their approach to the house. They were familiar with Susie's erratic and unstable predicament and they also knew that a hunting rifle would be on the premises. She began threatening and firing at them. They backed away, hiding behind their vehicles until, eventually, she was subdued and controlled. No one was hurt. After her arrest, she was denied bail as no one came forward or was able to offer assistance. She seemed rootless, a stranger among her own. In this and other communities, Susie had a history of erratic behaviour and criminal misconduct. She was deemed a risk to herself and others. Many had tried to help but she was on a road to self-destruction. The community could not absorb the threat she presented, and she was seen as an outsider. A conviction would mean she would be sent to a major city in the south to serve a jail sentence. This, I was told, distressed her even more than any conviction.

There was a concern, of course, of mental illness and insta-bility that soon played out. Facing several charges and unable to assist legal counsel in establishing a defence, the judge bifur-cated his decision, finding her not guilty on one charge but guilty on the others. As judgment was being passed, she sud-denly wailed and grabbed a pen from her counsel's hand and began stabbing herself in the neck. It was horrible for all of us assembled there. It was clear that her mental illness had never been adequately addressed. I suspected the reasons for that were the lack of infrastructure and services in the remote com-munities, coupled with her inability to stay in any one place long enough to get proper help.

One can only imagine the impact her violent actions had on those gathered in the makeshift courthouse that day. That impact became demonstratively real for one young 6-year-old girl who'd learned of it, while sitting patiently in a waiting area just outside the courtroom.

This young girl was the victim of sexual abuse and the main witness to testify in the next case on the docket. While the neck-stabbing drama unfolded, she waited for her case to be heard. Traumatized by the screaming and shouting that she could hear from the courtroom, she was speechless and unable to participate. That case was no more. Regrettably, it would have to wait until the next circuit. I hoped that the time and distance from these events would give this young girl a chance to recuperate her faith and trust.

A white man's justice

I initially pondered, as we 'visited' remote villages, whether it was appropriate to impose 'a white man's justice' on a community that might just not need us. It often crossed my mind that we may seem a little like aliens landing, striking fear and at times incomprehension as we went about our business, sometimes even carrying people off with us to far places. As it turns out, the fact that convicted persons would face a jail sentence 'south' was often determinative of a witness's cooperation. I sensed that these witnesses were credible and were telling the truth, but that they could not live with the outcome of contributing to a conviction. It was not uncommon to have a woman refuse to testify against a partner based on the fact he was the hunter and the family depended on him for their food.

As I became more experienced, my opinion gradually shifted, especially in relation to women who were victims of repetitive violence—unprotected without outside intervention of the rule of law. It became obvious that for many women, we provided a safety net where one did not exist.

To bring a sense of accountability and protection to an

otherwise helpless victim became a major raison d'etre. This was brought home to me on a particularly significant day in the Igloolik courtroom. A grandmother who was raising her 6-year-old granddaughter appeared before us. Grandparents raising children was not unusual in many communities where shared-raising of an oldest child is quite common. However, this particular child was the subject of abuse by her grandfather. The grandmother had been incredibly supportive in encouraging, yet protecting the child as a witness.

The grandmother worked with the RCMP with dignity and resolve knowing that our system would try to intervene to stop the abuse. Notwithstanding her efforts to protect the child against her husband, she understood she could not do this on her own. Working through a translator, she explained she had watched her otherwise-cheerful granddaughter suddenly change into a sad and anxious girl. Eventually, her granddaughter had confided the details of her grandfather's transgressions. She was angry, outraged and helpless to do anything without the intervention of the RCMP.

Susie's courtroom drama tragically prevented the resolution on that day for the family, but their willingness to access the justice system was demonstrative and reassuring. There was, it seemed, a breaking point when the criminal justice system could help.

Iqaluit was the most southerly city of Baffin Island that I visited. On my first winter visit, I was outfitted with a government issue Canada Goose jacket, an excursion coat available for staff to wear years before they became a status symbol. I would need it to brave the winter weather and winds. Juxtaposed against the small communities scattered around Nunavut, I came to think of Iqaluit as 'the big smoke'. Equipped with grocery stores, art galleries, hotels, movie theatres, coffee shops and restaurants, and eventually, even traffic lights, it was a bustling busy place. At times we returned from circuits at night, the city ablaze with lights after hours of flying in darkness. It was here that I saw my first display of northern lights.

I did many cases over the years in Iqaluit. The assortment of witnesses and attitudes was diverse. Often-times, I experienced an inexplicable and strange energy. For instance, I had a case involving a serious assault. While I was interviewing the victim, in passing he removed his hat and displayed horrible zigzag scars across his scalp. He had previously been attacked by a polar bear while out on the land. This assault by another male person became, in context, child's play. It really was insignificant to him, yet he showed up to testify. Interestingly, I learned later that Inuit who have survived bear attacks take on an aura and indeed special status in the folklore of their culture.

Northern communities

Taloyoak is the northernmost community of Canada's mainland, located on the south-western coast of Boothia Peninsula at the Northwest Passage in Nunavut. Like Iqaluit, Taloyoak is another community served only by air. At the time, its population hovered at about one thousand persons.

Remarkably, Taloyoak features 24-hour sunlight each day from May until the end of July. I visited during that time and experienced the phenomena of working until 2:00 a.m. and walking back to my room in daylight. I even saw children outside playing at that strange hour. It was actually energizing to have 24 hours of sunlight.

I remember going for a long walk with one of the women in the community who assisted with witnesses and victims. She walked me along the rolling dark tundra and rocky terrain to a gallery where the women made and sold their colourful traditional parkas or amautiit as well as their packing dolls made from boiled wool. She talked of the isolation, which she both loved but was, at times, frustrated by. The fragility of life in Taloyoak was striking, but these women were survivors and gathered often to support each other. I was left with an amazing feeling of the power of these women in their community.

Pond Inlet is situated on the northern tip of Baffin Island near the Eastern entrance to the Northwest Passage. It overlooks Eclipse Sound and the mountains of Bylot Island, which features a bird sanctuary.

My circuit to Pond Inlet was the most northernly and by far the coldest location I experienced—February being brutally cold that far above the Arctic Circle. We travelled commercial airline there, carrying with us a hockey-bag full of the week's docket and trials. The docket was voluminous owing to the previous circuit having been cancelled as a result of inclement weather. Plumbing problems at the Tununiq Sauniq Co-Op bumped my co-counsel out of her room and into the RCMP no-frills visiting quarters for a few days. In the 10-minute walk from the Co-Op to the RCMP station, we saw kids happy and playing in the snow oblivious to what was most certainly life-threatening cold. With the wind chill factor, the temperature dropped at night to -50 degrees Celsius. We made that trip as few times as possible.

The first day of court, I mentioned to the witness/victim support worker that my fingers had frozen in the brief trek from the Co-op to the recreational hall where court was convening. She promptly introduced me to a spectator in the court who measured my hands and returned to court the next day with fox-trimmed sealskin mittens, made to measure.

Amongst the many trials, I handled an impaired driving case I will never forget. There was no Breathalyzer or blood test in the case but the facts involved the accused who had been reported by a witness to be driving his vehicle erratically and had almost crashed. The witness knew the accused, so the RCMP attended immediately at the accused's house. They pulled up behind him just as he stopped his vehicle.

In his haste to disassociate himself from his vehicle, he had jumped from it without properly putting it in park. The truck continued on its route until one of the officers was able to stop it before it made its course down the fairly steep escarpment that abuts and forms part of the hamlet. The accused testified and admitted he had been drinking but insisted he had only had a few drinks and was not impaired.

He maintained he and his drinking buddy had even left a few ounces in the bottle they had opened that day. He said he was sober enough to drive, proof being he had not passed out. He wasn't really able to explain why he jumped from and left his truck running without placing it in park. The only cross-examination I had for him was to clarify the amount of alcohol consumed; three to four highball glasses without mix within a short time frame. Ironically for me, it was almost disheartening to have an accused render what appeared to be a truthful account yet not be able to raise a reasonable doubt. I think I actually regretted prosecuting him. However, earlier that week, the RCMP had driven me up to the top of this escarpment so I could take pictures of the stunning view of Eclipse Sound and the mountains on Bylot Island. It was alarming to think what might have happened had that truck continued on its driverless course.

I have many memories of places like Rankin Inlet, Cambridge Bay, and Hall Beach, which were among the towns or hamlets I visited as part of the Fly-In team. On many occasions, I also had the opportunity to prosecute cases in Yellowknife, a fascinating and diverse city, and a microcosm of our country. A growing city with a French community and impressive amenities, yet on the doorstep to remote Indigenous communities served by the circuit court.

The trips to the North were both exhilarating and terrifying. The need to get it right, to find the balance in the so-called search for the truth while respecting the dignity of those in the process and community was all encompassing. I could prepare for my trials, know the evidence and applicable law, but this forum in the North had many intangibles. It was so important to make and leave the right impression. I was part of the criminal justice system that flew in and flew out, leaving behind much to be talked about. We hit the ground running, and as I came to describe my criminal work experience, the North was also where the rubber hit the road.

Many of the people up there know one another. The complexity of prosecuting cases in the North is connected to the concern that what is said in a courtroom would affect the community. While, as lawyers, we are used to being recorded with our words serving to create a record, all this pales with the thoughts being recorded in the minds of community members who are present in the courtroom. Unlike in the big city where high school classes or the odd curious observer come to witness high profile cases unless they are the parties or supportive family members, in the North, court proceedings are attended by many who feel they and their community have a stake in what is to happen.

My experiences serving as Crown prosecutor in the North have changed my life, my relationships, and my view of criminal justice. Elders are the core of each community there. They embody, preserve, and enhance the culture and important traditions. They are the key to any acceptance of a circuit court. Learning to respect them enhances respect for the rule of law being viable in their communities. I can't help but think of how often in criminal justice 'in the south'—in the big cities—the demonstrative absence of an 'Elder' results in the missing compass in many lives.

Moreover, prosecuting in the North brings into focus the importance and success of sentencing circles in an age of the increasing need for restorative justice everywhere in Canada.

The RCMP are often included in the criticism of police forces in general, but they perform a remarkable and enlightened role in the communities of the North. Where they are

embedded, they are respectful, and respected. Their investment in serving, as well as protecting, is enormously important and commendable. In more than one community, I
experienced RCMP partners and families opening their
homes to Indigenous people to assist in education and life
skills, where needed. From tutoring to cooking classes to art
lessons, they blend in with the communities. It is remarkable
to see this accommodation of different cultures.

The landscapes of the nation find their art galleries in
the North. The beauty of its changing terrain from vast and
seemingly lonely prairies of snow and ice to the glacial lakes
and powerful escarpments is breathtaking.

Unhindered horizons exist in these places. The sky is
voluminous, and the world sometimes appears flat.

The cold and the adaption to it, the silent darkness, and
the heavenly galaxies are carved into and shape your spiritual connection to the earth. The people of the North, their
respect for traditions, their love and respectful use of their
natural resources, their ingenuity and their generosity of
spirit can never be forgotten by anyone who experiences it.

As I write this chapter, I am struck by the remarkable
acceptance of the Fly-In Court in the communities we visited and, I might add, of me as a woman practicing criminal law. In our big cities, if I may generalize, the criminal
justice system and the Court is shunned, isolated, avoided,
and misunderstood. It exists apart from everyday community life. In the North, on the other hand, it reverberates and
is felt by the many who gather to witness the account of the
events. There are no secrets, no strangers, and no isolation.
It is a part of life. Failure is accepted, in some way, as uni-
versal. Accountability, engagement, and restorative justice
are essential to the community's well-being. It taught me so
much.

On a mantle in my home is a sculpture that an Igloolik
artist, Marius Kayotak, made for me; a dancing drummer

— proud and fierce. I see it every day, and it reminds me somehow of justice in the far North of this great land. It is not blindfolded; it does not carry a scale or a sword; rather, it is rooted, treading the land while singing and celebrating.

Jennifer Briscoe was called to the Ontario Bar in 1985 and the Quebec Civil Bar in 1988. She served as a Prosecutor for the Department of Justice in Ottawa, then Montreal as well as a member of the Flying Team in Canada's North. She was onsite legal advisor for the Toronto Police Service and Counsel in complex mega prosecutions. She has served as an agent for the Public Prosecution Service of Canada.

TWELVE

John L. Hill

CARVED IN STONE
THE MISTREATMENT OF INUIT OFFENDERS

᠊ᐤ᠊

H IS NAME APPEARED as a prospective client on my list of 'those to be seen' on my next visit to Fenbrook Institution, a medium-security penitentiary located in Muskoka cottage country, north of Toronto. He was up for parole and wanted me to represent him before the Parole Board. Although I found the name hard to pronounce, I agreed to meet with him.

A young man in his early 20s, slim, with chiselled features and jet-black hair entered the lawyer interview room. I assumed the man bore the name I tried to say.

He corrected the pronunciation but added, "Yeah, that's me, but just call me T.J. That's what most of the guards call me here."

"Why T.J.?" I asked. "Those letters are not even in your real name?"

His answer was, "When I got here from Nunavut, none of the guards could say my name either. Some called me "Eskie" or "Mo"—I thought they were making fun of me. But they asked me more questions and I answered them. I told them I got five years and that before going to court I spent most of my time in my village by myself. I liked to hunt and trap. So that led to a new name ... "Trapper John." Some of the guards just shortened it to "T.J." and that stuck. A lot of people call me that now. You can too."

During my interview, I found that T.J. had lost a lot more than his name. He did not know where Fenbrook was. He simply knew he was shipped from Iqaluit where he went from court to the prison and it was in an area with lots of trees. Because of the distance, he had never received a visit during his entire stay at the prison. It had taken him a lot of time to adjust to the prison food that he was served. It wasn't that he found it tasted bad. He had just never eaten the diet that prisoners who come from the southern parts of Canada were used to.

There were about 30 other Inuit prisoners, and he could speak his Inuktitut language with them. They became his community while living in what he perceived to be a foreign land. Like many of his peers, he had become addicted to alcohol. Some of his friends had even died drinking antifreeze. He had attempted suicide before his conviction. The suicide rate, especially among young men, is disproportionately high in Inuit communities. He had become drunk one evening and sexually assaulted a young woman in town. Sexual assault was one of the main reasons young Inuit men come to prison.

T.J. told me that he was not involved in institutional rehabilitation courses or even in educational upgrading. He spent his time at the carving shack where he and many of his Inuit brethren were provided soapstone and encouraged to carve. He had learned how to carve as a boy and continuing the activity as a prisoner made the time go much faster.

A few weeks later, I chanced upon a trendy art store in Toronto. The store carried an impressive selection of Inuit art. I was struck by one very impressive piece. The $1,500 price tag attached to the carving was impressive as well.

"Don't let the price scare you," a young man behind the counter said in a low tone as I was fondling the price tag. "It's by one of our best young artists. The value of the piece is sure to increase. It would be an excellent investment. The profits go back into northern communities to benefit the Indigenous population."

Then I looked at the name inscribed at the bottom of the sculpture. It was a long seemingly unpronounceable name that I knew to be T.J.

A few weeks later, I again visited T.J. at the penitentiary. I asked him how much money he received selling his art.

"Nothing," he replied. "They give us the soapstone. We spend our time doing the carving. When we are finished, a man comes along and decides if he wants it or not. I have been able to keep a couple of pieces. One I even donated, but, like I told you, it just puts in the days."

A few weeks later, I heard Warden Mike Provan on the radio telling a CBC audience that the prison Inuit carving project was an excellent form of rehabilitation and a way to preserve Inuit culture. I saw it as exploitation.

NUNAVUT WAS A TERRITORY created in 1999 from land in the eastern Arctic and was given legislative powers much like a province. There are no penitentiaries in Nunavut. There was a provincial correctional centre on Baffin Island, but only prisoners serving a sentence of less than two years are kept there. Those convicted of longer terms were formerly transferred to a prison in Alberta that housed a large number of First Nations and Métis prisoners. Prison officials who administered correctional facilities in the south did not appreciate there could be cultural differences to be accommodated. By their practice they were saying, "Indians or Eskimos—what's the difference?"

With the creation of the Nunavut Territory, Fenbrook Institution was the new destination for prisoners from Nunavut serving in excess of two years. Since 1999, Fenbrook became their home. Nunavut prisoners who had been serving time in Alberta were transferred to the Ontario prison. There was even some attempt at cultural sensitivity.

The prison is built around a grassy knoll that is marked with three Inukshuks—traditional, piled stones used in the North as wayfaring devices. Visually, the monuments might add a degree of familiarity to Inuit prisoners.

In a 2003 interview with *Toronto Star* reporter Judy Stoffman, Warden Provan responded to the reporter's observation that in February with temperatures hovering at the -10 degrees Celsius mark, prison staff rarely ventured outdoors. Yet the Inuit men were outside dressed in thin cotton shells over short-sleeved T-shirts. The Warden answered, "They like it better here in winter," then continued, "The Muskoka summers feel stifling to them because they don't have sweat glands the way we do," concluding, "...also the trees and the pollen—they are not used to it, and it's hard for them. It is an artificial environment."

Provan admitted to the *Star* that before the Inuit were placed at Fenbrook, he had never ventured into northern Canada. "It was like something you'd read about in Farley Mowat books," the Warden said. But subsequent to the new arrivals being housed at Fenbrook, Provan became a frequent flyer to the far north and served on a correctional planning committee with the government of Nunavut. Provan admitted the experience changed his outlook:

> It was a bit of a challenge but we took it on and we started to learn about each other. We learned that the Inuit People are mostly lactose intolerant; there are no cows in the north and no root vegetables. If you fill them full of French fries and hamburgers, they get very sick, very fast. We fly in caribou, arctic char, seal, and bear meat. The men do their own cooking.

When I read Warden Provan's comments, I formed the impression that he saw the Inuit prisoners as something apart from the general population, a somewhat alien race. But maybe I was being too sensitive. Maybe the carving shack at Fenbrook is doing some good. Traditional prison industry trains people to work in factories. But there are no factories up north. Maybe the carvings would allow these inmates to develop a marketable skill.

The fact that the work was produced by Inuit carvers who committed deplorable crimes was never taken into account by the inventory coordinator of Arctic Cooperatives Ltd. The company supplies the soapstone and pays the Correctional Service of Canada for the art work distributed throughout Canada and the world.

Arctic Cooperatives publicizes a noble history of dealing with Indigenous populations. It says on its website that Arctic Cooperatives engages in community economic development. Each of the 32 Coops is independently owned and controlled by Inuit, Métis, and First Nations businesses. Their ventures include retail facilities, hotels, cable operations, construction, outfitting, arts and crafts products, and property rentals.

There is no doubt that the Indigenous groups can be very proud of advancing in a capitalist economy. But the website gives little indication that it is not just one Indigenous group exploiting another. It is an Indigenous form of trickle down economics.

Perhaps the use of the word 'exploit' is too accusatory. Arctic Cooperatives provides the Correctional Service with soapstone and then buys back carved artwork. Perhaps my original concern is that it is the Correctional Service that is being exploitative. Yet, I found that my concern for exploitation was shared by Dawn Marie Marchand, a Cree Métis artist. She voiced concern in an interview with the Aboriginal television network's APTN *National News* in 2016. The network's political program *Nation to Nation* had aired a story on a prison workshop at Warkworth Institution. The penitentiary at Warkworth, in a rural area east of Peterborough, Ontario, produces an assortment of items marketed as being, "Handcrafted by Canada's First Nations, Inuit and Métis people." The workshop is run by CORCAN Canada, operated by the Correctional Service of Canada.

The news report broadcast on APTN focused on "racially prejudicial" comments by a developer of training programs to be used by CORCAN in dealing with Indigenous inmates. Marchand, however, was more perplexed with the use that was being made of prison Indigenous labour. In a tweet, she objected to the use of Indigenous inmates providing "slave labour [for the profit of] the prison industrial complex."

A fur-trapping course was offered in 2008 but was discontinued the following year when a fur and shearing shop began operation. The course was designed as an Indigenous program that produced fur-trimmed sheepskin mitts. The popularity of the product was discovered when the items, first sold within the prison shops, found a market in Ontario stores. The stores then suggested that the market line be expanded to offer native-produced moccasins and drums.

In a 2016 APTN article by Jorge Barrera, the Indigenous instructor of the workshop at Warkworth, Karl Lech, speaks of the approach made by the retailers:

> They said, hey, this might be an idea for you. The guys might like to try this. A lot of them really enjoy doing moccasins. Not only that, it teaches them a lot of hand-stitching techniques too. They get to use scissors; they get to use fur knives. They get to use a lot of different tools."

Lech's family had been involved in the fur industry for over a century. He saw great merit in the suggestion. It would teach a skill that those who mastered it could use to set up shop once they were released Lech commented, "I had a couple of them say, 'This is really neat. When I get out, I'd like to make my family some moccasins.'" Lech continued, "It's perfect. It gives them some tools and they can do it. They can make a little extra money on the side when they get out. They can set up their own business."

Inmates at the time Lech gave his interview were paid $6.90 a day for their work. It was primarily a job for Indigenous workers. Lech assured the APTN reporter that non-Indigenous inmates could enter the program only if the list of Indigenous workers wanting a job was exhausted.

With a relatively low cost of labour, Jean-Philippe Crete, then a visiting fellow at the University of Toronto Centre for Criminology and Socio-legal Studies, looked into the retail price of the goods manufactured. Moccasins made from cow leather sold for $55 a pair, a 15-inch drum made from elk skin and cypress wood retailed for $100. Mitts sold for $70; headbands for $75, and dream-catcher key chains for $3.

Items were purchased from the Correctional Service and resold by retailers elsewhere. The Warkworth shop attaches a little tag to each item that reads, "Handcrafted by Canada's First Nation, Inuit, and Métis People."

CORCAN Industries was expected to turn a profit for the Correctional Service of $90 million for the 2017 fiscal year. The profit from selling Indigenous cultural products is only part of the total revenue. But whatever share Indigenous art makes up of the grand total, University of Alberta sociologist and criminologist Jean-Philippe Crete sees it as the product of pain resulting from the mass incarceration of Indigenous people.

In 2004, the Correctional Service of Canada published results of "The Inuit Needs" project. The study was a joint effort of Correctional Service Canada (CSC), Inuit Tapiriit Kanatami (ITK), and Pauktuutit Inuit Women's Association, designed to examine the institutional and community reintegration needs of Inuit federal offenders. The research involved questioning Inuit offenders, staff members, and inmate families. Among the conclusions reached was that there seemed to be a 'one size fits all' attitude in dealing with Indigenous offenders. The report summarized some differences in the treatment of the Inuit:

> Similar to the situation for First Nations and Métis people, Inuit are over-represented within the federal correctional system. Although Inuit represent about 0.1 percent of the Canadian population (Statistics Canada, 2001), they represent about 1 percent of offenders incarcerated in federal correctional facilities (approximately 99 offenders) (Correctional Service Canada, 2003a). In addition to their over-representation, the experience of Inuit, both during and after incarceration, indicates the need for targeted services and programs. Upon entry into federal institutions, Inuit are identified as 'Aboriginal'. Unfortunately, the use of this generic term tends to refer to the 'First Nations' population. Consequently, there are minimal programs and services geared towards the specific and unique needs of Inuit inmates.

This points to the fact that the needs of Inuit inmates are not properly met. They are expected to participate in programs that are not a part of their culture or way of life. For example, sweat lodges and sweetgrass smudges are based on First Nations culture. The Inuit Needs project goes on to say,

> Without some understanding of cultural differences between First Nations, Métis, and Inuit cultures, the appropriate services and supports for Inuit during their incarceration will continue to be unmet. Programs and services that address 'Aboriginal' offenders as a whole, rather than focusing on the diverse needs within each Indigenous culture, can hamper successful reintegration of Inuit offenders back into the community.

It is all too easy to believe that the difference in treatment of Inuit offenders and other groups is a product of racism.

Racism would suggest a deliberate attempt to discriminate against a visible minority. Rather, the failure seems to be an ingrained belief that all offenders should be treated the same, regardless of ethnic or cultural differences. An example of the way staff is very often blind to cultural differences is set out in the 2017 decision in an appeal brought by four penitentiary staff members against a management decision challenged under the *Canada Labour Code*.

The decision was handed down by the Occupational Health and Safety Tribunal Canada. It dealt with a complaint filed by Stuart Mungham and three other correctional officers working at Beaver Creek Medium Institution, the new name of Fenbrook Institution, when it merged with next-door Beaver Creek minimum security institution.

In late November 2015, An Inuit inmate, referred to as 'J', tried to see the Inuit Liaison Officer. The Inuit Shack Supervisor advised J that the Liaison Officer was not present, and J was told to leave the area. J refused. The Shack Supervisor activated her personal alarm. Thereafter, J left voluntarily.

The whole matter was investigated by the Correctional Intervention Team. The Team looked at J's institutional and criminal history, psychiatric assessments, and input from the Security Intelligence Officer. The Team concluded that there was no need to place J in solitary confinement. The appropriate resolution would be to have J agree to a Restricted Movement Agreement and be transferred to the new Tundra unit, where his cell could be monitored, prohibiting J from entering the Inuit Carving Shack. This would limit J's exposure to the Shack Supervisor.

The decision seemed too lenient to Correctional Officer Mungham, who worked in Tundra Unit and to three of his colleagues. They signed a refuse to work notice suggesting that J's presence in Tundra Unit posed a danger they should not have to endure. Their work refusal stated, "Due to the fact we feel unsafe due to inmate [J's] continued presence in population

... we feel unsafe due to the recent incidents he has become involved in...."

The issue became moot when J was released from prison on July 18, 2017. Nonetheless the officers continued to feel aggrieved because they felt the appropriateness of the employer's tools and guidelines as applied to J's situation did nothing to ensure worker safety.

Although not expressed in the decision, one can see that the source of the employer-employee impasse was the belief that a non-Inuit in such a situation would have been treated more harshly.

The difference in treatment given to J, an Inuit offender, and to similarly situated non-Inuit offenders can actually be seen as an indication that the CSC is taking steps to alleviate the problems identified in the 2004 Report. A summary from the report sets out why different treatment may be called for in such situations:

> Inuit offenders clearly have a broad range of crimino-genic needs *(ed.—criminogenic meaning producing or leading to crime)* when entering the federal correctional system and upon release to the community. Programs in place are attempting to address these issues. A large proportion of Inuit offenders have participated in programs aimed at addressing their diverse criminogenic needs. Further, those interviewed tend to feel that the programs have been useful. However, they also note that the most useful programs were ones that were designed specifically for Inuit offenders (such as the Tupiq program, an Inuit sex-offender program). For other programs, they tended to feel that the cultural aspect was missing. It is not clear whether all programs meet Inuit offenders' cultural or spiritual needs to the same extent. Although the programs target crimino-genic needs identified at intake, the offenders may not

respond fully to the programs unless they are given in an appropriate cultural context and in a way that is meaningful to the lives of Inuit offenders. Differences in offence characteristics, needs, home environment and cultural characteristics point to a need for different methods of intervention for Inuit offenders.

Although what some regard as lenient treatment in J's case, one must continue to remember that Inuit inmates are thousands of miles from their villages. Their contacts with friends and family—their support network—is severely restricted. A Federal Court case held that a non-Indigenous man from Penetanguishene, a community close to Fenbrook Institution, could not be transferred to a Kingston-area prison because it would restrict access to his support network. Yet our criminal and correctional systems see nothing wrong in displacing a man from a small isolated Arctic region to a heavily populated southern area totally different in culture and lifestyle.

Work doing carving may be a nod to the preservation of an Indigenous culture, but any skills learned will not assist in supporting reintegration once the inmate is released.

Perhaps our correctional authorities could do more to ensure useful skills training and rehabilitation potential. Dawn Marie Marchand, the Cree Métis artist, feels prison training should be more culturally relevant and teach skills useful upon release. In her APTN interview she said,

> If you go through the skills of trapping, the skinning, the drying, and stretching, *that* is going to teach you more about being back on the land, learning sustainability, learning how we did things like this. And then you learn how to make your moccasins.... There is nothing based on the land in supplying some leather and teaching how to do this for a couple of days. It is devoid of the actual land part.

Credit must be given to new initiatives to make more liveable Inuit communities. Crime prevention is a result of hope replacing despair. In October of 2022, Nathan Obed, president of Inuit Tapirit Kanatami (ITK) and Patty Hajdu, Minister of Indigenous Services made a joint announcement on Parliament Hill in Ottawa that the federal government will spend $11 million supporting ITK's efforts to develop a national strategy to prevent Inuit suicides.

What is missing from the plan is any suggestion that instead of moving federal inmates into a bewildering new world of southern penitentiaries, inmates should remain home to benefit from the support networks available in their home communities. That would also require large governmental expenditure. A new prison in Nunavut would be a costly enterprise. However, we have decided that a series of new prisons and healing lodges were preferable to imprisoning women from across Canada in one penitentiary in Kingston. Our courts are upholding the requirement that transfers must take into account the benefits of keeping an inmate's support network intact. Perhaps the provision of culturally appropriate treatment and skills development would allow Inuit offenders to carve out a new life.

&

John L. Hill is a lawyer who defends criminals and penitentiary inmates. He is a triple graduate of Queen's University, holds an Honours B.A. and M.A. in political science, a J.D. from the School of Law, and an LLM from Osgoode Hall. He writes columns for Law 360 Canada (formerly The Lawyer's Daily), and his book Pine Box Parole, *a recent book in the Durvile True Cases Series, is in development for a television docudrama.*

PART III

LAW ENFORCEMENT
OFFICERS

ERNIE LOUTTIT

SHARON BOURQUE

VAL HOGLUND

PAROLE OFFICER

DOUG HECKBERT

WITH

JENNIFER BRYCE

THIRTEEN

Ernie Louttit

THERE IS NO LAW AGAINST IT
CONSTABLE

꙳

1989. SASKATOON, SASKATCHEWAN

"Sniffers" is how some police officers referred to people who abused solvents by inhaling them. Lacquer thinner was the inhalant of choice. It was a shocking and eye-opening form of addiction for me to witness. There was a subculture of about 150 people, if not more, who sniffed lacquer thinner in Saskatoon. Most were youths. Some were as young as 10 years old, and almost all were Indigenous. I started dealing with them early in my career, mostly while responding to other crimes. They would be glassy-eyed and sometimes speechless, or at best mumbling, in answering my questions. Often their noses would be running, their balance and reactions out of sync, and they would fight to keep their 'soak'—the piece of cotton or whatever material they had poured the lacquer thinner on—when you tried to take it away from them. The smell was so overpowering it was impossible not to be affected by it when you were dealing with them. Sniffing was the most destructive self-abuse I had seen at that point, until in the later years of my career when meth came along.

At first, I just watched other senior officers deal with them because I had never seen this addiction before and I was still new, which, in policing, was the natural order of things. It became more personal once I was out on my own after field training. I was patrolling my area and was by a notorious apartment building where a lot of violent calls originated. All of a sudden, this older-model car literally flew out from behind a blind corner and crashed into the passenger side of my patrol car. I looked over and could not see the driver. I exited my patrol car and ran to the driver's side of the vehicle; it was still closed. Crumpled on the floor was a small boy. I pulled the door open and shut the vehicle off. I was immediately hit by the strong odour of lacquer thinner. I got the boy by the arm and pulled him out. I recognized him as the nephew of one of the adult male sniffers. He was glassy-eyed but came around quickly in the fresh air. He told me he was sorry because he couldn't reach the brakes once he got the vehicle in motion.

I called for the sergeant to come and document the accident. Then I put the kid in the back seat of my patrol car. I established he was only 11, so I knew I could not charge him. At best, I would turn him over to Social Services because, based on my previous experiences with his family, the solvent addiction was multi-generational, and I suspected no one would be able to take him in. The car was stolen and was towed from the scene after the sergeant wrote his report. While waiting for all of this to take place, I had been questioning this kid. "How does the sniff make you feel?" "How long did the high last?" "Where did you get it from?" He was straightforward for my first few questions, but refused to say where he had gotten it.

I had found a small glass juice container with a couple of ounces of lacquer thinner in it on the floor of the car where I had taken him from. I would not know the significance of it until later.

When the two social workers came to the station to retrieve him, they were matter-of-fact and businesslike, giving me the impression this happened all the time. They knew him, and he knew them. The drug dealers, pimps, wife beaters, and robbers I could deal with. An 11-year-old boy stealing cars while high on lacquer thinner was to me just one symptom of a much bigger problem. To be brutally honest, it felt like no one really gave a damn about solvent abuse. The abusers were mostly young First Nations kids—some, but not all, from broken homes and the children of parents with their own problems.

No Law Against It
I spoke with several detectives to see if I could get some direction or tap into what they were doing. It quickly became apparent they had little interest in what they said was basically a "patrol problem" and that they had more important matters to attend to. I went to my inspector and told him about my last call and asked what he thought could be done.

He replied, "There is no law against it, Constable. Just arrest them when you can."

The flippant and dismissive comments from the detectives and my Inspector when I asked about our police service's policy on dealing with inhalant solvent abuse was the motivation for starting an investigation which cemented my policing style for the rest of my career.

In the interest of fairness to some of the senior members of the Saskatoon Police Service in the late 80s and early 90s, these officers had been policing a city which consistently had the highest crime rate per capita in Canada for years. Other than the training they had received on the job, most had minimal or no further training. Post-incident stress and its long-term effects were seen as a weakness and were never talked about. Were there some racist attitudes among some of the members? Almost certainly. I just tried to work through or around those individuals.

In 1987, when I started with the Saskatoon Police Service, the population of Saskatoon was about 205,000 people with about 10 per cent being Indigenous: Indians, Natives, Aboriginal, First Nations; all terms used to identify them — and me—were still very much a part of the everyday language at the time. I had come directly out of the military after almost eight years and every one to me was just a civilian, even my own People.

I tried not to judge anyone or put much thought into other people's circumstances. I did not really know about Saskatoon or the people. After my first few years, I had definitely swung into believing the people struggling against poverty and constantly being exploited were the people worthy of my best efforts. One hundred fifty to two hundred solvent addicts in a city of 205,000 people does not sound like a crisis, but when the core of them come from a couple of neighbourhoods, the people there see it as one.

I started interviewing every person I dealt with who was high on lacquer thinner, usually after they were arrested for something else. Sometimes there were as many as 15 people at a sniffing party, which often took place in abandoned houses or low-rent rundown apartments. Almost all the contacts were during night shifts; I believe because of the stigma attached to sniffing solvents. Adults were usually uncooperative and quite often combative. They had amazingly high pain thresholds and often had to be overpowered.

The amazing thing about both the adults and the youths was how quickly they came down from their highs. In 20 minutes, they could go from glazed-eyed, non-verbal fighters doing whatever they could to keep sniffing or getting away, back to their normal selves. For some of the adult offenders, they just went back to being the same unlikeable criminals they were. The youths, both male and female, became teenagers again; some with a weak bravado, which quickly left them when you started asking questions which were not meant to trick them or charge them with new offences. They were, for the most part, honest and forthcoming with their answers.

I remember most of them by name. These are just three of the many kids this ultimately involved:

Quentin, a thin, 15-year-old boy who looked like a straight-A-student with his thick-framed, government-issued, 'Indian Affairs' glasses and a shy smile, had no explanation as to why he was sniffing lacquer. He was, however, one of the first to accidentally say where he and the other youths were getting their solvent supply by mentioning an address and then immediately clamming up.

Shelley, a 14-year-old girl from a troubled family, who dabbled in everything and was ruthlessly exploited by many men in her life, sniffed to block it out and hated it. She confirmed the address and gave me a name.

Kelly, a 15-year-old boy who came from a loving family and did not know why he started sniffing, confirmed what the other kids were telling me.

What emerged from these interviews was that the sniffers tended to group together, usually based on their age and social circles. Most, but not all, were sniffing to escape difficult circumstances. Some did it through peer pressure, and almost all of them hated it. They were looked down upon by everyone, even criminals, alcoholics, and IV addicts. Three adult males were identified as being the main sources providing the lacquer thinner. All of them lived in the neighbourhoods these kids lived in.

Taking flak

I was getting some flak for spending so much time on something that was not even considered a crime. It came from my supervisors and even some of the other patrol officers because they had to take some of the calls in my area when I was tied up. I recorded some of the kids I interviewed using a VHS camera, which was new technology to me and usually the exclusive equipment of the detectives. Night shifts allowed me access because there wasn't anyone around to say differently.

A local reporter came out with me on a night shift to do a story on solvent abuse and did an excellent job of trying to bring the extent of the problem to the awareness of the general population of Saskatoon. She interviewed an emergency room doctor who treated a lot of the chronic abusers who came in high with injuries. He explained the active addictive ingredient was toluene, an aromatic hydrocarbon which produces a euphoric effect when sniffed. It also, when mixed with acetone, affected the white brain matter of abusers; the running noses of solvent abusers was actually brain matter leaking out. The story ran, and in the days before the internet, it was basically one and done. I never received any feedback from the senior administration, good or bad.

To start, I decided to focus on the individual who had been identified the most often. He was a 38-year-old man. A big guy, six feet tall, weighing around 240 pounds. He often wore his hair in braids which highlighted his scarred face and small eyes. Other times, he wore a 'Billy Jack' cowboy hat. My suspect had a criminal record which was all over the map: assaults, theft, fraud, and driving offences for which he had never done any serious time. He had a big old North American car and lived in a large second-storey apartment pretty much central to my patrol area.

My interviews with the kids revealed my suspect was their main supplier of lacquer thinner. He would drive to different supply stores and buy large cans of it. He would then break it down into small glass juice jars and sell them for five dollars each. Sometimes he would take stolen medications or property in trade, and I suspected, sexual favours as well. He let kids 'camp out' at his apartment. Getting this information was like pulling teeth because a lot of these young people were dependent on him for their 'sniff' and had a sense of loyalty to him because of their addiction. I still did not have enough to charge him with anything. Getting the information was one thing; getting these kids to commit to anything prosecutable was a challenge.

Remembering the conversations with the detectives, the Inspector and the non-response to the television story, I felt I was on my own with this one. The parents of several of the young people were beside themselves, wanting to know what could be done about my suspect because, as almost always, people in the community knew more about him than the police did at the time. They were afraid of him and his extended family. In First Nations communities, there is a connectivity between their home communities and the people in the cities. The extent of it and how it factored into police investigations was just starting to dawn on me. The general mistrust of the police among some Indigenous people in 1989 did not help either.

I was still doing all the other patrol duties during all of this; the call load was always high. Domestic situations, robberies, sexual violence, shoplifting, and break-and-enters were constant sidebars keeping me, I felt, from my suspect, whom I had now become laser-focused on.

Off duty, I took to reading the *Criminal Code of Canada*, looking for something that fit. The most obvious section initially was 'administering a noxious substance,' but it did not quite fit because that basically addressed an offence like using chloroform to knock somebody out; that action would be direct and personal. None of the cited case law came anywhere close to what my suspect was doing: selling a legal substance knowing it was going to be abused and then taking advantage of the people who were abusing it.

I went to all the corrupting-children sections of the city, and the problem was that the suspect did not have the duty to care for these kids. He was not a guardian, parent, or a person in authority. I began to feel maybe the detectives and administration were right. There was no readily apparent accessible provision in the *Criminal Code* to apply in this situation, at least not in the first and second read-throughs.

It was then I came across Section 180. I think I may have skipped over it during my previous reading because I had never heard of anyone being charged with 'creating a common nuisance' before. Even now, 32 years later, I can remember how I felt. This obscure section of the *Criminal Code* was—I hoped—a potential solution to a problem that, until then, only a few recognized or were willing to accept to be a problem. Section 180 of the *Criminal Code* reads:

> Common nuisance
>> 180 (1) Every person is guilty of an indictable offence and liable to imprisonment for a term of not more than two years or is guilty of an offence punishable on summary conviction who commits a common nuisance and by doing so, (a) endangers the lives, safety or health of the public, or (b) causes physical injury to any person.

Using my tried and true two-finger method, I typed an 'Information to Obtain' and a search warrant, using all the information I had collected to this point. 'Search warrant vetting' by supervisors—a policy within most police services where a supervisor approves a search warrant before it can be presented to a judge—may have been policy in 1989. If it was, I was not aware of it. I had done several search warrants and no one had ever called me to task over the content or quality of them. As it was with this particular warrant, I think if it had been reviewed, I believe I would have been shut down.

I nervously attended the Provincial Court and, search warrant in hand, proceeded directly toward the judge's chambers. As the clerk took the warrant to the judge, I sat and wondered if the judge would even entertain my assertion, that my suspect was breaking the law by providing a legal substance to people who were willingly using it and, therefore, responsible for causing them harm. Most people have no idea of the process of obtaining a search warrant. You can't explain it to the judge; you are presenting the information in written form and then asking the court to grant it—you hand over the 'Information to Obtain' and the Search Warrant to the judge, and he reads it. It was a one-shot affair, and everything has to be there on the document. Warrant-writing has become a specialized skill since 1989 and good warrant writers are an essential part of all investigative teams.

After a few tense minutes, the clerk led me into the judge's chambers and without comment, the judge asked me to swear to the information and then signed the warrant. His only words to me were, "Good luck, Constable." It was a very good start, but I wasn't there yet.

The next trick was getting enough help to execute the warrant. I had just been warned about tying up patrol resources for search warrants the week earlier after conducting a stolen property warrant. It was actually a double warning because the detectives said I had preempted their authority as they were working on the same case. I was supposed to check with them before doing warrants.

Most of the experienced patrol constables liked doing search warrants, and they also had a sense of what I was trying to do because they too were dealing with the sniffers. Search warrants beat out having to take 'theft from vehicles' and 'break-and-enter' reports during the day shift. And besides, if anyone got into trouble over this, it would be me; I was the one who got the warrant. So, after a quick meeting in the parking lot to come up with a plan, we went to the suspect's address. The suspect and five other people, three of them youths, were there. Everyone was high on lacquer thinner, and the suspect mumbled there was no law against what they were doing. He probably genuinely believed this because he had been doing the same thing for years before I came along.

Everything the kids said would be there, was. Cans of lacquer thinner, small glass juice containers, all sorts of medications made out to people who were not present, were readily visible. Everyone was sorted out, and I arrested my suspect. He started struggling when we were at the top of a long set of stairs. Knowing how many lives he had ruined and would continue to if left to his own devices, he picked a bad place to pick a fight. I could feel his hate. He was devoid of conscience and evil to me. He made it to the Saskatoon Police detention centre in good order. Then, in keeping with how things were going within my service for me at the time, the detention corporal refused to book the suspect, saying he had never heard of the charge. There was a heated exchange between us which ended when I trumped his argument with the judge's signed warrant. The corporal told me I would not last long with my attitude.

Suspect Lodged, Court Pending

After my suspect was lodged in a jail cell, I began the long process of exhibiting the material I had seized before completing my report. I had no idea what would happen in court the next day. How would the Crown prosecutor deal with this—or would he even proceed? How would the defence lawyer react? What would the judge in the courtroom, where first appearances are made, say? I was switching over to nights, so I would not know until I got back.

I don't know the exact sequence of events that took place or the details of how it unfolded, but God bless everyone involved. When faced with a period in remand after the initial arrest, the suspect pleaded guilty to creating a common nuisance and was sentenced to a year in jail. The local paper wrote a short story, and the arrest came to the attention of the Police Service Administration. The Police Service was portrayed in a positive light, so I did not face any trouble for stirring the pot again.

With this win under my belt, now the real work started. I began re-interviewing some of the kids I suspected were abused by my suspect. It was difficult because of the misplaced loyalty they had to him, their addictions and, in some cases, the lasting effects of solvent abuse which had impaired their cognitive abilities. Within a couple of weeks, I had laid charges of sexual assault and sexual interference on this man. He had no preference for gender and abused both. I did this entirely on my own and was never offered any assistance or advice from anyone except encouragement from my fellow patrol members.

The local paper in Saskatoon, *The Star Phoenix*, printed more stories when the charges were laid. I did not realize it at the time, but the paper was my best ally back then, bringing this otherwise largely ignored problem out into the public eye. I was at the station leaving a report on a day shift when one of the sergeants came to me. He said the head of the Morality Unit was at the daily briefing with the Chief of Police and other senior administrators; he was taking credit in the paper for his detectives making the arrests. The sergeant asked if this pissed me off. I told him I didn't care as long as my 'Pied Piper' was off the streets and in jail. I was not there for the glory. I was there to make a difference.

Laying charges and successfully prosecuting offenders is sometimes very difficult when your witnesses are reluctant to come to court for a hundred different reasons. In the end, I secured only one conviction against my suspect which netted him a two-and-a-half-year sentence for sexually assaulting a boy from the same reserve he was from.

During my testimony at one of the preliminary hearings, the suspect kept staring at me and pointing to his head then at mine. I knew he had shot himself in the head years before and I knew he was indicating that was what he was going to do to me. The presiding judge asked me what I thought, because he had witnessed the gestures too. I told him what I knew: threats in court are very subjective, and in spite of this, I believe everyone knew what was going on, but there was nothing anyone could really do about it.

There were a crazy number of things going on out on the streets throughout this period of time, but this case was especially important to me. I had many more difficult and controversial cases as my career went on, but this sniffing story is the one that immediately came to mind when I undertook to write this story, because of the lasting impact it had.

Other officers used my template for the common nuisance charges to take out other adult males who were providing lacquer thinner to youths. It took about two years of hits and misses before solvent abuse ceased to be a problem in Saskatoon. Between 1987 and 1991, a lot of people, including youths, died by misadventure, substance abuse, suicide, or murder. Many more are still dealing with the long-term neurological effects of solvent abuse to this day, but by 1991, except for the occasional diehard adult addicts, the issue of solvent abuse in Saskatoon was done. I take great pride in my contributions to bringing this to a satisfactory end.

Mission Driven

In the military, especially the combat arms, one tends to get very mission-driven; I certainly was. I saw a problem and worked on it until it was done. This case cemented the way I policed; though, I believe it was already in the mold just waiting to solidify. The indifference to this form of abuse was certainly a motivator; challenging indifference became a central theme through much of my career. Challenging leaders to lead. I avoid the term 'racism' because once you say that word, it causes people to turtle; they get defensive and dig in deeper. No change occurs this way. Indifference and racist attitudes are close cousins and leaders need to be on guard, always, and recognize neither is acceptable.

With the exception of a 15-month stint in the Street Crimes Unit, I ended up spending my entire career in patrol. I worked in the central and west part of Saskatoon and was, as much as a cop could be, part of the community. I was a consistent presence, which—depending on what side of the law you were on—was either a good or a bad thing. Towards the end of my career, I often would tell stories that were based on my experiences. I used this as a leadership technique for individual constables and would wind up with an audience of several people. On more than a few occasions, they ended with one of the constables saying, "Sarge, you should write a book." So, write a book I did!

As it was, I knew I had reached capacity for my ability to deal with trauma and its cumulative effects. I always believed when you say the words, I am going to retire, you are 'done'. I started writing my first book on my back deck. Handwritten in Hilroy old-school exercise books, the stories started to come together until, eventually, I had the workings of my first book. My general-purpose form went in after I found a publisher, and I retired from policework in 2013.

Since then, I have written three books and spoken to thousands of people from all walks of life about leadership and my experiences. It helped me to deal with the effects of the job, and in retrospect, I now see clearly what a violent world I had lived in. I found myself more relaxed and contemplative now. Almost every ex-police officer can tell you after leaving whatever force they were on, we never really see the world exactly the same way again. There is a depth of knowledge about people in all sorts of circumstances which remains imprinted. Sometimes cynical, but more often than not, accepting and just a little bit wiser, acknowledging no one is perfect and there are more good people than bad. The job carries on without you.

In 2019, retired for six years, I was in a Sobeys store in Saskatoon with my wife when a woman started walking toward us very purposefully. This situation can be unsettling; as all ex-police officers can tell you, it is hard to keep track of all of the people you have dealt with over your career. Angry people can just appear seemingly out of nowhere to give you the gears over something you had been involved in years before. This lady stopped short and asked, "Are you the guy who wrote the book, *Indian Ernie*?" I said I was. She explained she was a public health nurse in the centre of the area with the highest number of solvent abusers in the late 1980s and early 1990s. She said staff was overwhelmed with cases and then it seemed, all of a sudden, it was done. She never knew what happened until she read my first book. She thanked me and left. We drove home, smiling.

Lead whenever you can.

Ernie Louttit was born in Northern Ontario. He is a member of the Missanabie Cree First Nation, raised in a small hamlet called Oba on the CNR mainline. He joined the Canadian Armed Forces in 1978 at 17 years of age. Ernie served with the Princess Patricia's Light Infantry and the Military Police until joining the Saskatoon Police Service in 1987. Ernie Louttit retired in 2013.

FOURTEEN

Sharon Bourque

A FULL-CIRCLE EXPERIENCE

ﻌﻟﻌ

Tân si n'tôtem'tik Sharon Bourque *nit'siy'hkâson.* Hello my friends. My name is Sharon Bourque. I am Métis and was born and raised in northern British Columbia. My mother is of Cree and Scottish ancestry and is from Peavine Prairie, Alberta. My father is of Cree and French ancestry and is from Lac La Biche Mission, Alberta (the Mission). I am the elder of two girls. My parents separated when I was 13 years old. Mom moved out of the house, leaving dad to raise my sister (8 years old) and me with no immediate family supports. Dad believed that to get ahead in life, we needed an education and that meant graduating from high school.

What I remember is that I did not get to experience my teenage years like my other girlfriends, as I went from being a 13-year-old girl to becoming a mother to my younger sister. I went to school to learn and also played on the school sport teams, but when I got home, my role switched from being a teenager to that of a mother role. I prepared the meals, cleaned the house, and did laundry while looking after my younger sister.

I looked forward to summer, as Dad would take us girls to the Mission for summer holidays. We swam every day in the lake with our cousins, picked berries with Grannie, and went to Church on Sundays. These were happy times where I could just be a kid and not worry about anything.

Yet, as I reflect back on my childhood, we did not live the Métis way of life. My dad, sister, and I did not live in a Métis community. The town we lived in was a small farming community and was predominately white. Although Dad acknowledged our Métis heritage, he explained that times were tough for Indigenous Peoples back in the 1970s, and he did what he thought was best and that was to have us blend into mainstream society. Today I am a wife, mother, daughter, sister, auntie, friend, advocate, educator, and helper. I am also a retired police officer.

My Own Voice

I started off by telling you who I am and where I come from. It is good to know where you come from as it makes for better relationships with other Indigenous People. It also creates space so that we have something in common—our Indigenous relations. This is something that I learned early on in my career as a police officer and which I carried with me into my second career in education. I speak and write truly from my own experiences and perspectives and do not represent Indigenous Peoples' voice. The only voice I can represent is my own, and this is where I place myself.

My journey into policing as a Métis woman came with its fair share of challenges. A story that has always remained particularly vivid in my memory is an investigation early on in my policing career that came full circle into my career in education. For me, this event feels like it happened yesterday.

Before policing, my goal was to become a physical education teacher just like my English teacher/volleyball coach who was my role model and mentor. Instead, a high school career fair completely changed the course of my career plans. Out of curiosity, I had attended an RCMP information session. I remember walking into the classroom and seeing all boys—I was the only female in attendance. Needless to say, after the presentation by the male RCMP officer I was hooked, and my goal was, henceforth, to become a police officer.

After graduating from high school, I moved to Edmonton to pursue a career in policing. I began working as a civilian member with Edmonton Police Service, because I believed this would be the best setting to gain experience, knowledge, and understanding of the police culture. I worked hard and had a few female police officer friends and role models that I looked up to. It took me many tries with my police applications to get accepted. I endured a lot of hard work and tears but I believed in myself, persevered, and made it through. I received the good news from my female police officer friend and mentor who was pregnant with her first child and who worked in the recruiting section. Shortly after receiving the news, I met with the recruiting sergeant who congratulated me and shared that they had two concerns about me; they were concerned about how I would do academically and that I would get fat. I remember this conversation like it was yesterday.

After completing recruit training, I was assigned to South Division Patrol and was partnered to work with the most senior member in the squad. In the police vehicle he said, "You should be at home, barefoot and pregnant." He continued to say that I had two strikes against me, "You are female, and you are Native."

Needless to say, my journey into policing was a tough go from the get start. The hurdles that I had to overcome to prove that I had what it takes were emotionally, mentally, physically, and spiritually draining. I never did fit into the box, but I got the job done and I did it well. A constant message that I have told Indigenous youth during my policing career and now in education is, "Be proud of who you are and where you come from. Don't change being who you are so that you can fit into the box."

After working three and a half years in South Division, I transferred to Downtown Division Patrol. The reason? I wanted to work downtown as there were a number of Indigenous People living in the inner city. I had also just started my Native Studies degree at the University of Alberta and I wanted to learn more about Indigenous Peoples and their history and how I could better serve them. I was also on a personal journey to learning more about myself as a Métis woman.

The Crime

In 1991, I investigated an impaired driving case, which involved a stolen vehicle. I was working first watch, just my briefcase and me. It was 0630 hrs. and I was driving eastbound on Princess Elizabeth Avenue in a marked police vehicle approaching Kingsway Mall in Edmonton. I observed a four-door car pull out in front of me. The vehicle was straddling both the number one and number two lanes and was driving under the speed limit. It then drifted over to the curb lane and would speed up, then slow down. This pattern continued until we came to the intersection at 106 Street. The vehicle stopped briefly, then made a left turn onto 106 Street, northbound while the traffic light was still red.

I notified control that I had a possible impaired driver and requested a stolen vehicle check, which came back negative. I then activated my overhead lights to do a vehicle stop; however, the suspect's vehicle continued driving north bound on 106 Street and made a left-hand turn onto 118 Avenue, west bound on a red light, making no attempt to stop for it. The suspect's vehicle then made a right-hand turn, north bound, as it had nowhere else to go and immediately pulled into a vacant parking lot and stopped. I advised control of our location and started to approach the suspect's vehicle on foot when it began driving away from me at a low speed.

I ran back to my vehicle and notified control. The suspect's vehicle made a left-turn, south-bound, onto the road and began to drive at a very high rate of speed, which I estimated to be 120 km/hr. It was like a scene out of *The Dukes of Hazzard*. The suspect's vehicle went airborne and hit the light standard head on with such force that the bottom of the light standard—cement and all—came right out of the ground. Time slowed down. The suspect's vehicle landed upside down in a parking lot. When I got out of the police vehicle and approached the suspect's vehicle, I could hear a girl's voice crying, "I want my Mommy."

There were two female occupants in the vehicle. There were broken beer bottles all over the ground. EMS and Fire responded with the jaws of life, along with members of my squad who took over the collision investigation. After the driver was extracted from the vehicle and placed onto the gurney, I followed her and the paramedics to the ambulance where she was placed in the back. Once inside the ambulance, I arrested, chartered, and cautioned the driver of the vehicle (suspect) for impaired driving and rode with her to the hospital.

Once the suspect was placed in the examining room in the Emergency Department, I continued with my police investigation. Despite the vehicle having shown up negative earlier as stolen, I learned from a fellow squad member investigating the collision that he had spoken to the registered owner of the vehicle who confirmed that the vehicle had, in fact, been stolen. I explained to the attending doctor that I had reasonable and probable grounds to believe that the suspect was impaired by alcohol and because of her physical condition, it would be impracticable for me to obtain a sample of breath from her and that I would like to do a blood sample. The doctor examined the suspect and advised me that he was of the opinion that the suspect was unable to consent to the taking of samples of her blood. I advised the doctor that I would be applying for a telewarrant to obtain a blood sample from the suspect. A telewarrant is a warrant that is requested by telephone to a judge. This was my first and only time doing a telewarrant during my entire policing career.

I provided information, on oath to the judge, that I had reasonable and probable grounds to believe the suspect had, within the preceding four hours a) committed impaired driving as a result of consumption of alcohol, b) the suspect was involved in an accident resulting in bodily injury to themselves and a passenger, and, c) that the attending doctor was of the opinion that the suspect was unable to consent to the taking of blood samples and that taking the blood samples would not endanger the life or health of the suspect

I confirmed that 'Tina' (a pseudonym) the driver of the stolen vehicle was 14 years old and her female passenger was 13. After obtaining the telewarrant, I observed blood samples being taken from the suspect by the doctor. The vials of blood were turned over to me. I immediately returned to police headquarters and turned the vials of blood in to the Forensic Identification Section. After completing my investigation, the appropriate charges were laid and the case went to Youth Court. The accused pleaded guilty and was sentenced. In most cases, this is where the story would end. But not in this case.

A Surreal Experience

In 2006, I was working as a School Resource Officer at seven inner-city elementary and junior high schools. The Principal at one of the junior high schools asked if I could drop off a suspension letter to a parent, as the family did not have a telephone. I went to the address of the 14-year-old grade 9 student to deliver the letter. I knocked at the door. The student answered and it was apparent that he was not happy to see me. His Kokum (grandmother) then came to the door at which time I identified myself and stated why I was there. Kokum looked at me hard, then shouted to her grandson, "Oh my God. It's her. She saved your mother." Kokum then called the mother who came out from another room.

The mother was Tina, the driver of my stolen vehicle/ impaired driving file from 1991. She told me if it hadn't been for me, she wouldn't be alive today. This was a surreal experience. Something I will never forget. To this day—and it has been 30 years—I can still paint a clear picture of what happened, how time stopped when the vehicle went airborne, hit the light standard head-on and then flipped over landing on its roof. Then, how time sped up.

Reconnecting with Tina through her son is an experience I have never forgotten and never will. Was it fate? I don't know. On November 9, 2006, I officially retired from the Edmonton Police Service so that I could continue with my last year of studies at the University of Alberta. My plan was to retire after 25 years police service and to embark on another career in education. In June 2008, I received my combined degrees in Bachelor of Arts in Native Studies and Bachelor of Education. Shortly after, I was hired by Edmonton Public Schools as a teacher and began working in the Aboriginal Education Unit as a teacher consultant.

Coming Full Circle
By 2014, I was working at a local high school as the First Nations, Métis, and Inuit (FNMI) Coordinator/Counsellor. My role was to support the achievement and well-being of Indigenous students who self-identified as First Nations, Métis, or Inuit. This also involved visiting local junior high feeder schools and connecting with the grade 9 FNMI students.

During registration at one of the junior high schools, I was sitting with a grade 9 male student and reviewing his registration forms. While scanning the form I recognized the name of his legal guardian, who was his Kokum. I asked if his mother was Tina. He said, "Yes. How do you know?" Tina's name was not listed on the form. I said here is my business card. Give it to your Kokum. She will know who I am. Later that day, I received a phone call from Kokum, and we briefly reconnected. Kokum was, of course, the mother of Tina, the driver (accused) in my impaired driving/stolen vehicle investigation from 1991. Life had not been kind to Tina. She'd lived a hard life and had been killed by her partner in a domestic violence situation. Kokum was now raising the children.

As I reflect, I realize I have come full circle. My journey has included learning about who I am as an Indigenous person—a Métis woman, in the male-dominated profession of policing. I am grateful for the skill set that I acquired during my policing career. These skills have been transferable into my various roles within education since retiring from Edmonton Police Service in 2006.

Because I love to learn, I continued with my education studies at the University of Alberta and completed my Master of Education Degree in Theoretical, Cultural and International Studies in 2013. I have been blessed to work in a variety of roles in education as a teacher, consultant, assistant principal, FNMI Coordinator/Counsellor and now as a Graduation Coach. My passion has always been about making a difference. Being a role model and mentor to Indigenous youth; supporting, mentoring, coaching and advocating for them. Challenging? Yes. Rewarding? Yes. I have no regrets with the career paths I have chosen. Life is what you make it to be.

Sharon Bourque is Métis and was born and raised in northern B.C. She is a retired police officer (Edmonton Police Service) now working in education. Sharon's passion has always been working with, supporting and mentoring Indigenous youth. After retiring, Sharon received her Bachelor of Education, Bachelor of Arts in Native Studies, and Master of Education degrees at the University of Alberta.

FIFTEEN

Constable Val Hoglund

THE UNWITTING CRIMINAL: ALONE BUT FULL OF HOPE

I was gobsmacked at the Truth and Reconciliation display.
I was dumbfounded by the photos, articles, and racist phrases and slogans
depicting atrocious scenes and events I never thought could have
taken place in Canada. Not the Canada that I knew.
Throughout this story, brace yourself to witness for yourself some of
these horrifying racist phrases.

"GOOD MORNING, EVERYONE," my sergeant addressed
our squad that filled the boardroom. He typed on the
boardroom keyboard, pulling up the list of the individuals in
our holding cells. I work in the Human-centered Engagement
Liaison Partnership (HELP) Unit of the Edmonton Police
Service (EPS). HELP Unit is a collaboration of police officers
and social agency navigators. Our team provides wraparound
supports to vulnerable people who cause high social disorder.

"Do you recognize any of these names this morning?" the
sergeant asked in his usual compassionate tone. My squad
scanned the TV screen for familiar names. It was a priority
in our unit to assist justice-involved people who struggle with
addictions, mental health and homelessness.

"Hey, Sarge, can you scroll back to the first name on the
list, please?" I recalled a name from the past. My squad and I

were 'on parade', a meeting that police officers conduct before hitting the streets. As my sergeant scrolled up, I looked across the table at my civilian partner, Joy, and gave her a we-need-to-help-this-girl look. Joy was 24 years old and, like me, treasured working with young people.

"Maggie," I affirmed out loud to my sergeant, "I worked with her six years ago when I was in Youth Unit. It's amazing she is still alive." The sergeant clicked on her name to pull up her charges. I informed my team that Maggie was addicted to hard drugs and was involved in some dangerous situations. "I would like to visit her before her bail hearing, so she knows how to get a hold of us if the judge releases her."

My supervisor agreed and then somberly spoke, "Looks like she may be staying inside for a bit. She is facing some pretty serious charges. On the bright side, however," he proposed, "Maggie is qualified to be on your caseload if she wants to work with you again."

As the sergeant proceeded to the next name on the list, I let his voice grow distant as my thoughts drifted back to when I used to work with Maggie. My heart sank. I knew this girl's story all too well. I was eager to help her again, but the butterflies in my stomach implied I wasn't going to like what I was going to see.

The crime

After parade, I sat down in front of my computer to review Maggie's file. My sergeant was right. She was in custody for some really serious charges. As I read the report, and watched the video footage, I rubbed my eyebrows and sighed. Everyone involved was lucky to be alive.

On July 3, 2021, at 11:30 p.m., two teenage boys were cruising down Jasper Avenue, enjoying a Sunday evening drive in downtown Edmonton. The small car they were occupying was equipped with a dashboard camera. As the boys were proceeding through a green light at the common intersection of 101

Street and Jasper Avenue, an uncommon ringing pierced their ears when a truck careened into the passenger side of their car. The trajectory of the boy's car was terminated by a pole, pinning the driver's side door shut. Both airbags deployed, and miraculously, the boys sustained only minor injuries.

A stolen truck had barrelled through a red light and had barely missed pedestrians in the crosswalk. After colliding with the boy's car, the truck ricocheted into a marked police car that was stopped at the intersection. The lone police officer had been on his way to a special duty event. He, too, was fortunate and only suffered a swollen left forearm.

As Maggie drunkenly stumbled out of the driver seat of the truck she had stolen, her heavily intoxicated body attempted to flee from the scene. A bystander apprehended her and waited for a non-injured police officer to take over the arrest. Maggie was unhurt in the collision. Maggie was 22 years old.

The true crime

Slaughtered their buffalo.

Maggie was born to Indigenous parents in 1999, beginning her life on their First Nations reserve in central Alberta. She is the youngest of a least a dozen siblings and half-siblings. She grew up without experiencing a nurturing family life. She lived with her mother until she was a mere 8 months old until social workers became concerned about Maggie's well-being. The deeply worrisome facts revolved around her mother's substance use, violence between Maggie's mother and father, and a lack of supervision.

To prevent physical harm to Maggie, she was placed in kinship care (with family). After four unsuccessful placements on their reserve, 3-year-old Maggie was apprehended due to neglect. In 2003, a social worker obtained a Permanent Guardianship Order (PGO) to become Maggie's legal guardian. Consequently, Maggie's mother chose to remove herself from Maggie's life, turning down visits offered by the social workers. Maggie never knew her father. This innocent and disregarded child had no healthy family members around to take care of her; thus, she was placed in a foster home in Red Deer.

Disrupted families for generations.

For the next two years, Maggie was displaced from one foster home to another like property. In 2005, at the tender age of 6 years old, this unloved child was shipped to Edmonton, forced to start over at her eighth placement.

Adult Maggie has conveyed to me, "In Edmonton, my foster mother cared for me a lot. She also fostered my elder brother of two years. I joined figure skating, baseball and Tae Kwon Do. I drew and read a lot in my spare time. I had my own room, my own style, and my own phone, in case of emergencies, at 9 years old. It was pretty cool."

Maggie and her brother lived with the Edmonton foster family for three years until her brother became too hard to handle. Maggie didn't approve of a lot of decisions that her foster mother made, but, looking back now, Maggie understood having to give her challenging brother back to the care of the social workers. In 2008, the Edmonton foster mother divorced her husband and moved Maggie and herself in with the foster mother's parents to a town in central Alberta.

When Maggie was only 9 years old, a social worker brought her to see Maggie's biological mother who was in the hospital in a coma. Reportedly, Maggie's mother had fallen down a set of stairs and hit her head. Her mother was hospitalized in and out of various stages of consciousness, for 10 years. She couldn't talk or move, but she could cry.

In 2010, after living with her Edmonton foster mother's parents for over a year, Maggie's foster mother moved in with her boyfriend and Maggie to another small town. In 2012, although Maggie did not have a relationship with her biological father, it was the year to recognize his passing. In that same year, at 13 years old, Maggie wanted freedom, and she no longer felt supported by her foster mother. Maggie moved to a group home in Lac La Biche.

The Edmonton foster mother was a very strong and independent person who taught Maggie to also have a strong personality. Maggie said, "I think that's probably where we clashed. I became closed-minded and often thought I wasn't good enough. I lied a lot. I even lied about lying."

Maggie's biological mother was transferred to Montana, USA, her birthplace, in 2014 to be with her family during the year of her passing. Even though Maggie did not have a relationship with her biological mother, Maggie and her social worker attended the funeral across the border.

In early adolescence, Maggie started smoking cigarettes, consuming drugs, and drinking alcohol. Social workers documented 18 placements after Maggie was moved to Edmonton; 25 in total after she was born. When I spoke with the social workers recently, they admitted they moved Maggie too often.

Cut off their braids.

During some recent conversations I have had in person with Maggie, she has quietly expressed to me, "I moved to many different group homes throughout my teenage years, until my addiction to meth grew, and my care for life grew less. I remember having one particular social worker who helped me understand the parts of my life that I had no control over. She was helpful. Many social workers quit."

It was distressing to me that Maggie could articulate her

destructive path like reciting a nursery rhyme. This was her transcript and she had no say in her life's unfair teachings. Maggie told me that almost all of her family members were involved in drugs and gangs. I had a lump in my throat the size of a grapefruit. This hard-worn young woman continued. "I was a runaway in my teenage years. I ran from everything to anything that served me no purpose. I had a habit of lying and stealing. The street had me in survival mode."

Maggie continued quietly while staring straight ahead, "These cycles took me to jails at a young age. In my head, I was fighting for the next high. From 2017 to 2019, I was homeless, addicted, suicidal, on probation, or in jail. I survived back and forth from Edmonton to Calgary. This continued into my young adult years."

The Concealed Crime

Genocide.

In 1990, I joined the Edmonton Police Service, at the naïve age of 20 years old. I had no knowledge or understanding of the horrendous abuse of Indigenous Peoples.

"You're only arresting me because I'm Indian," I would hear often. "No, I'm arresting you because you committed a crime," I would retort back my textbook response.

Savages. Cleanse their souls.

How on Earth could I have understood what had happened to Indigenous Peoples when the Canadian government hadn't taught the history of those genocidal acts? Because it wasn't history. The oppressive actions of ridding the culture of Indigenous Peoples were current. A residential school was operating in Saskatchewan and didn't close until 1996. Many non-Indigenous Canadians did not know about this sad, dismal period in Canadian history. If they did, it wasn't spoken about.

At the beginning of my policing career, there were no cell phones in every pocket like there are today. My home phone was a rotary phone. The internet wasn't established until 1994. I was an uneducated and oblivious rookie.

The Canadian government commenced apologizing for their involvement with the Catholic Church in 1998 to former students of residential schools, limiting it to the students' suffering from physical and sexual abuse.

Violations of language, culture, and spirituality.

Another apology was made by Prime Minister Stephen Harper in 2008. Then, in 2014, the Truth and Reconciliation Commission (TRC) came to the Edmonton Shaw Conference Centre, acknowledging this horrendous chapter in our country's history. I recall walking over from Police Headquarters to the TRC. I had no idea what to expect. I had seen the advertisement for the TRC at work that had encouraged staff to attend.

I was gobsmacked. In the large open area outside of the conference rooms, there were expansive displays. I was dumbfounded at the black and white photos and articles depicting atrocious scenes and events I never thought could have taken place in Canada. Not the Canada that I knew.

Residential Schools.

I had never heard of them.
I numbly walked into a few of the conference rooms, sat down, and watched movies in outright horror.

Children kidnapped, beaten, raped.

There were no means of containing my raw emotion. A waterfall of tears streamed down my cheeks for hours. I met up with my daughter's school teacher, and we spoke of how Canada's appalling secret had been veiled from Canadians for so long. The teacher was aware of some of it and had attended the TRC so she could educate her students more accurately.

Purposeful attempt from the government and the Catholic church to eradicate all aspects of Indigenous cultures and lifeworlds.

The words rang in my ears.

The public facility was crowded with human beings, but each room was disturbingly quiet. Deeply injured souls moved catatonically from one presentation to another. Lingering glances of sadness, empathy, anger, and confusion projected from face to face, no matter what the skin colour. Some mouths gaping open. I'm certain mine was.

I called my husband on my way home, distraught, and veritably confused. I felt as though I was suffering in the first stage of grief: denial. I asked him rhetorical questions, "How could this have happened? How does all of EPS not know? Why weren't we taught this in recruit training?"

Starvation, torture, imprisoned.

Confining the criminal

• • •

I Did So Silently

My mother, no matter who came into her life,
the power of addiction always overtook.
And those who meant something drifted away.
I lived the first three years with a jumble of memories.
I remember the day I was taken
by Child & Family Services.
I was seen by a man and a woman
I had never met before standing in my house.
My reaction was to cry and freeze,
but I did so silently.
I was questioned as to who was watching me.
I was told later of the way in which I was found.
Unclean. Lice crawled through my head.

—Maggie

• • •

It was back in 2014, when I worked in the high-risk youth unit, that I had the distinct, unforgettable pleasure of meeting Maggie. She was a 15-year-old, beautiful, Indigenous girl, standing five foot nine inches tall, with long silky hair and pretty hazel eyes. She carried herself with a happy disposition, and considering everything she had been through, Maggie radiated sweetness. She was enthralled with my furry partner, a therapy dog named Hershey. Maggie loved dogs.

Maggie was humourous, soft-spoken, full of hope, and spirit. Astoundingly, she was always polite with me and spoke highly of police officers. She was also vulnerable and easily taken for granted, leaving her mistrusting of adults and the world, rightly so. Maggie's behaviours matched the environment that she grew up in and what happened to her while growing up. No choices.

Kill the Indian in the child.

I rarely heard from Maggie, barring incarceration. I believed she found shelter where she could, whether in a relationship or with friends. When Maggie was in jail, she wrote vivid yet distorted compositions about her chaotic life. She wrote about longing for love in her challenging relationships. She would call me and recite those traumatic writings over the phone. Sometimes she would narrate them softly, but most times, she would recite the words like a rap song. The verses always haunted me, knowing how much misery this victimized young girl had experienced.

Maggie's writings were more than a cry for help at the time, they were a reverberating release of her entire young life. Maggie remembers being abandoned when she was about 4 years old. Every person who subsequently let her down was a grim and painful reminder that she was all alone. I saved her writings for years, but regrettably, have lost track of them.

Illegal for an Indian child to attend any school other than
a residential school.

It is devastating for any inmate to phone someone on the outside, only to have them not pick up the call. In the Youth Unit, when my squad was on days off, many of us would carry our work phones with us in case we saw a call coming in from the youth jail. Hello, is anyone there? I remember stepping away from many family barbecues saying, "I gotta take this call, be back in 10 minutes." Sometimes the inmate didn't even have 10 minutes, more like 4. It was a slight amount of time out of my day and a key amount of time for the young person who was reaching out.

Because Maggie liked to write, I connected her to a local author who wrote a biography about her own recovery from addiction. Maggie and the author spoke over the phone a few times when Maggie was in jail. Then, on one occasion, I arranged for Maggie's social worker to bring Maggie to meet the author. It was an empowering meeting for Maggie, and I cherish the photo of the three of us, and my furry partner, that day. Sorrowfully, I lost touch with Maggie after I tenured out of the Youth Unit.

Buried without graves. Gone. Forgotten.

Resulting crimes

From 2016 to 2020, Maggie had 40 documented occurrences with the police … exploitation … destruction of property … victim of assault … missing from group homes … found in river by fire department … warrants … using and selling drugs … wandering in streets … stolen property … sleeping in public places … drunk driving … and in 2021, Maggie had 20 more documented calls for service.

Healing the true crimes

Generations of suffering will take generations of healing. I now know what 'roots of crime' means and how important it is for justice practitioners to not only understand it, but practice it.

Anxious about seeing Maggie for the first time in six years, her situation was even worse than I suspected. Patrol constables had found her sleeping on a bench near a mall on a late October evening in 2021. She had 10 outstanding warrants, including the stolen truck collision charges that she was out on bail for.

As my partner Joy and I opened the heavy steel door in our holding cells, Maggie was sitting on the floor looking up at me. Gaunt. Dirty. Odiferous. She had swollen, discoloured hands and fingers from the harsh effects of homelessness. The deprived young woman was scratching at the lice in her hair. I wanted to hug her and tell her it was all going to be okay, but we both knew that hug was going to have to wait. All we could do was pump fists, tap toes, smile at each other, and catch up on the last six years, looking into each other's familiar faces. She asked about Hershey, of course. I promised she would get to visit him soon.

Maggie served four months in jail. As much as I dislike seeing susceptible people locked up in prison, it does accommodate important and sometimes life-saving, rehabilitation. In Maggie's case, she was off the streets, could detoxify from drugs under medical supervision, and had a warm roof over her head while entering winter. She had clean clothing, could regain her hygiene, and had a steady supply of meals each day. Maggie had access to a phone and she was in a known location where we could visit her regularly. The institution's social workers, her defence lawyer, and Joy and I could all work together with Maggie to implement a safe and healthy release plan.

Punished for their sins.

Maggie decided she wanted to go to a facility that provided counselling, addiction treatment, and a cultural component. The day I picked Maggie up from jail to go to treatment, a guard said to me, "We wish Maggie the very best. We are going to miss her and her sense of humour." Maggie humbly thanked her, cracked a joke, and smiled. I was proud of her.

I had a few gifts for Maggie when we arrived at the treatment centre. I told her, "Joy is really disheartened that she couldn't make it today, but we bought you a plush toy dog because we know how much you love animals."

Maggie hugged the cute stuffy and named him Rupert. I had two sets of clothes for her to change into as her street clothes weren't salvageable. After the intake with the nurse, I gave Maggie an earnest hug and told her that Joy and I would visit every Wednesday.

"Okay, and thank you for your support. It means a lot to me." Maggie was always very grateful and humble.

Two weeks into treatment, though, Maggie wasn't engaging fully in what was expected of her. She was sleeping in, was tardy for her classes, and wasn't taking treatment seriously. She was also focusing unnecessarily on drama that was going on with a few other residents. The conversations that Joy and I had with Maggie were frivolous, and we determined that our lassie wasn't altogether invested in the programming. Joy and I brainstormed on the way back to the office about how we could motivate this forlorn young woman who had a prolonged and arduous start to life.

Prior to our next visit, Joy and I had a plan. We printed off 8 by 10 pictures of the three demolished vehicles involved in the collision, that our lethargic girl had just done penance for.

"I did this?" Maggie was stunned.

She held the pictures for a long time remaining speechless, scarcely recalling the scene at all. Maggie believed the collision had occurred on a country road north of the city.

Immediately after that visit, in the beginning of March 2022, Maggie progressed, trusting the process of her treatment plan. On our fourth visit, Maggie's assigned counsellor was pleased to give us good news, that Maggie had delved into her past, shared her story with the group and was now surpassing everyone's expectations.

Maggie declared to Joy and me, "There's nothing for me out there. I need to learn how to be me while I'm in here. I'm sorry I wasn't taking treatment seriously. Would you like me to read you what I wrote?" Music to our ears! This time Maggie had written poetic rhymes of acknowledgment, acceptance, and forgiveness.

After our following visit, Joy suggested to me that we reward Maggie for all of her hard work and bring her a police hoodie. "The Police Association office has some nice green-coloured dog unit hoodies," Joy reminded me. Joy was right; when we gave it to Maggie, she loved it and put it on right away.

"You earned it, kiddo. But you may want to be careful wearing it in here, as it may be looked upon as an unpopular item," I jested. Maggie giggled, agreed, and said she will wear it to bed to sleep in. "Good idea," I said as laughter billowed from us all.

When participants are in treatment, they are free to leave whenever they wish. As a backup plan for Maggie, we reached out to a city-wide addiction's worker, who could work with Maggie if she chose to leave treatment. However, Maggie stayed for two more months. Joy and I brought Maggie more clothing, personal items, and at her request, chocolate and instant coffee. We also brought her loose tobacco and fabric prints so she could offer protocol for the Elder at cultural ceremonies. Maggie was doing so well in treatment that she was invited to stay longer. But this heightened young lady had other plans.

"I feel stable for the first time in my life. I want to get a job." Maggie had been in treatment for four months. "I've learned a lot, and I'm ready to get out there and put my new skills to use."

Joy and I knew of a horse ranch in central Alberta that needed a volunteer in exchange for room and board. We knew Maggie loved animals. We also knew that horses have a special place of honour in the cultural heritage of Indigenous Peoples and are important in their cultural healing. Joy and I hoped that the best place to start a new channel in Maggie's life was on a horse ranch.

Joy and I showed Maggie the website of the horse ranch, and she was thrilled. It was the end of May when we brought Maggie for a tour of the ranch and an intake interview. Maggie loved it, and the owner was happy to give our eager girl a chance. That night when we brought her back to treatment, Maggie felt alive, organized, and confident.

A week later, when we retrieved Maggie from the treatment centre to drive her back to the ranch to stay, she had her bags packed and was waiting for us. We posed with her for photos of her receiving her treatment certificate. She gave a few last-minute hugs to staff and friends, then, as she was loading her bags in the back of our truck she wisecracked, "Look at me having all my shit together." We all chuckled. Joy and I knew she was very pleased with herself for completing treatment and was excited to volunteer on the horse ranch, but we also knew she used humour as a coping strategy. Another new home. More strangers to take care of me.

As we drove Maggie to the horse ranch, Joy and I said, "You're getting an early birthday present from us. You're gonna need a pair of cowgirl boots if you're gonna be scooping up a bunch of horse plops." Maggie took one look at her new boots and grinned from ear to ear.

"Poop-scoopin' 101, here I come!" Maggie glowed as she shimmied into her new sense of freedom. Our faces ballooned from laughing with Maggie the entire road trip.

While Maggie was participating in valuable therapy at the horse ranch, Indigenous Peoples experienced long-overdue healing of their own. Pope Francis fulfilled a penitential visit to Edmonton in July of 2022 to reconcile with Indigenous Peoples for the Catholic Church's role in residential schools. During his tour, I was assigned to the Sacred Heart Church and the Commonwealth Stadium and I was impressed with the peace provided.

Maggie worked on the horse ranch for the summer and scooped a lot of poop, cleaned saddles, groomed horses, caught horses, saddled horses, and rode horses. She also participated in equine counselling sessions and learned how to do other chores around the ranch such as gardening and riding the lawn tractor to cut the grass.

Over the years, Maggie missed out on meaningful relationships with her many siblings. After the ranch, Maggie moved in with her older sister in southern Alberta whom she has always wanted to be closer with. Her sister has her own struggles too, but it was important to Maggie for the sisters to be reunited. Maggie is now working two jobs and learning to be a cook.

Maggie texted me the other day, "I hurt my finger at work." I'm overjoyed that all that is hurting on this determined, loving young woman is her squished finger. No more drugs. No more dangerous crimes. No more homelessness. Maggie's latest update is that she has rented her own room from a nice lady in town. Her first month's rent was sponsored by a local church. Maggie is learning to be independent and has looked into furthering her education through the Advancing Futures Bursary program.

Joy and I were honoured to provide Maggie with consistent weekly, and sometimes daily, support for eight months. To this day, we delight in seeing her updates roll in on a text. Whether it's a funny story, or a question, not only do we happily reply, we feel gratitude that she chooses to keep in touch.

I often get asked, "What's it like working with the homeless? That must be hard." Now you know.

❧

Val Hoglund is a senior constable with the Edmonton Police Service. Her husband and children are Métis and she feels gratitude each day to be part of a Métis family. She is a Certified Restorative Justice Facilitator and is also an Equine-assisted Personal Development Coach. She has concentrated her 33-year career on helping children, youth, and families. The highlight of her career was when she was in Youth Unit, partnered with a therapy dog. Val was the recipient of a provincial team award for her work in the Youth Unit.

SIXTEEN

Doug Heckbert

I KNOW WHO
KILLED MY BROTHER

IFIRST MET Joseph when he was referred to me by one of my friends who knew that, as a former parole officer, I was writing chapters about people who had been convicted of crimes and who had been on parole or probation. He said Joseph worked for him on a construction project, that he had come to know Joseph quite well, and was impressed with him as a worker. Joseph, who is Indigenous, had told my friend that he was on parole. When Joseph learned about my writing, he was interested in talking to me about his life.

I texted Joseph and we made arrangements to meet at a coffee shop near where he lived in Edmonton. I wanted to hear directly from him that he was in fact on parole, that he really did want to have his story told and that he would be comfortable having me do so. I wanted Joseph to hear from me that his story would be told without disclosing his identity.

We first met in the evening after he returned from work. Joseph struck me as energetic, intense, somewhat impulsive, and cooperative. He was well-spoken, and he spoke quickly, spicing up his sentences with lots of swears and with interjections like, "You know," "Man," and "Bro"—most of which have been edited from his interview. Joseph was of slim build, five feet eight inches tall, had short dark hair, and a neck full of tattoos that disappeared into his t-shirt to emerge on his fore-arms. His jeans were tight-fitting, and he wore a black ball cap and running shoes.

He wanted to get started on our interview right then and there in the coffee shop. I directed that we would meet later in a quiet place where our conversation would not be overheard. In my view, a coffee shop was no place to talk about one's personal history or crimes. Joseph agreed, and we decided on a day and time to meet in the local library not far from his apartment. Our follow-up interviews were held again in the library and at his apartment.

Here is how he described his early years:

I was born in Fort McMurray, Alberta. My dad is from the east coast. My mom is from Fort Mac. She grew up on a reserve then moved off the reserve to go to Fort Mac—that's where my mom met my dad in the early 80s. They were together for a while and then I was born. My mom told my dad that Sam, my step-brother, was his son, but later on it turned out he wasn't. They divorced when I was 2 years old. They got a blood test for me and him; my brother wasn't his and I was. My dad wasn't letting me go with my mom when they separated. I've been with my dad since I was 2 years old. My dad raised me by him-self and did the best he could up until I was 14. My dad didn't want my mom to be part of my life either because of the way she was like. She would say something, then never show up. I never got anything for my birthday or anything like that. When I was 10, he met the woman he is with now; and he moved her out west, out here. When I was 14, they packed up and moved back east. Dad asked me if I wanted to move with them and I said, 'No.' I told him I wasn't going to move out there—I didn't know anybody back east and I didn't like her at the time. I was always looking for his approval; and I never had it, you know. I always thought I was useless. But my dad never told me I was useless; my stepmom used to always drive that into my head.

Joseph decided to remain in Fort McMurray as a teenager, rather than go down east with his dad and stepmom. His dad arranged for him to stay with a guardian, and Joseph pretty well had the run of the place. He came and went as he pleased with few rules or expectations from adults. It was during this time that Joseph became involved with buying and selling drugs.

So I stayed in Fort Mac when they left. My dad would come up here to work and visit me once in a while. He didn't leave me in a bad place, just left me with a guardian who let me do whatever the hell I wanted to do, as long as she got her $600 a month for housing me. It was all good. My dad would give me $100 a week for school. I was a bad kid and would take that $100, buy dope, and then sell it at school to make more money and then get a part time job. I said I was working, you know, but I wasn't. Oh, I'd work for two weeks then quit. Dad knew what I was up to, but he turned a blind eye. That went on until I graduated. I didn't graduate with the best marks, but I did graduate. I struggled with most classes but that's because I didn't do the work. I didn't want to help myself, I guess.

The guardian became a mother figure for Joseph for the three years he lived with her. He became close to her son Rory too, whom Joseph came to see as a brother over time.

The guardian was a good family friend. She used to

be my baby sitter when I was a little kid. She was nice. She passed away when I was 22, she died of cancer. She was pretty much the only mother figure I had in my life. She used to decorate for weddings, taught me a lot of stuff like that. Yeah, I would just come and go on the weekends, no need to call in or anything, show back up on Sunday evening and go to school. She'd cover my ass; lied to my dad. She was pretty solid like that, but I could have taken a few kicks in the ass, I guess.

When Joseph became an adult at age 18, it seemed like the patterns in his younger years had become fairly well entrenched and he carried on doing the same things.

When I turned 18, my mom started coming around in my life. It kinda made things worse. She made false promises, so I'd close the door on her and let her back in here and there. She was always around, in close vicinity, but she had never made herself a part of my life. After that, at 18 when I graduated from high school, my dad gave me a thousand bucks; told me to start my life. So I took that $1,000, bought a bunch of dope, started selling dope even more. I was doing all right for a while then the ship went south, went downhill. He got me in the union which was good. I've been in the union, ever since, but I'd just use it as a fall back—do a shutdown here and there, make twenty or thirty grand. I wouldn't work the rest of the year—just sell dope. I did that for a lot of years.

Joseph's drug use started when he was 15, in grade 9 at school. That quickly turned into drug abuse when he started selling drugs, in addition to using. His abusive use of drugs lasted for eight or nine years until Joseph was in his mid-20s.

I was handed a dope phone at 15 years old. They gave me a phone that profited $1,600 on a Thursday night—pay day night. 'Here's the phone; come on back when you need some more'. I was hooked. I was a 15-year-old kid going to high school in grade 9. I had $1,600 in my pocket on Friday morning, going to school. Gold chains, the nicest clothes.

I didn't know what to do, you know; I was lost, got sucked in, you know. And later on in life, I'm sitting there, (Some of this shit my dad still doesn't know) but I'm listening to him and there's this program about biker gangs on TV. They grab the kids when they're young and they corrupt them young. It's the guys under them that corrupt the young guys and suck them in. That way, the gang keeps their hands clean.

Then one day my dad said, 'Come on I'm gonna take you pipelining'. I was already too far gone. I was always on the dope, making three grand a week, drinking it, snorting it, and gambling. That's where my paycheck went for a good three years. I could have bought a house, had my truck paid off. I had to learn that stuff. Some people never learn it. I was lucky to wake up when I did.

I was always working and dealing—half and half. I was flying under the radar—working part time as a teenager and being a bad kid at the same time by selling dope. I never had a steady job, right, until I hit the pipeline and then it was always good.

My guardian's son, Rory—I've known him since he was in diapers—was struggling. I loved him as a brother—I considered him a brother. He was lost. His mom had passed, right. I was on the dope and I was sending him money so he could just get dope and then sell it. You know, I'd get my cut. I said fuck it—I got tired of it. Then I got sucked into the home invasion.

Up to this point, Joseph had lived a contradictory life. For years, he bought, sold, and used drugs extensively but was never caught. He had completed high school, and he worked about half the time, thus maintaining a front of respectability, of being ordinary. He saw his mom and his dad from time to time but stayed aloof from them. As he grew older, he was getting tired of the lifestyle. It seems he started to give some consideration to making a lifestyle adjustment, although just what that would look like was still unclear.

It was his relationship with his 'brother', Rory to whom he felt a loyalty and a protectiveness that he believes got him directly involved in the home invasion.

One day, Rory picked me up at camp at five in the morning. I'll never forget that because he got the truck stuck in the mud on the camp road. Had to get it towed out. Big ruts, in the spring. I quit that job, hopped in the truck in the middle of the night and said, 'Let's go'. I had a big bag of dope waiting for me. We had rented this house in a town not far from the city for like two months.

We upgraded to a bigger house and we had some more guys with us and then everything was going smooth. I went away with my mom to my grandparents' 60th anniversary. While I was gone, someone home-invaded my house and stole everything—all the clothes, tied my brother Rory up, beat him up bad—didn't kill him, didn't stab him; I'm surprised. So, we were left broke. A couple of days later, Rory come up and said he knew some guys who had some shit (valuables) and I told him, 'No man— we'll get it back. We're not going to go and do that.' A week went by. I was drunk. It was like midnight. Him and another guy came to my room. For two hours straight, they come up and down, up and down, hounding me to go. And then I gave in because I wasn't letting him go alone. I loved that kid to death. So I went. Before, I had told his mom I would protect him at all cost—I promised her before she died.

That night, Joseph and the others left the community they were living in, and drove to a nearby community.

All I did was just walk into that house, that's all. I didn't have a weapon, I didn't take anything. I seen somebody got stabbed, and I just got out right away. There was an altercation. I vaguely remember going in 'cause I was so messed up. I remember seeing that guy get stabbed and then it was like I sobered up real quick and saw what I was doing and then just ran out.

Joseph ran from the scene of the home invasion and several of the others were quickly arrested by police. An extensive investigation by police was launched and police eventually determined that Joseph was involved. The pressure on him was building. He continued using, and he felt like his life was a mess. Then came the overdose. An overdose occurs when there is so much drug or mixture of drugs in the body that the body is functionally poisoned and, to protect itself, its systems shut down. Basic physiological functions like breathing and pulse are compromised to the point that death is a real possibility. Overdose is a critical physiological condition.

I was getting more and more screwed up. Then I went to a rodeo with a bunch of dope—I did an ounce of cocaine for myself in a day and a half, which was unheard of. I had an eight-ball left so I swallowed it, then it blew up in my stomach and that's how I ended up in the hospital. That was the overdose—that's what pushed it over to the edge. That one bag blew up in my stomach. It ruptured my guts—I was puking blood. My nose was a faucet, bleeding like it blew up. I was hallucinating, couldn't stop throwing up blood—it was just like someone cutting a vein, just coming out. I looked at my hand; I was totally covered in blood, right down my arm.

Once the ambulance got there, they tried to put an IV in me. They moved the rig for 10 minutes, trying to poke and get the IV in me. They got the IV in me. The cops showed up first, and I told the cop, 'Yo, my phone is not working'. I was like, 'can you call my dad? Call him and tell him I am sorry.' The cop wouldn't call him—wouldn't call my damn house. You know what I'm saying? I still don't get it. You know, what the hell? Call! It was practically my last dying wish for someone to call my house and nobody did. Only the nurses called when I got to the hospital in Edmonton. They called home when I was in hospital. They put me in that room to die. I woke up when I seen my dad cry after I got out of the hospital from the overdose. He drove across the country in four days to come and see me. He said, 'I don't ever want to see you overdosed again.' He was crying, said he was supposed to die before I die. It's going to be a hard day.

My mom showed up at the hospital the day after I overdosed. My dad got a hold of her somehow, so she left work and drove all the way to Edmonton and got there when I was in the emergency room. They put me in a room to die. They told me I was going to die. They told my mom they don't know why I am still alive and that I'm gonna die. My eyes are rolling in the back of my head. I just remember they put me in the room to die, man. My system was dying, starting to fail, and she come in there with my step brother and one of my uncles. They rubbed me with holy oil and prayed for a few hours. Then the doctor come running in and said, 'Okay, we're going to take him into surgery'. They took me in and they told me I might not wake up. I said there was a good chance, whatever. I'm already this far gone—you might as well try.

I was told I was a walking miracle. God has big plans for me. That's what I was told. The doctor at my overdose couldn't believe it. Every blood vessel in my face was collapsed, my whole face was purple-veined, everywhere. My eyes were just black. I weighed like about 120 pounds. I don't ever want to see anyone's face like that again. I never want to look at myself like that in a mirror. I looked at myself the next day in a mirror and said I should be dead.

Up to now, Joseph had not been too interested in or involved with his Indigenous heritage. He was aware of his background, but it had not been an important part of his life. That now was about to change.

I pulled through. My mom, my brother Sam, and my uncle told me they seen life come back into me. Then, after that, she took me to see a medicine man. A couple of days later, she took me to a ceremony. We offered him tobacco. I got doctored. I asked to be forgiven for everything I'd done in the past. I didn't want those demons with me anymore. I didn't eat anything white or anything. I took some medicine, and it wasn't white; and what I threw up were big chunks of white—I don't know what the hell it was.

The medicine man was quick to scoop it up and go bury it in the woods. It still boggles me to this day. I asked for the demons to come out, and I seen some shit come out—it is pretty crazy. I didn't believe in that stuff up until that day. My dad told me it was sorcery, but, at the end of the day, that is my heritage. That got me a little culturally attached. Later, I would go see that medicine man once in a while when I was on day parole.

When I went to jail, I stayed away from cultural stuff until I got to minimum security, an Indigenous healing centre in Edmonton, and then I started going to cultural programs, sweats, and other ceremonies."

When a person is arrested by police, the officers make an immediate decision whether to release the person on a summons or appearance notice, or to keep the person in custody to ensure their appearance in court. Keeping the person in custody until their court appearance is a common police decision when the charge is a serious one, such as a home invasion.

After Joseph turned himself in to police and was then immediately arrested, he appeared in court where his case was adjourned a number of times. At one of these appearances, Joseph's lawyer submitted an application to the judge to have him released on bail, also known as judicial interim release, rather than continue to keep him in custody. The judge, after hearing from Joseph's lawyer and the prosecutor, eventually approved the application and released Joseph on bail. A number of conditions were imposed: uphold a curfew, abstain from non-prescription drugs and alcohol, report changes in address or employment to police, not to be in possession of sharp items with sharp edges, no contact with co-accused, and attend court when required to do so. These conditions are to protect the public and to ensure the accused person's appearance in court.

> Like I said, I pulled through that and then went back on the pipeline and this time I was with my dad the whole time. I went working for a couple of months then got a phone call from the cops about the home invasion and turned myself in. So I went down there. Everything was on the table. The other guys had talked. The cop left the room. He left his binder on the table on purpose. I reached over, turned his binder over, and I opened the pages. There were pictures of me—what I was wearing, everything, a bunch of statements.
> Then I made bail. My dad was scrambling to get bail

money. He hit every ATM he could find to get the bail money. He bailed me out. I was on bail for two years before I got sentenced.

While on bail, his case slowly wound its way through the courts for a period of two years. Joseph complied with all the bail conditions, and he was steadily employed for most of the time that he was on bail. Many people experience an event so profound that its memory stays sharply in their mind forever. For Joseph, one such event was the death of his little brother.

In that time on bail, my little step-brother Rory died. He got shot. You know, I'd told him to change his life, 'Change your life man, it's not worth it.' A year or so after I'd been on bail, I got a phone call—he's dead. Someone shot him in the head; someone kicked in his door and shot him."

When I think about it now, this is another stepping stone in my life. If I wouldn't have changed, if no one had been willing to help, and I didn't help myself, I would have been sitting right next to him, and who knows what would have happened? I might have been the one who got shot, or I would have seen him get shot. I would have grabbed the gun, and I would have shot back. I probably would have killed them all.

And to this day, I know who did it. I know where they are right now. I've seen them. But I don't blame them—they have to live with that. You know, I don't have that weight on my shoulders. They do.

Joseph was sentenced in 2016 to four years imprisonment for the home invasion charges. He began the sentence in a medium security penitentiary where he spent a year working in the institution's employment program. In 2017, he was transferred from the penitentiary to an Indigenous healing centre. Here, he was classified as an inmate for five months, then was released on day parole for six months. On day parole, Joseph worked in a cafeteria and as a construction labourer during the day, returning to the healing centre at night.

> When I got sentenced, I went to a medium security penitentiary for about a year. After that, I transferred to the healing centre. That place was good. My Elder was good. I went and grabbed a spirit name, an animal; went fasting for three days in the woods. Built a nice round hut out of willows and pine branches. I made this door that I could prop open with two sticks on the side. I had my one door; you're not supposed to cover it, so I left it open. So I could have a fire in my hut which was dangerous but I still had a fire going 'cause it was cold. All I had was sleep—no water, just a sleeping bag, a foamy, and my fire. And I had to stay in the circle—my boundaries that I tied my cloth in that area. Some other people would come and bring me firewood when I needed wood, right? People came and checked on me. Three days. On the third day, I was starting to hallucinate, I can tell you that much. My lips were just pasted. I remember being so dehydrated that I couldn't pee. Just this little bit would come out—yellow and green. Holy shit, my kidneys are going to fail. It was good, a good time. After, I drank lots of water, and we had a sweat. I'd go to sweats every week when I was in there. When I got on day parole, it was once a month for sweats. I did five months there at the healing centre and then six months day parole, then full parole to the street.

It has now been about four years that Joseph has been clean and sober. Two years of that time were while he was on bail and under the watchful eye of police and court officials. During the past two years, he has been under the watchful eye of prison and parole officials. During the entire time he has been involved with the criminal justice system, he has not been found to have committed other crimes. It seems he has been able to refrain from using drugs and alcohol—a remarkable achievement considering his previous extensive use of substances for eight or nine years.

Also, during this time, he faced a traumatic event—the shooting death of his 'little brother', Rory. In my view, he made a wise and thoughtful decision not to 'get back' at Rory's killer. This, too, can be seen as a remarkable achievement, given his previous criminal involvement.

> Since I've been doctored, you know, I've had the urge to do drugs about twice. There is a lot of things that I wouldn't have given a care about and now even a year after I went back to my dad's, some of my old friends there on Christmas Eve, they were all drinking and I wasn't allowed to drink. They were all drinking and then one dude shows up with a big bag of dope, throws it on the table, started chopping out lines for everybody. I got up and left. 'Look boys, I gotta go.' Still my friends, you know, but I know when to distance myself. I know when to leave. That's a tough choice for a lot of people. I was a heavy user. I would use anything—I didn't care. You put a drug in front of me—I didn't care, okay, let's do it.
>
> In the past, I didn't care if I lived or died at one point. I didn't care about anybody around me, I didn't care about my family. I thought they all abandoned me. Well, kinda was abandoned. I've got to think of this from every perspective I can. That's how I was taught. That's one thing my dad taught me. That is try to think of every worst-case scenario. The one time in my life I didn't listen to him, and that's how I ended up in jail. I always crossed my toes—everything. I made sure I thought of everything—what could happen if I did this or that. That time, I put my life in someone else's hands, and I'll never do that again.

Joseph is living in an apartment with his girlfriend. They met at a church service while both serving time in different prisons. This relationship has lasted for about two years.

> I have a girlfriend now—a fiancée. She's good. She has been on parole. She went to jail. I met her at church on a pass. I was on day parole and I was allowed to go and visit her. But only 'cause I was doing so good. I'm happy I met her. Sometimes, she struggles. She's been done parole for a while now. She has her moments. That's fine. She doesn't use. We're not perfect but we're making the best of it. They say two wrongs don't make a right, but two wrongs are making it right now.
>
> I prayed for a long time to meet somebody who knew the same stuff as me and has the same outlook on life. Someone I can relate to.

Joseph has developed a certain philosophical view about his life. He is not angry at anyone. He does have some frustrations with the justice system, based on how some officials dealt with him, but Joseph has come up with a way to put his life into perspective.

> Maybe I should have taken some alternative routes, made better choices. It is what it is. I can only do so much. I tend to laugh and joke about this, but you know, my brain—I'm 28 years old, but my brain is older.
>
> After I almost died from the overdose, I tell my dad I love him almost whenever I talk to him. He's the same thing. It takes a real wake-up for everybody. I'm just a labourer out here now, struggling, but I'm doing okay. I'm a foreman now, but that's only 'cause I'm sober. The trust—it took me a long time to rebuild

my name. I'm happy now, you know, better job all the time, no worries.

My life has been a roller coaster. Now, I think about things, second guess, and anticipate what is going to happen. I try to think things through, trying to look at the downside of things. Some guys do the first thing that comes to their mind; they don't give it a second thought. That's how you fail. It is hard to do. I don't risk it, man. I know better. It's not worth it. I've come this far, and I'm not going back.

In 2018, Joseph was released from the healing centre on full parole to serve the balance of his sentence in the community under the supervision of a parole officer. There are a number of conditions relating to his release on parole: report to the parole officer, a lifetime ban on possession of weapons, and no contact with known drug users. If he 'screws up' and does not successfully serve his sentence in the community, he will be returned to a prison, likely the medium custody penitentiary where he started his sentence, to finish the remaining portion of the four year sentence in custody.

Since then, I have reflected on Joseph's case—might there have been other things that the Parole Board and his parole officer could have done to assist in his reintegration to the community? The Board had imposed conditions on Joseph to spell out what he could and could not do, thereby protecting the public. The Board did not spell out additional conditions designed to help him lead a law-abiding lifestyle.

It was obvious to me in hindsight that conditions related to Indigenous culture could have been helpful to Joseph. However, the Board, at the time of their decision to release Joseph on parole, did not order him to attend ceremony and sweats.

In my view, parole boards have a tough decision to make in cases like this: do they impose such conditions on a parolee or is it the responsibility of the parolee to take part in such activities of their own volition? Similarly with parole officers: should they direct their clients to take part in cultural activities or is this more appropriately a matter of personal choice? To what extent do parole officials build cultural practices and ceremony into the Treatment Plan?

ஃ

Doug Heckbert has been a probation officer and prison case-worker with Alberta Correctional Services, parole officer with the National Parole Service, staff trainer and program director with Native Counselling Services of Alberta, and instructor with MacEwan University. His book Go Ahead and Shoot Me and Other True Cases About Ordinary Criminals *is book 7 in the Durvile True Cases Series.*

SEVENTEEN

Doug Heckbert and Jennifer Bryce

GETTING FPS# OFF OUR BACKS

ِؐ

Editors' Note: In his 2020 book Go Ahead and Shoot Me! *(True Cases Series book #7), Doug Heckbert wrote about 'Paula,' a pseudonym for a woman who has, since then, bravely disclosed her name and identity as Jennifer Bryce. Jenn's disadvantaged early years were similar to the women in Hon. Kim Pate's, Constable Val Hoglund's, and Sharon Bourques' chapters in this book, but Jenn's (aka Paula's) focus was how to free herself from her FPS#. In this chapter, we excerpt the original story, then add details of Jenn's life transformation.*

Jennifer Bryce is a Métis woman, 50 years of age who, as we shall learn, spent 22 years in and out of the criminal justice system, both as a youth and as an adult. She expressed the hope of getting FPS#s (Finger Print Section numbers) "off people's backs." This is a number assigned by the national police service to people charged with and/or convicted of criminal and quasi-criminal offences. Jennifer was known by her FPS# for many years, and her last FPS entry expired 12 years ago. She began "wading through stuff" by outlining some childhood experiences:

Some of my earliest memories were the smell of alcohol, arguing, violence, fighting, all around me. I don't have a lot of memories from age 10 and under. I remember feeling displaced all the time—on-the-run. My folks were into their addictions. Although I self-identify as Métis, it was never spoken about in my upbringing as dad did not live his life as a Métis man. By age 12, my parents had separated and that changed the course of my life. I was a little kid, I needed love. The only thing I knew how to do was to reach out in a negative way.

As she reached age 13 (she was now old enough to be considered a young offender), her behaviour became increasingly problematic. By 16, she was in youth court:

...I could roll into a car dealership with a hustle, like, 'I'm graduating this year and my folks are buying me a brand new ride and they told me to come down here to check it out'. I was very good at what I did! That's how I got about half of the vehicles I ever stole. The dealer would put a dealer's plate on a vehicle, hand me the keys and I'd go for a ride. Later, I would get the keys, steal a vehicle and then get involved in a high speed chase. Once I put a plate on a new vehicle and took it for a two-day test drive. Then, the cops saw the vehicle and the chase was on. The police caught up and surrounded the vehicle with guns drawn. When they opened the door and recognized me, one officer ripped a strip off me; he was so mad. 'You f'n little brat!' he screamed. Needless to say, I was charged as a youth with theft of auto, break and enter, and endangering the public.

Now, Jennifer had earned her FPS#, one that would follow her for the next 20 years:

I entered the youth system. I figured I was old enough to defend myself, that I was a big girl now, so I stepped up my level of criminal activity. The judge asked my mother if she wanted to take me home, and she stood up and said, 'No—you guys take her. I don't want her anymore'.

Jennifer entered the youth justice system at 16, and she spent the next two years in custody, beginning in a group home and ending two years later in secure custody.

By 17, I was big and bad. In court, the judge asked me what I wanted to do. Since I was big and bad and tough, plus having some youth time left, I chose to do adult time. I was sentenced to eight months in an adult prison.

Jennifer's FPS# followed her into the adult justice system. Her first adult sentence of eight months turned into imprisonment for two years:

I experienced crazy people, trauma, riots, fights, staff being injured, inmates injured, being caged because of my behaviour. I would freak out when they locked me up, do anything to pound out the door or scratch the window, anything to get out. I felt like a mouse in a cage, trying to eat its arm off. This was a whole new level of trauma.

Staff working in correctional centres have really tough jobs. They have to control inmates in order to protect the public, the staff, and other inmates, as well as help inmates prepare for release, better equipped to live a law-abiding lifestyle. Thus far, staff had decided the best way to deal with Jennifer was to keep her locked up. This met the criteria of control and protection but did not meet the criteria of helping people adjust in a positive way, especially in the face of her fast-approaching release date. Jennifer explained that staff then developed a new correctional plan for her that focused on getting her re-integrated into the general inmate population and into the community: upon her release, Jennifer stepped tentatively into the community. She hadn't spent much time in the community in the last four years. A lot would have changed. How would she adapt? She explained:

> Now I'm 20. I've been in jail since I was 16. I've got nothing other than a few friends. I was living a double life— crime, drugs and violence was more normal to me than going to school and getting a regular job and training. I was back in jail seven months after release—for assault. I didn't drink before, but now I drank for three people for a good 10 years.

Jennifer somehow stayed out of trouble with the law for the next four years, bouncing around from town to town and then settling with a friend:

> I started taking pills with the alcohol. You don't feel anything. It was Ts and Rs (Talwin and Ritalin) back in those days. Alcohol gave me that excuse to pound the shit out of people. That's how I operated for quite a while up to 1994, after I had been out close to four years, no more charges. One time I was drinking and got into a fight, beat somebody up real good and ended up getting charged with assault. So, I hit the justice system again.

This time, the court was lenient with Jennifer and took her youth record into account; she received a suspended sentence and probation. As she said, "They were still giving me chances."

> That's when I went in and robbed a convenience store. I was half in the bag, walked in there and robbed them. I was

sentenced to 18 months and sent to the same jail where a female guard worked, who had previously romantically creeped me out. This was traumatizing. The people who were supposed to be reforming me were actually re-victimizing me—locking me up in a cage, talking my ear off about love, how beautiful I am—all this weird stuff.

Jennifer began journaling, putting her thoughts and feelings down on paper. One theme she journaled about was this female staff member, now a senior official at the institution, who continued to creep Jennifer out, and now, another female inmate as well. Someone found her journal, read it, then wrote a letter of complaint to the warden. The warden attacked her credibility and announced she was being transferred out. Just hours before the transfer, two guards who Jennifer liked and trusted suddenly took her to a room in the institution and locked her inside, instructing her to pick up the phone and call the number written on a piece of paper. Jennifer briefly wondered what was going on, but she trusted these two staff, so she called the number. In Jennifer's words:

> I called the number, and it was the frick'n Ombudsman. They wanted to know what was going on, so I told them—I opened up a real can of worms. It felt so good to finally tell my story. Finally, somebody believed me and was listening. I reflected on whether I really wanted to go ahead with this. I said to myself, "F'n right, let's open it up." I took responsibly for it. I was using her back—tit-for-tat. I was surviving.

Jennifer was transferred to another adult correctional facility in another jurisdiction. She took a few programs like anger management, addictions, and a 30-day treatment program. She also worked closely with the Ombudsman and was released right after the Ombudsman's investigation was concluded. Upon release, Jennifer moved to another city to live with a friend, a woman who showered her with gifts and encouraged her drug abuse. She decided to end the relationship the only way she knew how—fighting back. So, she took the friend's credit cards and removed several thousand dollars via ATMs. Police were called, and Jennifer was charged with theft of the credit cards but received a suspended sentence and probation. After court, her friend, the victim of the credit card theft, took Jennifer shopping and gave her $5,000 cash.

> I started getting into poor man's heroin. I got introduced to downers, to morphine. It numbed me; I couldn't feel a thing. I was in a relationship with a drug user as well, just motoring along in my addiction; and it progressed from cocaine to opiates. This kept me right into the life of crime—I was addicted and had to have it. I never got busted with anything—I just didn't get caught. I was going into stores to steal shit, steal someone's wallet. I didn't have the guts to go do a robbery, so I stayed with petty thefts—ten bucks here, twenty bucks there.

Jennifer hit the pen again on an armed robbery charge. What happened next was one of those things that planted a seed in Jennifer and got her thinking about new influences, new directions for her life. She explains,

> I started working with an Indigenous Elder. She talked about culture and ceremony. I was mad at God for quite a few things and I was confused about spirituality and culture and ceremony. I connected with the Elder, and we created an awesome relationship. She was a beautiful mentor. She helped me understand so many things about myself and where my life was headed. I started going to ceremony, and I started doing sweats. I was the fire keeper. I started thinking about spirituality and looking

at Creator, at medicine, prayer, and ceremony—all this
stuff really works.

She eventually reached a turning point in her life. She got
to work by taking programs whole-heartedly and finally admitting her addiction. Jennifer took some core programs, worked
with a women's organization's worker, and a trauma therapist.

> I quit all drug activity, well, for the most part *(a giggle
> here)*. I stopped engaging in shenanigans; I stopped beat-
> ing people up. I threw myself fully into programs and
> talking and shedding layers, sharing. I used that time to
> do good things for myself and for switching my whole
> vocabulary, my thinking processes. I engaged with the
> new Elder who was there, doing culture and ceremonies
> that worked.

Jennifer walked out of the penitentiary better equipped
than on any of her previous imprisonments. She went looking for work, something she had not done for many years. She
found employment—milking cows. She explains what a great
job this was for her:

> I got connected with this farmer. He took time to see me
> and planted some seeds in my life. I worked for him for
> just 10 days; however, we had conversations, shared a bit
> of our lives and the family loved me. They knew I was
> rebuilding my life and they gave me a hand up. They didn't
> care what colour I was or how many tattoos I had. They
> didn't see that. They seen me and they seen my spirit. This
> was part of my launching pad; they helped me a lot.

She came to a conclusion: she wanted to give back to
the people who helped her. In looking for work possibilities,
she spotted the web page of a human service agency that was

looking for staff at the courthouse in a small city. Jennifer continues,

> They wouldn't hire me because of my criminal record, but they said I could volunteer with youth at the courthouse to build up my skills. I would bring my co-workers coffee and donuts, started meeting lawyers, having conversations with judges. I love talking with my clients, guiding them, and learning about the justice system on a whole new level. I get to form relationships with people, and I have my own caseload. I get to help them, love them where they are at today. Now I can give to people who need it—I can see what they need. I needed that too, damn it, so here! I'm going to cry in joy and give you what I got.

Word spread among the community agencies about "the new girl" at the courthouse. A manager from another human service agency asked her for a resume. Jennifer reflects,

> I knew I could reach people on a different level. I had the energy, the ideas, and the passion to do more. I thought I could write programs based on my own experience, like self-worth because my self-worth was blown for 40 years. It took me time to build it up again and to understand my energy. My employer totally backed me. I figured I was going to get my own business licence because I knew in my heart to aim at the communities that don't get what we have in the city, to rural people, youth, whoever needs them. I had this stuff all wrapped up inside me, I wanted to give it away. I knew as a human service provider that you don't get rich but you are enriched in working with people with love, in spirituality.
> In 2018, I bought a business licence. I had done a lot of healing after losing my dad. All of my past comes

flooding in for me and that brought me to now when I was back in the human service field. I'm sober, I am cancer-free, and making all these connections. I registered my company, getting the name from what dad used to call me, my nickname.

Now, Jennifer has started on another path. She transitioned her skills and go-getter attitude from a court worker, housing worker, and a trauma worker to that of a business woman.

I always will remember my FPS#. It is entrenched in my mind, but my vision is clear. I'm free of resentment and being pissed off. I use that number to teach and to guide, to use pieces of me, to bring people to reality. I use my passion to take my story to people. I want others to feel it. But you know that it's real; there was a price paid to live that story.

This was Jenn's story as she spoke with me for *Go Ahead and Shoot Me!*, when she was still known by her pseudonym of 'Paula'. There were laughs, lots of laughs, when we got together recently to reflect on some of the things that happened to her and the goofy things that she did. There were some tears, times when the memories washed over her, overwhelmed her.

As I reflect on Jenn's story, I wonder why we, as a community, seem to find it so difficult to pay attention to how we might respond to addiction, crime, and chaos in a preventative way. We seem to be content to 'call the cops' and 'throw away the keys'. Is this out of sight, out of mind? We as a community pay a hefty price for this attitude. Surely there are better ways that would yield better results.

I am impressed by Jennifer's resilience. She overcame circumstances that would destroy others. In her case, I think there was a little girl, bursting with enthusiasm, but had no one around to steer her, guide her, to mentor her. Where was her extended family? Where was her community? She turned inward on herself and had over 20 years of turmoil, chaos and anger. But, she overcame these forces and learned how to manage herself to become a valued employee and a contributing member of the community.

Her story is remarkable—several times she said she does not know why she didn't die. She overcame challenges and barriers to be at a point now in her life where she is poised to take on the risk of being in business, to be on her own in the human service field, with all its risks and rewards.

2022 was an eventful year for Jennifer. She was a speaker at the Canadian Criminal Justice Association's World Congress on Probation and Parole in Ottawa, Ontario. She spoke about her 22 years in the youth and adult criminal justice systems and the Indigenous Elders, judges, police officers, and correctional officers who planted seeds in her mind that she could live without addictions, crime, and chaos. At Congress, Jennifer met one of her former guards from the penitentiary for women where she served one of her 'pen bits'—both were stunned to see each other, then amazed and overjoyed at how much Jenn had changed since then. Her presentation was electrifying as she spoke to attendees from Canada and abroad.

Also in 2022, the Native Counselling Services of Alberta (NCSA) asked Jenn to join the HELP team that pairs Edmonton Police Service patrol officers with an Indigenous navigator. Jenn now arrives at 7:00 a.m. for her shift. In her words:

Usually, we smudge before parade. We have a cultural room in our office and we use that cultural space to go in and smudge in the morning. The officers are also smudging with us as well. Here, there is diversity and there as balance. We smudge, parade, and then gear up for the day. At parade, the police term for a morning meeting, our sergeant goes through where we are to go; provides updates on any of our clients, like who is struggling with addiction, homeless, or in jail; lets us know of any information that will impact our shift; lets us know who is paired with who and lets us know what appointments we have—there are some clients that are assigned to me.

I make sure my backpack is full of warm clothes, snacks. Socks, gloves, hand warmers; bottles of water and granola bars are in the vehicle. I carry gift cards and cigarettes—a great relationship builder in the Indigenous community. I also carry a smudge pan and sage and matches—that is, again, part of who I am. We carry naloxone kits because we deal with overdoses every day.

The calls to assist patrol are social disorder calls, and we don't schedule these, so we are always unsure of just what we will be facing. This has been a healing journey for me, getting to see the men and women behind the uniform, who they are as people, getting to see the trials and tribulations they had.

That's the beauty of what Jenn has developed with EPS, bringing social agencies together with police officers. It's back and forth, a healing journey, a working relationship. There's respect there and equality. Jenn continues,

I have a participant who has been referred to me so I go look for him at the shelters, last known locations, building relationships with the community because I'm looking for my guy. We see people in those negative conditions, and with the assistance of the HELP team, they are more inclined to stay out of trouble. They meet our unit and say, 'Holy shit! You get what I'm talking about, where I'm at'; then they start to heal the relationship with that officer.

Jenn offers a glimpse of what lies ahead for HELP:

People across Canada and from the US are coming to check us out. People are seeing that this is really working—Wow! What's up with this? If we can build those relationships back with police and start modelling to our community members, great work is being done. HELP will be expanding to all divisions—a really cool thing!

Jenn recently received an invitation from Saskatchewan to speak to staff at the group homes, youth detention facilities, and correctional centres where she served sentences as a youth. She was also asked to join a women's drum group, based at the University of Alberta to use drum teachings to work with Indigenous women in federal prisons. Members of the community, may they be drum circles or dairy farmers, can support Indigenous offenders, indeed all offenders, no matter what their FPS# shows.

ॱऀ

See Doug Heckbert's bio on page 256.

Jennifer Bryce is now the proud owner and operator of Lil' Bear Resources, Edmonton, which offers one-on-one mentoring as well as youth and adult personal development programs to promote healing and positive outcomes. Among the services offered are Restorative Justice, Crisis Intervention, De-Escalation, Suicide Prevention and Awareness, Mental Health First Aid, and Life Skills Coaching.

INDEX

Anderson, Jethro 124–125, 129, 130
Anderson, John 52–66
Arawak Nation 65
Arbour, Hon. Louise 90, 99
Arctic Gas pipeline project 12–34
Arnot, Dave 174
A. Silverman, Justice 160
Athabasca Chipewyan First Nation 2
Auger, Grace 53–58
Baptiste, Alvin 107
Baptiste, Debbie 111
Barrera, Jorge 194
Batten, Jack 77
Bayly, John 71–79
Beardy, Coleen Tenona 121
Beresh KC, Brian 1, 163–174
Berger, Beverley 6
Berger, Erin 6
Berger, Hon. Justice Thomas R. ix, 6–7, 11–34
Big Canoe, Christa 118
Blackfoot 5
Blais, Judge Ray 174
Bloodvein First Nation 134–145
Bourque, Sharon 217–224
Boushie, Colten 105–115
Brennan, Declan 160
Brillon, Wylie 49
Briscoe, Jennifer 175–187
Brown, Rosemary 48–49
Bryce, Jennifer 257
Bushie, Reggie 117–132
Buxton Museum 2
Canada Labour Code 197
Chipewyan 13, 17
Convention on the Rights of the Child 142
Cote, Bernice 40
Cote First Nation 36, 45

INDEX

Crete, Jean-Philippe 195
Criminal Code of Canada 42, 44, 61, 99, 134, 140, 141, 209–210
Davis, Justice C.S. 41–44
Deer, Dr. Frank 3
Deloria Jr., Vine 64
Doctrine of Discovery 2
Doug Heckbert 241–268
Dunn, Catherine 7, 133–145
Dyck, Jenny 159–160
Ear, Marty 51–66
Eden, Dr. David 121–124
Ernie Louttit 203–216
Fiddler, Alvin 118
Fontaine, Nahanni 144
Foreman, Sharon 173
Gerretsen, Hon. John 124
Gerussi, Bruno 35
Ghanji, Dr. 56
Gibbons, Richard 172, 174
Gitxsan First Nation 147, 149
Goodwin, Jamie 119
Gordon, Robert 120–122
Gunanoot, Simon Peter 148
Gwich'in 13, 17
Haida Nation 48
Hajdu, Patty 200
Harper, Robyn 124–125, 128
Harper, Stephen 231
Heckbert, Doug 7
Henderson, Stuart 152–153
Hepner QC, Alain 54
Hill, John L. 189
Himadam, Peter 150
Hoglund, Constable Val 225–240
Hoglund, Val 7
Homicide Act 43

INDEX

Hughes, Honourable Commissioner Ted 144
Iacoubucci, Justice Frank 119–132
Indian Act 35, 39
Innuksuk, Henry Suviserk 68–79
Inuktitut 13, 17
Jewett, Pauline 46–49
Johnson, Corporal Andrew 54
Jones, Lorna 84–101
Joseph Saulnier 147–162
Kahnawake 3
Kasechewan First Nation 119
Kayotak, Marius 186
Keeseekoose First Nation 36
Key First Nation 36, 40
King, Berenson 118
King, Rhoda 118
Kirby, Constable, James 150–151
Labelle, Baret 51–66
Labelle, George 54–58
Labelle, Sheila 54
Labelle, Sherman 51–66
Langenham,Mikle 68–69
Lech, Karl 194–195
LeClair, Max 147
MacDonald, Blanche 46–49
MacDonald, Constable D. B. 41
MacDonald, John A. 109
MacIntosh, Alex 147–164
Mackenzie Valley Pipeline Inquiry 11–34
Many Fingers, Crystal 5–6
Marchand, Dawn Marie 193, 199
Martland KC, Brock 156
McRae, Dr. Shelagh 121
Mi'kmaq 65
Moe, Premier Scott 108
Montgomery, Bob 4–5

INDEX

Morgan, Don 109
Morrison, Hon. Nancy 6–7, 35–49
Morrisseau, Kyle 124–125, 129
Mountain, Antoine 6
Mungham, Stuart 197
Murphy, Chris 107–109
Murray, Kim 119–122, 125
Nekaneet Cree Nation 98
Neve, Lisa 81
Nishnawbe Aski Nation 121
Northern Frontier, Northern Homeland ix, 19
North Slavey Dene 13, 17
North-West Resistance 1
Obed, Nathan 200
Panacheese, Paul 124–125, 128
Pate, Hon. Kim 7, 81–101
Peacock, Rolanda 119
Peirol, Paulette 88
Pierre, Jacy 121
Pierre, Marlene 122
Pîhtokahanapiwiyin, Chief Poundmaker 1–2
Poitras, Colette 3
Policha, Judge Joe 169–172
Poundmaker First Nation 167
Provan, Warden Mike 191–200
Purewal, Justice Nina 160
Red Pheasant Nation 105, 111, 166
Reid, Bill 48–49
Reilly, Hon. John 51
Riel, Louis 1
Robinson, Lloyd 53
Roleau, Judge Charles 166
Royal Alberta Museum 2
Royal Commission on Aboriginal Peoples x
Royal Commission on the Incarceration of Female Offenders 47–48
Royal Ontario Museum 2

INDEX

Rudin, Jonathan 117–132
R v Bunes 58
R v Gladue x, 53, 61, 63
R v Ipeelee x
R v Bastian 43
R v Stanley 105–115
R v Williams 61
Saulnier, Joseph 7
Scalplock, Tammy 54
Sergeant, Dr. David 22
Shyba, Dr. Lorene 1–7
Sinclair, Phoenix 144
Slaven, Chief Judge Jim 72–79
Smallwood, Chief Justice Shannon ix–xi, 6
Smith, Adam 33
Smith, Ashley 97
Soonias, Rodney 166
South Slavey Dene 13, 17
Spillett, Leslie 144
Stanley, Gerald 105–115
Stanley, Leesa 105, 112
Sterling Brass 40–46
Stoffman, Judy 192
Stoney Nakoda First Nation 5, 51–66
Strang, Curran 124–125, 130
Strang, Ricky 117–132
Suchowersky, Dr. 56
Sunchild, Eleanore KC 1, 105–115
Tlicho 13, 17
Tootoosis, John 174
Trudeau, Prime Minister Justin 2
Truth and Reconciliation Commission Report
        x, 82, 99, 121, 130, 231
Vertes, Hon. John Z. 7, 67–79
Wabasse, Jordan 124–125, 128–130

INDEX

Wake, Drew Ann 6
Wampanoag 65
Wesley, Mandy 120
Wesley, Ricardo 119
Wesley, Trudy 5
Wet'suwet'en First Nation 149
Williamson, Dr. Robert 73
Williamson, Jean 73–79
Worme, Don 90
Yakeleya, Raymond 1–7

Books in the Durvile True Cases Series

Series Editor, Lorene Shyba MFA PhD

1. Tough Crimes: True Cases by
Top Canadian Criminal Lawyers
Edited by C.D. Evans and Lorene Shyba

2. Shrunk, Crime and Disorders of the Mind:
True Cases by Forensic Psychiatrists and Psychologists
Edited by Dr. Lorene Shyba and Dr. J. Thomas Dalby

3. More Tough Crimes: True Cases by
Canadian Lawyers and Judges
Edited by William Trudell and Lorene Shyba

4. Women in Criminal Justice: True Cases By and About
Canadian Women and the Law
Edited by William Trudell and Lorene Shyba

5. Florence Kinrade: Lizzie Borden of the North
Written by Frank Jones

6. Ross Mackay, The Saga of a Brilliant Criminal Lawyer:
And His Big Losses and
Bigger Wins in Court and in Life
Written by Jack Batten

7. Go Ahead and Shoot Me!
And Other True Cases About Ordinary Criminals
Written by Doug Heckbert

8. After the Force: True Cases and Investigations by
Law Enforcement Officers
Edited by Det. Debbie J. Doyle (ret.)

9. Pine Box Parole: Terry Fitzsimmons and the
Quest to End Solitary Confinement & Other True Cases
Written by John L. Hill

10. Indigenous Justice:
True Cases by Judges, Lawyers & Law Enforcement Officers
Edited by Lorene Shyba and Raymond Yakeleya